ASCENDANCE
OF A
BOOKWORM
I'll do anything to become a librarian!

Part 1 **Daughter of a Soldier Vol. 3**

Author: **Miya Kazuki**

Illustrator: **You Shiina**

Temple

North Gate

Guildmaster's House

Gilberta Company

The Merchant's Guild

The store that buys magic stones

Central Plaza

West Gate

The Market

Craftsmen's Alley

Ehrenfest

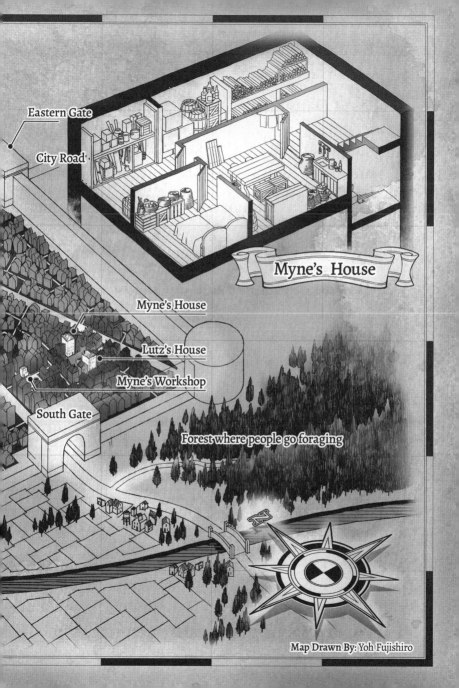

Eastern Gate

City Road

Myne's House

Myne's House

Lutz's House

Myne's Workshop

South Gate

Forest where people go foraging

Map Drawn By: Yoh Fujishiro

Part 1 Daughter of a Soldier Volume 3

Ascendance of a Bookworm: Part 1 Daughter of a Soldier Volume 3
by Miya Kazuki

Translated by quof
Edited by Aimee Zink

First published in Japan in 2015
Publication rights for this English edition arranged through TO Books, Japan.

Find more books like this one at www.j-novel.club!

President and Publisher: Samuel Pinansky
Managing Editor: Aimee Zink

ISBN: 978-1-7183-5602-3
Printed in Korea
First Printing: January 2020
10 9 8 7 6 5 4 3 2

Part 1 Daughter of a Soldier Volume 3

Prologue

"Myne has finally succumbed at the Gilberta Company. Prepare a room and a magic tool," said the messenger sent by the guildmaster, who was in the Merchant's Guild.

Freida's light-brown eyes narrowed sharply. *I knew this day would come,* she thought as she looked up at the butler beside the messenger and ordered him to begin preparing immediately.

"I believe that my grandfather will have sent a messenger to the Gilberta Company as well. It will not take long for Benno to arrive here with Myne. Let us be as ready for them as we can. I will enter grandfather's room myself." Freida touched the thin chain that hung from her neck at all times and pulled it up. Attached were two keys. One was the key to her grandfather's room and one was the key to the safe within it.

With her attendant Jutte at her side, Freida entered her grandfather's room and opened the tightly locked safe within. Inside were the magic tools that he had purchased from nobles using the full extent of his fortune. Originally there had been ten, and now there were only a few. They had been necessary to save Freida's life from the Devouring, the same sickness Myne had.

Her grandfather had used these tools to buy time while he used his connections as a widely influential merchant to eventually secure an agreement with a certain noble, saving her life in the process. But it was impossible to tell when a noble might change their mind. The leftover tools might one day be necessary to save Freida's life once again.

Freida, touching the bracelet on her wrist given to her by the noble, closed her eyes.

"Are you certain about this, my lady?" Jutte spoke to Freida, having sensed her slight hesitation.

Freida sliced away her brief bout of indecision and reached inside the safe. "Quite certain. Myne is the first friend I've ever had, after all. If a magic tool is the price for getting her to join our store, then so be it."

The necklace-shaped magic tool in her hands was so old that it would likely fall apart if handled improperly. No matter how much money you offered to a noble, the only magic tools they would ever sell to commoners were similarly old and on the verge of breaking. The nobles were ripping them off for sure, but it was that or death.

"Myne will understand." Myne had created a new kind of hairpin, one sewn from thread. There was no mistaking that she had designs for many other new products in her head. She was a veritable golden egg, so valuable that the Gilberta Company — one with a sharp eye for profit, rapidly rising in status and wealth within Ehrenfest — would temporarily register her just to secure their hold on her. Freida wanted that golden egg fiercely. Her senses were screaming at her to get Myne on her side immediately.

However, her heart wasn't filled only with greed. Myne was indeed Freida's first friend, a girl her age, sick with the same disease and working toward the same career. Freida wanted Myne by her side. She wanted for them to support each other, even after she was forced to leave and live in the Noble's Quarter. She wanted that with all her heart.

If Myne wanted to survive, she would have to form a contract with a noble, just as Freida had. The Gilberta Company would be no help with that, but the guildmaster of the Merchant's Guild would. If Myne were to join them, they would be able to secure a more favorable agreement for her.

"If Myne is staying with Benno out of gratitude, we need merely make her feel more gratitude for us. Saving her life will do just that." It would be nice if that gratitude alone were enough to make Myne switch sides, but human emotions were not changed so easily. In which case, she just needed to remove her other options. Freida would make as many plans as it took to get her hands on what she wanted.

"My grandfather told Benno that each of these were worth a small gold and two large silvers each, but in truth, they are worth two small golds and eight large silvers. Benno had said that Myne could pay for them, but will she still be able to if the price is so much higher?"

"What will you do if she cannot pay?" murmured Jutte in a neutral tone.

Freida smiled. "She will need to join the Othmar Company. Even a large gold in losses would be worth Myne's employment."

Discussing the Devouring with Freida

The feeling of being swallowed by heat and slowly devoured was familiar to me. I focused my mind as much as I could just like last time to try and resist it. *I haven't even made a book yet, come on!*

But despite mimicking what I had done in the past to survive, there was simply too much heat this time. No matter how hard I pushed, it just pushed back harder.

I kept on fighting away, swiping away at the heat with as much courage as I could muster, when suddenly it started getting sucked away in a certain direction. The Devouring heat around me started swooshing away, like a vacuum cleaner was sucking it all up. *Alriiight! Get out of here!*

I was so amused by the shrinking heat that I shooed it away with my hands like a dog, pushing more into the vacuum cleaner, when suddenly I heard a large snap. Immediately the heat stopped leaving me. No matter how hard I pushed, it just bounced back.

...Um? Did I break the vacuum cleaner? Did I maybe do something really bad just now? Oh no. For a moment I reeled in horror within the greatly reduced fog of heat. Naturally, there was nobody to tell me what had happened. I was all alone. But I was also alive and could think about it later.

It felt as if there was about half as much Devouring heat as before. It wasn't too hard to push the diminished heat into me and put a lid on it. I packed it all tight inside of me, like stuffing something into a cardboard box, and pushed it into a closet.

When I was finished, I felt immense relief and noticed my mind slowly rising out of the depths. ...*Where am I?*

When I opened my eyes, I found myself in a world I didn't recognize. First of all, it was dark. I thought for a moment that it was just that the sun had set, but it was only dark around my head. I could see light filtering in by my feet, which helped my vision adjust, and eventually I could see that I was lying in a bed with dark-green curtains hung all around it.

The curtains by my feet were pulled to be half open. Basically, I was in a canopy bed with thick drapes about half a foot or so away from the sides of the bed that were meant to block light and prying eyes. Only a rich person could afford so much cloth for something like this.

...*Oh wait, did I reincarnate as a noble this time?!* The bed itself was of a much higher quality than my old one, too. It wasn't stuffed with straw, it was made of something soft and had a warm sewn sheet on top of it with a warm blanket too. Both felt nice to the touch. Honestly, this bed was just incredibly comfy. In my Urano days I had slept in a spring bed with a down-filled quilt or comfy blanket depending on the season, but a year of poverty had changed my standards completely. In fact, it honestly felt weird that straw wasn't poking me from beneath the sheets and flying out everywhere as I rolled around in bed.

...*Straw beds are warm too. Eventually you get used to fleas and bed bugs biting you. Eventually. But it's been a long time since I've slept in a bed that felt this nice. I want to sleep even more now.*

The bed I slept in with Tuuli was narrow enough that I had to be careful not to roll into her, but this one was wide enough that I could roll around as much as I wanted. I rolled to one side and saw a chair and a small table with an unlit candle beside the bed. There was nothing in this room I recognized.

Or there wasn't at first, until I noticed something. My hands and hair were my own. I grabbed some hair and held in front of my eyes, which allowed me to confirm that I was still Myne. ...*Well, I guess I didn't reincarnate again. There goes my theory about where this place is.*

I searched my memories to try and remember what had happened before I fell unconscious. Which reminded me that Benno had sent a messenger to the guildmaster before I passed out.

"...Aaah, I guess this is the guildmaster's house, then?" I remembered that he had magic tools that could do something about the Devouring heat, and that Benno had made a deal with him, so this was definitely the guildmaster's house. That explained why everything was so fancy.

"Excuse me, is anybody there?" My body was too heavy for me to sit up, but I wanted to get a grasp on my surroundings. Still at the edge of the bed, I reached out and pulled the curtains a bit. They wavered, and a woman who must have heard me passed through them.

"Please wait just a moment." She left it at that and left. Unable to move and still confused, I remained wrapped in the blankets. My body steadily warmed up and my eyes began to droop.

...*Oh no, I'm sleeping again.* As I started drifting off once more, I heard the door open and shut, then heard footsteps coming my way. I snapped back awake, like a seasoned slacker reacting to their teacher's footsteps.

The curtains rustled and Freida entered with a lit candle shining on her light rosy hair. "Have you awoken, Myne? How much do you remember about what happened?" Freida set the candle on the stand and sat on the chair by the bed. I tried to sit up so we could talk, but Freida gently pushed me back down. "The heat must have put an enormous burden on your body. Please, rest."

"Thank you. But I feel like I'll fall asleep mid-sentence if I keep lying down, so…" I got up and sat cross legged as Freida smiled and shook her head, telling me not to push myself. "Ummm, okay, how much do I remember? I remember up until the heat burst out in Benno's store and swallowed me up. There was so much of it I was being overwhelmed, and then it all got sucked away somewhere. Did you do that, Freida?"

The heat had never been sucked away like that before. She had likely used one of those magic tools Benno was talking about to save me, which meant an expensive magic tool had probably been destroyed in the process. I felt the blood drain from my face, and in contrast Freida nodded several times with a warm smile.

"That is mostly correct. I packed as much heat of yours as I could into the old magic tool. It broke due to that, but I imagine it took much of your Devouring heat with it. How do you feel?"

"Great! I feel a lot better. But aren't magic tools really expensive…?" I asked, my face pale.

Freida informed me of the price with an extremely amused smile. "Indeed. The one that just broke was worth two small golds and eight large silvers. Benno said that you would be able to afford that, but I wonder if that's truly the case."

That pretty much confirmed that Benno knew the price of the magic tool when he paid me for extra information on the rinsham. The price he paid would be too much of a coincidence otherwise. … *Wait. Didn't he offer to pay two small golds at first? That wouldn't have been enough. Did he think I would make up for it with paper sales?*

Feeling some degree of unease toward Benno's actions, I looked at Freida and nodded. "…I'll pay."

"So you do have enough, then…? Then you've escaped me once again." Freida opened her eyes wide, then pouted a little with frustration. "If you had been unable to afford it, we would have had you register with the Othmar Company rather than the Gilberta Company. Grandfather told Benno that the magic tool would cost a small gold and two large silvers, so I thought for sure you wouldn't have enough. It seems that Benno thought one step ahead of us."

…Good job, me, for turning down the two small golds! And Benno, the best decision you ever made was raising the price just high enough that it would cover this! The day I join a store that lays traps for me in life-threatening situations is the day my fragile self succumbs to sheer anxiety! I patted my chest in relief and Freida got a serious look in her eyes.

"If I may use an example, that magic merely sucked some water out of an overly full cup. There is still water in the cup, waiting to be refilled, and as you grow older the overall amount of water will increase."

I nodded. Half a year ago it was worse than a year ago. A month ago it was worse than half a year ago. Now it was worse than it was a month ago. The Devouring heat was getting increasingly difficult to manage, and I was only fine now thanks to the magic tool. There was less heat within me now than before, but I knew better than anyone that it would refill and get worse over time.

"The problem is that the bigger the cup gets, the faster the water increases. I can imagine that it will only take a year at best before it is filled up entirely again."

My senses told me that she was telling the truth, likely due to her own past with the Devouring. I nodded and Freida continued on in a flat tone, her expression looking as if she was intentionally cutting out her emotions.

"Therefore, Myne. Think well and choose. Would you rather live and die as a noble's slave, or would you rather live with your family and rot away in a year's time?" I blinked in surprise, not understanding her, and Freida gave a troubled smile. "Magic tools are generally held only by nobles. My grandfather purchased these old, nearly broken ones by fishing through his connections and paying exorbitant sums, but I believe that outside of the ones we own, you won't find any other magic tools for sale."

"Whaaaat?! A worthless, nearly broken magic tool still costs two small golds and eight big silvers?!" I opened my eyes wide in surprise, and Freida slowly tilted her head after blinking several times.

"I believe that is a reasonable price considering it saved your life. A properly working magic tool will run you a price of several large golds. For a commoner with the Devouring to survive, they need to sign a contract agreeing to work for a noble in return for a magic tool, and subsequently work the rest of their life as the noble's slave to pay back the debt," explained Freida as if it were just common sense, implying that she had received the exact same explanation several times in the past.

"…Is that what you did, Freida?"

Freida's expression blossomed into a smile. "Indeed. I have already signed a contract with a noble. Although I am allowed to live at home until my adulthood ceremony, upon coming of age, he will take me as his mistress."

"Bwuuuh?! M-M-M, Mistress?! Do you know what that word means?!" I hadn't expected to hear such a word from such a cute, pretty little girl. My mouth flapped open and closed like a fish, which made Freida look confused herself.

"…Judging by that reaction, you know what a mistress is?" That wasn't a word that most six- or seven-year-olds knew. And under normal circumstances, they would never casually say that they planned to become one themselves.

"The initial discussions involved me becoming the noble's second or third wife, but an official marriage would be quite complicated due to lines of succession and competition between wives. In particular, my family has more money than a laynoble, so an official marriage would likely lead to undue strife according to my grandfather."

"Gaaah?! Guildmaster! What kind of things are you telling this kid?!" I let out a shout and Freida's expression hardened a little.

"Myne, I am saying this for your benefit. Choosing to live means choosing to live in the world of nobility. If you do not maneuver carefully, you will be killed for other reasons even if magic tools save your life. Information is critical for protecting your life. Choosing not to heed these warnings will only put yourself in danger."

"I'm sorry. I am the fool. It's me." As always, my innocent Japanese brain was not equipped to deal with the challenges presented to me. This was an entirely different world from the one where I had lived in relaxed peace. I apologized immediately and Freida forced a smile.

"Do not worry. Our situations are fairly out of the ordinary. My grandfather is the guildmaster of the Merchant's Guild and through his work has connections with many nobles. He was capable of selecting ideal circumstances for me thanks to those seeking favors, help, and so on."

"Ideal circumstances…?" I tilted my head in confusion and Freida beamed a sincere smile, clearly glad that I had asked.

"There is a store waiting for me in the Noble's Quarter. I am not being given just a floor in my master's estate or something of the like, but rather an entire store to call my own. My family will have to fund it all, but I am quite looking forward to doing the business I had given up on with my Devouring." Freida smiled like a blooming flower, eyes shining with excitement for her future.

"...I see. You're not sad that you don't get to marry someone you love?"

"Dear me, Myne. What are you saying? My father would decide upon my master regardless of any other factors. Even if I were given choices, they would be carefully selected choices and I would have no true agency."

Riiight... What's common sense to me isn't common sense here. I forgot that fathers tend to pick marriage candidates here. It all has to do with which families know which families.

"My family is quite satisfied that I will be establishing a base of operations for them in the Noble's Quarter, and although thirty percent of my profit will be going to my master, the store will be physically distant from him to such an extent that I will avoid much hassle that would otherwise pose significant problems. That was the best deal possible."

Although I knew it was standard for this world, seeing Freida speak of her future as a mistress with an excited smile made me feel conflicted.

"My family had leverage with nobles in the form of financial support, but does yours? You might face a future where my position as a mistress is outright enviable. Think hard, think well, and choose a life that you can live without regrets."

Aaah... I understand. I'm sick with the Devouring too. I need a noble's protection just to survive. Freida's telling me to plan ahead for the next time that the Devouring heat becomes too much for me. I'll need to choose whether to become a noble's slave or die with my family.

"Thank you. I'll think hard about what I want to do. I'm glad you told me all this."

"Certainly. I imagine you have no other associates with this knowledge? If you ever have any concerns about your Devouring, feel free to consult me. I believe I might be the only one who will ever truly understand what you're going through."

The Devouring was such a rare disease that few knew about it. It felt nice to finally have someone I could talk to about it.

"Thanks for all your help. I think I need to get home now, though." I could tell the room was getting steadily darker; the sun would likely be setting soon. My family would worry if I didn't get home soon.

I tried to get up since we had finished our conversation, but Freida once again gently pushed me back into bed. "Fret not, you may continue to rest. Your family just saw you during their last visit."

"Last visit? Wait, how long have I been out?" I blinked in surprise at the implication that a day had passed.

Freida put a hand to her cheek and thought for a moment. "You were brought here yesterday at noon, and the sun is about to set today. You must have been quite exhausted, considering how long it took you to awaken even after your fever fell. We decided that you may stay here until the baptism festival the day after tomorrow, regardless of when you wake up."

It seemed that a lot had gone down between Benno, the guildmaster, and my family while I was asleep. Just imagining how my family reacted to hearing about me passing out made my stomach hurt.

"Judging by his attitude today, I imagine that Lutz will be visiting right in the morning tomorrow, perhaps with your family in tow. Close your eyes again and rest for today."

"Thank you, Freida."

"Be sure to make a firm decision before speaking of this with your family. And... if you feel better tomorrow, shall we make the sweets as promised?" Freida stood up and quietly left with the candle, leaving my vision in darkness.

I mulled over what Freida had said and thought hard about my future, but my body desired rest and my eyes started to droop despite the fact I was sitting up. I snuggled into bed beneath the covers and, without resisting the comfy covers for even a second, fell asleep on the spot.

Making Cake with Freida

The next morning, I left the bed for the first time and looked at the room I was using. *Wooow... It's like a hotel.*

The canopy bed was in the corner of a decently sized, simple bedroom with just a table, three chairs, and a fireplace. But the floor had a thick carpet covering it, and there were curtains over the wavy glass window for privacy. The room may have looked simple, but it was clear that a lot of money had been spent on it.

Also, there was a servant girl standing by the chairs near the door. "Good morning. You may wash your face here. I will guide you to the dining room when you are ready."

"O-Okay."

She handed me a clean cloth and showed me where warm water had been prepared for me to wash my face with. The perfect hospitality honestly made me a little nervous.

"Forgive my rudeness, but as your normal clothes would look improper in this home, we have prepared a different outfit for you to wear." She took out an outfit that seemed to be one of Freida's hand-me-downs. My heart raced at the opportunity to wear clean clothing not made of patchwork for the first time in a long time. Then she brushed my hair for me, but I put my hair stick in myself. The servant looked at the stick curiously, but said nothing and promptly finished getting me ready.

By the time we reached the dining room, Freida and the guildmaster were already waiting for me. I first had to thank the guildmaster for all he had done for me. "Thank you very much, guildmaster. I appreciate your kindness and hospitality."

He responded to my gratitude with a nod. Freida briskly walked up to me and touched my forehead, then my neck. Her cold hands sent a chill through my body that made me flinch, but Freida ignored that. "Good morning, Myne. I see that your fever has gone down."

"Morning, Freida. I feel great. Like, so much better than I did before." *Oh, she was checking my temperature.* I thanked her with a smile and she returned a happy one of her own.

We walked to the table together and the guildmaster let out a hmph. "It's good that you're well again, but don't expect us to sell another magic tool. We're saving them for Freida in case something happens to her."

"Grandfather!"

"He's not wrong, Freida. He bought all of them for your sake. I'm just thankful that he let me use even a single one of them." The guildmaster had obtained the tools by using all of his connections and his wealth. I had paid for them, sure, but the fact that I was even given the chance to do so at all was nothing short of a miracle.

"Myne, you would do well to think hard about your future." He gave me a sharp look that felt like it pierced right through me and I nodded with a tiny gulp.

"In any case, we need to report this to your family," said Freida. "Is there anything you want to tell the messenger before we send him?"

The word "messenger" threw me for a loop, but then I realized that of course the guildmaster and Freida wouldn't go to my place themselves. Sending a messenger was normal for them. I turned to face said messenger.

"I want to thank Freida for all her help, so could you tell them to bring some (simple all-in-one shampoo) with them?" We still called the rinsham by its full name at my place, but it wasn't an easy phrase to memorize. The messenger's face kinda scrunched up as he struggled to remember.

"All sinble what...? Erm, forgive me, but could you state that once more?"

"Ummm, it's a hair-cleaning liquid. They should understand you if you just say rinsham. Thank you for doing this."

"Hair-cleaning liquid, rinsham. Understood."

I saw the messenger off after making sure he knew where I lived, then noticed the guildmaster looking at me while stroking his beard. I got the feeling I had seen a similar foreboding smile in the past.

"Freida. Myne certainly owns a lot of interesting things, doesn't she?"

"She does. I'm quite disappointed we missed the opportunity to obtain her knowledge in exchange for the magic tool."

It was scary being surrounded by the two of them in a situation where I had no allies. I felt like a rabbit in a lion pit.

"You know! I think I'll go ahead and pay for the magic tool! With money!" Fearing that they would make up some excuse to raise the price, I immediately tapped my guild card against the guildmaster's and finished paying him.

"He actually paid you that much... Curse you, Benno," murmured the guildmaster in frustration. It seemed that Benno had managed to weave through the guildmaster's web of traps with outstanding guile. *Good job, Benno! You saved me!*

"Eat as much as you like, Myne."

"Absolutely." I couldn't stop smiling if I tried. 'Cause I mean, we were eating white bread for breakfast! White bread, made out of flour! I could put as much honey as I wanted on it too, which was crazy.

After having my fill of the sweet and tasty bread, I went after the soup. It had a nice salty flavor, but it felt like the broth was lacking in vegetable flavor. They were definitely boiling them and then tossing out the water. That destructive practice was thoroughly ingrained in the culture here. But the eggs and bacon tasted great, and they even had fruit for dessert. It was a hearty breakfast fit for Japan and I loved it. Breakfast at the guildmaster's place was great.

I elegantly picked away at my food as the guildmaster looked at me with furrowed brows. "Who taught you those manners, Myne?"

"Nobody? This is just how I eat." I had read several books on manners and experimented in restaurants back in my Urano days, but I hadn't actually studied them anywhere, so I wasn't lying.

The guildmaster's brows furrowed deeper and it was clear on his face that he was doubting me, but I tried not to worry about it and just finished eating. Worrying about it would only hurt me.

The guildmaster left for work after breakfast and soon Freida and I were informed of visitors. My family had apparently dropped by just to see me before going to work themselves.

"Myne! Nguuh?!" Dad started to race toward me, but Mom got in between us and pushed him aside.

"I'm so glad you've woken up, Myne. I thought my heart was going to stop when Lutz told us you collapsed in Benno's store and were taken to Freida's home."

"Sorry for worrying you. Freida used to have the same sickness as me and we needed her help to get me better." I knew for a fact that my mom would pass out herself if I told her that they used a magic tool worth two small golds and eight large silvers on me.

"Miss Freida, thank you very much."

"Mom, did you bring the (simple all-in-one shampoo) to thank her?" That was the only thing I could think of that we could use to pay her back other than money, and since her baptism was tomorrow, now was the perfect time to get her all cleaned up.

"Mhm. Though I'm not sure how much she will appreciate this stuff. Tuuli?"

"Thanks for saving Myne, Freida," said Tuuli as she handed Freida a small jar.

Freida took it with a smile and curtsied by lowering her hips a little. "You're quite welcome. I'm just glad to have helped."

"We're seriously thankful," said Dad. "Lutz said that she was in a pretty bad spot. I don't know how to thank you for saving my daughter. Myne, since you're feeling better already, will you be coming home tonight?" Dad's eyes were pleading with me to come home early. I would have said yes so my family wouldn't have to keep worrying about me, but Freida stood between us with a smile.

"No, Myne will be staying here until my baptism so that we may keep an eye on her in case her condition worsens, as agreed upon yesterday. I would not like for our plans to be changed so suddenly."

"...Alright."

"Thank you for all your help, and sorry for the trouble." Mom did a similar curtsy gesture involving lowering her hips. Wondering if that was this world's equivalent to bowing, I took a step closer to get a better look when all of a sudden Tuuli hugged my head with both arms.

"We have to go to work now, but don't bother these nice people and do all sorts of weird things like you do at home, okay?"

"I know that, Tuuli. I'll come home after the baptism. Good luck at work."

My family left quickly, busy as they were, and Lutz came right after as if he had been waiting for them to leave.

"Heard you finally woke up. How's your fever? Did it really go down?" He touched my head and neck just as Freida had, checking to see how hot I felt. His hands were — almost unbelievably — colder than Freida's.

"Aw, Lutz! Your hands are way too cold!"

"Ah. Sorry."

"Well, don't worry. I'm all better now."

"...For a year at best, right?" Lutz, knowing the circumstances of the magic tools and my Devouring, frowned to show that he wasn't celebrating just yet. But still, I had been in such a tight spot that even a year felt like a huge relief.

"I can use that time to think up a bunch of stuff and search for a solution. I'm going to make a book. Definitely."

"That's all you ever say, Myne. But alright. I'm gonna go tell Benno about this. He was saying yesterday that he might come see you this afternoon."

The moment Benno was brought up, Freida's expression morphed into a solid pout. She had been listening to my conversation with Lutz from behind, but that was the last straw.

"I'm afraid that won't be a good time for us. We'll be busy making sweets at about that time. Isn't that right, Myne?"

I got the feeling that letting Freida and Benno meet right now wouldn't be a good idea. I was the most likely to suffer and I could already imagine myself sitting helplessly between them as sparks flew through the air. It wouldn't be good. "Sorry, Lutz, but could you tell Benno that I'll drop by the store later?"

"Sure, but… what're you making? Something new?" It seemed that Lutz was more interested in our cooking than in Benno.

I laughed and shook my head. "I don't know, we'll have to talk to the chef first."

"Oh my, you won't be deciding yourself, Myne?" said Freida, confused. But I couldn't plan a recipe without knowing what ingredients and tools were available. Not to mention that if the chef was friendly, we could enlist their help to make more difficult things, but if they were not so friendly, we would have to settle for something simple.

"I can't decide on anything without knowing what ingredients and tools they have here."

"Does the same not apply to Lutz?" Freida pursed her lips, not satisfied with my explanation. But Lutz and I lived in similar conditions, eating similar things and using similar tools. It was an entirely different situation from Freida's place.

"I didn't make anything for Lutz. I just told him the recipes." In Lutz's place, his family used their own ingredients and made the food themselves. "Right, Lutz?"

"Yeah. Myne's too small and weak to do any cooking herself."

"We should be done by later afternoon, I'll save some for you if you want to try it out."

"Really?! Heck yeah, count me in!"

Freida, with her competitive spirit burning fiercely at Lutz, glared at the door for a bit after he left and then looked at me unhappily, her cheeks puffing out cutely. "You coddle Lutz too much."

"I don't think so. Really, it's the opposite. He takes care of me way more than he has to," I said, making Freida pout even harder. To be honest, I didn't know why Freida was so unhappy about all this.

I faltered a bit, feeling awkward, and Freida shot a pointed finger in my direction. "Very well then, I will take care of you myself."

"Wha? Why?"

"You are my very best friend, but I am not your best friend. It's infuriating."

Wow... What a cutie. I wanna poke her puffed-out cheeks. Now knowing that Freida's unhappiness was born of jealousy, I couldn't help but giggle a little. "Okay, think about it like this. We can do girl things together that I could never do with Lutz. Would that cheer you up?"

"Girl things?" Freida tilted her head in confusion. Her main hobby was counting and earning money. Trying to play with dolls together would probably just lead to a discussion about profit margins on toys or the like. That would be fun in its own way, but we didn't have that much time to play together.

"We could bathe together, wash each other's hair, roll around in bed and talk, all sorts of girl things. I couldn't do any of that with Lutz, right?"

"My, how wonderful. Shall we go to the chef, then, so we can first discuss what sweets we will make?" Freida took my hand and guided me to the kitchen. Standing there was a plump-looking woman, who had seemingly just finished cleaning up after making breakfast. She seemed to be about as old as my mother and resembled Lutz's mom, Karla.

"Leise, Leise. About the sweets today..."

"Yes, yes. You're going to make some with your friend, right? You've already mentioned it more times than I can count."

"May I ask what ingredients we have to work with here?" I asked, making Leise raise an eyebrow.

"Ingredients? Just what're you planning on using?"

"Ummm, flour, butter, sugar, and eggs. We don't have any sugar in my home, so we usually use jam or honey as a substitute, but maybe you have some here?" The kinds of sweets one could make varied heavily based on available ingredients and tools. There was a good reason why I mainly just made pancakes and french toast variants at Lutz's place.

"We've got sugar."

"Really?! Wow! U-Um, also, do you have an oven?"

"Yup. Can't you see it?" Leise shifted a bit and a large firewood oven came into view. My heart bloomed with growing anticipation.

I looked up at Leise, squeezing my hands tightly in front of my chest. "That means you have pans for cooking in an oven too, right? Do you have scales?"

"'Course we do." Leise shrugged as if telling me not to ask questions with obvious answers and I honestly wanted to jump for joy.

"Yes! That means we can probably bake a (cake)!" Recipe after recipe for sweets came to mind. There were more than a few recipes I had memorized down to the exact measurements.

...*Wait. I know the recipes, but I don't think people around here measure weight in grams. What should I do?* I had forgotten this crucial fact in my excitement, but ingredients and tools weren't enough to make sweets. You needed to measure the ingredients down to the wire.

I had made the parue cakes in Lutz's place like normal pancakes, going by instinct and thus getting pancakes of different size and thickness each time. That was fine since the boys just wanted quantity, not quality, but real baking needed precise and accurate measurements. Freida was letting me use an entire firewood oven here, I couldn't let myself fail. Trial and error was out of the question.

Mmm… Is there anything I could make that doesn't need precise measurements? I tried thinking of sweets I could make without knowing any units of measurement, and soon remembered something that I had read about in a book on French confectioneries.

"Ummm, I'm going to make (pound cake)." Pound cake in French was *quatre-quarts*, which meant four quarters. It was a cake made using four ingredients of the same amount: flour, eggs, butter, and sugar. I could make pound cake without any precise measurements as long as I had a scale to weigh each ingredient.

"I've never heard of that. What kinda food is it?"

"It's a sweet made from mixing together an equal amount of flour, eggs, butter, and sugar."

"You're actually gonna make something like that?" Leise's eyes widened in surprise, so much that I faltered and backpedaled immediately.

"…Well, I don't have to if it's not okay."

"It's fine, but are you sure you know what you're talking about here?"

"Yes."

We set up a time for our sweet-making and Leise started preparing the oven, so we left the kitchen and started hunting for aprons to wear while cooking. Freida had never helped with the chores before and thus had never worn an apron. Eventually a maid found two for us and we put them on, wearing large handkerchiefs folded on our heads to hold back our hair. We were ready to go.

Once it was time to cook, we returned to the kitchen. Upon seeing us, Leise burst into surprised laughter. "Goodness, young miss. Looks like you're pretty enthusiastic about this."

"Indeed. I will be doing the cooking myself this time."

Naturally, they didn't have a cake pan, so I decided to use a small circular metal pot instead.

"Okay, how about you share this recipe of yours with me now? I won't know how to make it unless you go through the steps."

"Okay. First, we measure the ingredients and heat the eggs and sugar until they're as warm as our body temperature."

"And how are we gonna do that?"

"Um, I was planning on filling a larger bowl with hot water and putting the pan in it."

"Ah, water-heating. Alright then, we should heat the water before measuring the ingredients, then." In a world without gas stoves and such, hot water couldn't be made so quickly. That was obvious, but since I had never made sweets in this world before, it was hard for me to notice ahead of time.

"The most important thing is that the sugar and eggs are mixed together thoroughly to the point of foaming a bit. Once that's happening, put in the flour and mix it all together with a chopping motion. Then, put in melted butter and stir gently so as to not break the foam."

"Melt the butter, alright. We start baking once it's all mixed together?"

"That's right."

Leise, having gotten a grasp on the recipe, took out a scale and put it on top of the counter. The next step was measuring the lined-up ingredients. She taught me how to use the scale while Freida and I tried to balance the ingredients on them, then she started heating the water in the meantime.

We measured the eggs and sugar first, then Leise mixed them together with fervor as the water beneath heated it all up. The foaminess of the mixture would change the size and flavor of the cake for the better. Meanwhile, Freida and I measured the butter.

"Once everything's measured, we put butter on the sides of the pan so the cake will be easier to take out." We smeared butter in the pot and I decided to sprinkle some flour on top as well. Without cooking paper, this was our next best option.

"Let's sprinkle flour on it next. It'll be more fluffy if we let lots of air inside." Making sure not to get it all over the counter, Freida and I sifted the flour. In the end, I gave it three sifting passes.

"My my. The eggs used to be yellow but now they're getting white, and bigger too." Freida enviously watched Leise beating the eggs.

It was clear she wanted to try beating them herself, so Leise gestured to the bowl and mixer with a grin. "Want to try, young miss?"

"Oooh?!" Freida immediately began beating them with happy enthusiasm, but got tired out and gave up before long. It took a lot of strength to hand-mix cake ingredients. It was too heavy a burden for us Devouring girls.

"Myne, is this about right?"

"It is! Now we can add the flour." I prepared the bowl by sprinkling in a layer of flour, then poured in the rest while using a wooden spatula to separate chunks and mix everything together. "You just keep mixing it like this. We'll put the butter in next. Has it melted yet?"

"Yup, I put it next to the hearth while the water was heating up."

"Leise, please take over here. My arms are at their limit."

"Good grief. Neither of you girls got any strength to ya." Leise took my place with a grin. She put in the butter and got back to mixing.

Freida brought over the pot we were using as a cake pan and watched us finish the mixture, eyes gleaming.

"Once we pour the mixture into the pot, we need to pick it up and kind of drop it to push out the extra air. We don't want too much."

The pot was heavy enough that I left all that to Leise. She picked it up without hesitation, clearly having never expected for a moment that we would be able to do it ourselves.

"Now we just have to bake it in the oven and we're done."

I didn't know how to use wood ovens, so it would be best to leave this step to Leise. She set the pot into the hot, crackling oven and shut it tightly. "It should finish baking while we're cleaning up," Leise said.

While helping Leise clean up in such a clumsy and ineffectual fashion it could hardly be considered helping, a nice sweet scent began drifting through the air. It was so cute how Freida was wiggling eagerly in front of the oven, asking whether or not it was ready yet.

"Not yet," I answered, feeling nervous myself about whether or not we had succeeded. We had used a lot of valuable ingredients to make this pound cake, and on top of that, it was the first time Freida and I had made sweets together. Failure just wasn't an option for me.

"...I think I'll check on it." Leise opened the oven and peered inside. The cake had risen nicely. However, the backside of it seemed darker than the front.

"Leise, it looks like the back half of the cake is cooking more. Could you turn it around for me?"

Leise spun the cake around and pushed the pot back in. Personally, I wouldn't stick my hand into that hot oven even with the thick mitten-esque gloves she had. I was moved by the skill and courage it took to be a professional chef.

After shutting the oven tightly again, Leise looked down at me. "How do you tell when it's done?"

"You can stick a thin, pointy stick made of something like bamboo to check. Do you have something like that?"

"Mmm, yeah, but they're for skewering meat." She rummaged through a shelf and produced two long iron skewers, like the kind you would use to stick through meat and vegetables together at a barbeque.

I had never used a skewer to check if a cake was done before, so I honestly didn't know how well it would work. *That'll poke a big hole in the cake, but um, I guess we don't have much of a choice here. I used chopsticks to check once in my Urano days, so it should be fine.*

Leise stuck a skewer in and then pulled it out, revealing some wet dough stuck to it.

"Looks like it's not cooked on the inside yet."

"How can you tell?"

"There's a little dough stuck to it, right? It'll be done cooking once the skewer comes out clean."

The top of the cake was kinda turning dark brown by the time the inside was cooked, which meant the oven was probably too hot. But unlike the ovens I was used to, it wasn't that easy to control the heat. I would have to rely entirely on the experience and instinct of those trained in these matters.

"I think I'll be more careful with the oven next time," murmured Leise as she took the pound cake out of it. Once the pot was outside, I could see a fluffy well-cooked cake inside that looked just like a castella.

"Simply amazing!"

"Yup, it sure looks good."

The two of them both looked at the finished cake with shining eyes, and I felt an indescribable sense of satisfaction welling up in my chest.

"These usually taste better if you wrap them in tightly wrung, damp cloth and leave them out for two or three days, but we should be fine taste-testing this one first."

Leise chopped the cake into fine slices. I grabbed a piece and tossed it in my mouth. The nice thing about taste-testing as a chef was that you got to eat a little before everyone got attracted by the smell.

"Mhm, this is exactly what I was going for."

Once I was done, Leise — who was very used to taste-testing things — did the same herself. Freida had been hesitating to put a bit of the cake into her mouth, but after seeing Leise eat some, she hurriedly threw it in.

"Goodness!"

Two pairs of eyes widened in surprise and Freida and Leise spun around to look at me simultaneously. They had a predatory look to them that reminded me of the guildmaster this morning, and I got the feeling that I might have put myself into real danger. It would probably be smart to flee before they asked me any weird questions.

I grabbed Freida's hand. "Freida, let's eat this at teatime, or after a meal. Now's a good time to take a bath." We hadn't really done much in the way of helping her bake, but due to us sifting flour, our sleeves were fairly dirty. We had plenty of time, and the sooner I cleaned her up with rinsham the better. So with all that said, we left the kitchen.

But I stopped in the door and turned around, not wanting to forget to thank the chef. "Thank you for your help, Leise."

Taking a Bath with Freida

When I left the kitchen with Freida's hand in mine, the maid from before was waiting outside. "Please take a bath before wandering all over the place, if you would."

"My my, it seems Myne and Jutte think alike," giggled Freida as she walked on.

Jutte had already prepared hot water for us, having predicted that we would get dirty while baking sweets. She held a box containing a change of clothes, towels, and the jar of rinsham as she guided us to the bath. "Please follow me."

My eyes widened as I saw Jutte walking down the stairs. Benno's office had a staircase leading up, so the fact that there were stairs dotting her home leading down to the store wasn't surprising at all. But would it be okay for me to go down there myself? I stealthily asked Freida for confirmation. "...Won't these stairs take us down to the store?"

"Don't worry."

Jutte passed by the first floor door leading to the store and kept going down. Upon reaching the basement, we found two doors. One was a finely crafted, decorated door and one was a normal door. Jutte opened the decorated door and we went inside.

It led to a room with floors so warm that I questioned whether or not it had heaters beneath them. There were two large wooden benches with cloth spread on top of them. They looked like massage benches.

"Now then, please take off your shoes and clothes."

It seemed that the room was a massage parlor slash changing room. At Jutte's urging, I took off my clothes. Freida took off her clothes as well with Jutte's help.

We then passed through another door, which led to a decently sized bathtub. It was about the size of a single family onsen in Japan, and two to three adults could fit inside with stretched legs.

"Bwuuuh?! What is this?!" I hadn't expected to see such a fancy bathtub and reflexively let out a cry of shock, which echoed throughout the room.

The floor was made of white marble and the tub, made of similar material, was wafting with steam. At the tip of the tub was a statue of a girl holding a jar, and hot water was flowing out of it. Water overflowed from the tub at the same speed as new water was poured in, so the water stayed warm. The ceiling was tiled and a window, positioned at the top of the wall, let sunlight inside. That light reflected off the white marble and gave the room a bright atmosphere.

I froze in the doorway in shock, which made Freida laugh in amusement and pass by my side to get into the tub. "Ahaha, surprised? My grandfather recreated the design of a bathing room he saw in a noble's villa. I do not normally use it, but as my baptism is tomorrow, he gave me special permission."

"There are actual bathtubs here..." I had not entered a bathtub in over a year, and now one stood before me. And it was larger and more decorated than my old Earth bathtub.

"The design came from another country. And it seems to be popular among nobles for their health and beauty." Jutte entered the room with her clothes still on. Her apron, made of a harder material made to absorb water, was useful for wrapping around her skirt and keeping it up. And so she did, wrapping her skirt up so that it wouldn't get wet.

Jutte was clearly about to start washing Freida, so I hurriedly took out the rinsham. "Jutte, please use this when cleaning her. You kind of like, shake it a bit, and…" I explained how to use the rinsham, but Jutte just looked down at Freida with a troubled expression.

"Jutte, I think it will be fine for Myne to wash my hair today."

"A-Are you sure you're fine with that?"

Jutte moved aside, so I started cleaning Freida's hair. Meanwhile Jutte rubbed soap onto a towel and began cleaning Freida's body.

"When you have a lot of hot water like this, you can put it on your hands and rub it into your hair directly. Rub your fingers against your scalp, carefully so your nails don't scratch anything."

"That tickles, but feels quite nice."

I could imagine that Jutte kept Freida well groomed. Her hair was smooth and a little silky to begin with. Perhaps this rinsham was wasted on her. It might be the case that nobles are already so concerned with cleanliness that rinsham won't sell that well. *I might need to report this to Benno,* I thought while cleaning Freida's hair.

"Once you've cleaned all of it, you rinse your hair. Do so thoroughly to get all the rinsham off your scalp," I explained, after which Jutte washed the bubbles off Freida's body with a bucket. With her body now clean, Freida walked to the tub and entered it with a splash. I waited to see what she would do, and soon she rested her head on the edge of the tub with her hair hanging off the edge. Jutte took her hair and carefully rinsed it.

...Oho, so that's how she does it. I'm glad I didn't offer to rinse it and then dump a bucket of water on her head. That would have been bad.

Jutte finished washing Freida's hair while I was still processing what she was doing. It was nice to be somewhere with easy access to hot water.

Freida was done being cleaned, so I reached out for the rinsham to wash my own hair. Freida left the tub with her eyes shining and walked over. "I would like to try washing your hair as well, Myne."

Um... Should a rich girl really be doing that kind of thing with a commoner? I glanced at Jutte to see her reaction. She let out a quiet sigh and sat next to me too.

"Very well, my lady. We can clean her together. I would like to get practice using this rinsham as well."

She says practice, but I bet she means that she wants to be there to guide Freida along before she makes any mistakes. I owe you my life, Jutte.

Small and large fingers rubbed my head as they washed my hair together. It felt ticklish, but I couldn't let myself laugh. I held it all in.

"Your hair is so nice and straight, Myne."

"It's kinda annoying since it's hard to wrap up with a string. That's why I use a hair stick."

"It is quite odd to see hair wrapped up in a stick, now that you mention it."

"Well, it was my last resort. I just didn't have anything else I could do."

Once my hair was fairly clean, Jutte left the rest to Freida and started washing my body. I couldn't escape since Freida was still there, so I just sat still and let her clean me.

"And now you're clean, Myne." Freida, sounding satisfied, let go of my hair after giving it all a good rub. But before I could grab the bucket, Jutte quickly picked it up.

"Now then, please enter the tub so I can rinse your hair."

"I-I can do that myself."

"You are our guest. Allow me."

Beaten down by her unwavering smile, I got into the tub and rested my head on its edge just as Freida had done. My hair hung down and Jutte delicately rinsed it for me. Her gentle hands and the warm water touched my scalp. I could imagine that Jutte always helped Freida bathe. She was experienced and skilled, so much so that I nearly fell asleep. *Aaah… This is like a spa. Feels so good.*

"Hm, Myne. How do you wash your hair without a bathing room?" asked Freida, snapping me back to reality.

This isn't a spa. I can't fall asleep. I searched for where Freida's voice had come from and saw that she had gotten into the tub as well and scooted next to me, with her head in a similar position. I looked at the steam drifting up to the decorated ceiling tiles and explained how I usually washed my hair.

"I usually fill a bucket about as half as big as yours and mix the rinsham into it. I then dunk my hair into the bucket and rub it while it soaks. Once that's done, I wipe it with a cloth several times to get the liquid out before brushing my hair."

The rinsham needed to be diluted enough that some staying in my hair wouldn't be a problem, and I needed to wipe it with a towel a bunch to get as much of it off as possible. That was the only way to survive in an environment without a bunch of hot water. My life would be so much easier with a bathing room like this.

"Do you own this rinsham, Myne?"

"No, I sold all the rights to Benno. He should be putting it on the market soon."

"I see…" Freida looked like she wanted to say something, but before she could, Jutte finished rinsing my hair.

"Was that enough?"

"Yes, thank you. It felt great." I sat up to say my thanks and Jutte stood up.

"Then I will be taking my leave to prepare for later. Enjoy your bath, you two."

After watching Jutte leave the bathing room, I sunk down into the water all the way to my shoulders. I splashed some hot water on my face and let out a deep sigh. *Fwaah. This is heaven, just heaven.*

"Goodness, Myne, look at that smile. Do you like the bath that much?"

"Of course! I would take a bath here every day if I could. Just having enough hot water to dip into like this is like a dream to me." I nodded hard with a big smile, but Freida didn't seem like she was that happy. "…Do you not like this bathtub, Freida?"

"I don't dislike it, but it's so hot, and my head always spins once I'm done."

"Oooh. You're overheating. You should leave the tub sooner," I answered on reflex and Freida blinked in surprise.

"But I'm just staying in as long as I do with the normal tub."

"The water in normal tubs get cold really fast, but that statue is pouring new hot water in here constantly, so you'll overheat and feel bad if you stay in just as long. Why don't you try leaving sooner this time?"

"I think I will."

Freida and I left the bathtub fairly early. Or at least, it was early from my perspective, but it looked like Freida had warmed up pretty thoroughly. Her whole body was flushed pink.

"Do you feel okay? Is your heading spinning?"

"I'm fine this time."

Jutte offered to give us massages with scented oil once we were done, but I declined. It sounded interesting, but in my case, I wouldn't have a bathtub to enter afterwards. I had no idea whether Tuuli would be able to wipe it all off me once I got home.

I put on my clothes, brushed my hair, and watched Freida getting a massage. "I can't believe you get massages, too. That's so fancy."

"I don't like them much myself, but my grandfather said I will need to be used to them once I join noble society."

Ah, okay. Freida doesn't like the baths or the massages much, but she does them anyway as practice for when she needs to join noble society. Her life will go very differently depending on whether or not she's used to these things when the time comes.

"...That's fair. You should get used to them since you have the opportunity. Practice and experience will make a big difference in the long run."

"That is why our home has much copied from the villas of nobles."

I had wondered why Corinna's home differed so much from this one, but now I see that it wasn't just the result of the guildmaster being more wealthy. The food, bathing room, furniture, and so on were all a level above in price so that Freida could get used to living the life of a noble.

"He sure loves you a lot, huh?"

"…He's investing for the future. My grandfather is doing much to ensure that my store in the Noble's Quarter runs smoothly and that his efforts up to this point do not end up wasted." Freida pursed her lips, looking a little unhappy. She was probably right, but it was hard for me to say he would have done what he did without love.

"Your dream is to own a store, isn't it? He's supporting your dreams. And when he ordered your hairpins, he looked just like a grandfather who would give the world for his granddaughter."

"Did he?"

Hm… I wonder if Freida's lonely? She couldn't go outside much due to her Devouring, and getting cured meant being bound by a contract with a noble. With her future sealed as a noble's mistress, she had to live in preparation for living in an environment not suited for making friends. She needed the strength and calculating intellect to survive in noble society and she needed to learn everything it took to run a store before reaching adulthood. There was no doubt that she spent each day immersed in studies.

It wasn't in the cards for her to live for her own sake. Her life, future, and the expectations of her family were all no doubt putting immense pressure on her young shoulders. Not to mention that despite the money they were spending on her, Freida's family was expecting a return on their investment in the future, so she couldn't exactly rely on them too much.

…Maybe that's why she's clinging to me so much? We both had the Devouring, were dipping our toes into trade before our baptisms, and according to Lutz, we even were similar about going crazy for our hobbies. There was no mistaking that we were more similar than your average pair of kids. Perhaps all that is making her want me to become a part of her life.

"Amazing, Myne! My hair's so silky now!" I'd drifted off into thought until the massage finished, and Freida, now with her clothes back on, ran a hand through her hair and let out a cry of excited surprise.

Jutte looked happy too as she brushed Freida's hair. "Indeed, it turned out quite nicely."

"I'm glad you both like it. I hope it was a good enough thank you present for the magic tool."

"Dear me, Myne, you paid for that tool. Far be it from me to accept a present on top of that."

I smiled at Freida's very merchant-like reply and shook my head. "I thanked you because I wanted to. If the guildmaster hadn't gathered those magic tools for you, I wouldn't have been able to buy one with the money I had."

With our leisurely bath over, we returned upstairs and smelled something nice in the kitchen. It seemed that Leise was giving the pound cake recipe a round two. "This is one recipe I don't want to forget, y'see," she said.

I smiled at Leise's confident smile. I would love if that recipe caught on and cake became more commonplace, so she had my support. Freida looked pretty excited to see a second pound cake.

"Since you're making a new one, can we eat the one we've already made? I would like to enjoy some tea with Myne."

"Sure, I'll take it right out."

Lutz arrived just as we were preparing tea in the dining room. "Heya, Myne. Sure smells nice in here."

I laughed to myself, imagining that Lutz had come all this way after smelling the cake, but he narrowed his eyes and peered at me.

"Myne. You been pushing yourself today? Don't go too far just 'cause your fever went down. Get in bed soon. You'll get sick from exhaustion."

"Bwuh? Huh? What? I'm feeling fine." I patted my face in confusion and Lutz shook his head, brows furrowed.

"You're just so excited you don't notice. You're not doing great."

"My my, but we just absorbed her Devouring heat with a magic tool and all we've done today is make sweets and take a bath," Freida listed what we had done today in my defense.

"…Alright, I see. You're a healthy person who got stuck with the Devouring. But Myne? She's sickly even without the Devouring. She passes out so much it's hard for most people to tell whether she's passing out from the Devouring or from exhaustion," said Lutz, sighing and rubbing his temples.

Freida and I reflexively looked at each other.

"Is that true, Myne?!"

"You're not sickly, Freida?!"

It seemed that we both assumed too much about the other. Freida thought I would be fine if just my Devouring was cured, and I thought that Freida was just as sickly as me, so doing what she did would be fine for my health.

"I dunno what you mean by taking a bath, but I'm guessing since this is a new place you've been trying to see and do everything."

"Ngh… I haven't done that much." Under normal circumstances I was always gripped by anxiety about my health, and it was true that I had been avoiding thinking about it by using Freida as an excuse.

"I can see on your face that you've done too much. Don't forget how weak you are. 'Cause I mean seriously, you can't get much weaker."

"Do you have to keep calling me weak like that? It's kinda mean."

"It's the truth. And think about it, aren't you going home tomorrow? Do you know how mad your family will be if you get another fever here?"

If I got sick in the guildmaster's home after playing around too much, I would be throwing dirt in the face of their kindness. Dad's excitement would get stomped on, Mom would yell at me for being such a burden on Freida's family, and Tuuli would shake her head in disappointment, asking why I couldn't sit still for just one day.

"Oh noooooooo…"

"I see your point. I cannot allow her to fall into ill health again under my care. Myne, please rest for the rest of today. Okay?" said Freida with worry in her voice.

I answered with a nod. "Okay. Thanks for warning me, Lutz. And… Freida, sorry, but could you share some of the (pound cake) with Lutz?"

"Yes, of course. Jutte, please take Myne to her room."

Once I entered the guest room and got in bed, I immediately felt just how exhausted I was. My whole body felt heavy and way hotter than could be explained away by the bath. It was the first time I had ever cooked under intense pressure and taken a consistently warm bath in this body, so I hadn't understood my limits. …*I'm impressed Lutz noticed just like that. I should expect nothing less from him.*

By the time the soft blanket had warmed up from my body heat, I had already fallen into a deep sleep.

Freida's Baptism

I woke up to quite a stir outside my room. A maid other than Jutte was sitting in the chair by the door, waiting for me to wake up. She was fairly young, probably not even twenty years old, and seemed friendly. I climbed off the bed and pulled aside the surprisingly heavy curtains to get out. She smiled as she saw me push through.

"Good morning," the maid greeted me. "How are you feeling today?"

"I'm not sick, but I don't feel great either. So I'll be quiet today until my family comes to get me."

She let out a quiet laugh. "Dinner last night was quite something. Everyone was talking about the dessert you and Mistress Freida made. The entire family wishes to meet you now, Myne. They are all quite determined to get you working here at our store."

Ahahaha, um. That's pretty bad. Did I narrowly escape a terrible fate thanks to sleeping early? Should I maybe not take a single step out of this room? Even this maid just added that my future would be safer if I joined their store... She's one of them. I can't trust anybody. Nowhere's safe!

"Um, it sounds like there's a lot going outside the door..." I looked at the door to change the subject and the maid's smile broadened.

"With breakfast over, the young lady is being prepared for her baptism. I will guide you to the kitchen once she is finished changing."

To be honest I was pretty hungry since I hadn't had any dinner last night, but my stomach hurt just thinking about eating with Freida's presumably overbearing family around. I'd lost my appetite for just about anything.

"Um, could my food be brought to this room? I don't need much since I'm not feeling well, and eating around so many new people would make me really nervous. I'd probably have trouble eating anything like that."

"Ahaha, that's fine. I'll be right back with it." After changing me into a pair of Freida's old clothes, the maid left the room. I crouched to the floor and cradled my head the second I was alone.

...This is bad. Who could have seen this coming? I knew that the guildmaster and Freida had their eyes on me, sure. But what's this about their whole family being after me now? All because of some pound cake? They have a whole lot of sugar, so that must mean that they make tons of sweets. Or maybe — and I don't even want to consider this possible — but maybe sugar is a new product that just entered the market and sweets in general haven't been developed in the culinary world yet? That can't be what's happening here, no way.

I heard the maid returning with food as I agonized on my knees. I immediately stood up and put on a poker face as she entered the room.

"Please enjoy your meal."

They must have remembered what kind of food I liked, as breakfast was once again white bread with honey and jam on the side, plus sweet fruit juice. There wasn't as much soup as last time, since I didn't like it that much, but there was plenty of bacon and eggs. My weak points had been sniffed out in no time.

Once I finished breakfast, I decided it would be safest for me to stay holed up in my room until my family came, using my ill health as a shield. The guildmaster and Freida alone were threatening enough; I couldn't deal with their whole family all at once on my own. If I could, I would have summoned Benno and Lutz to my side for help.

I was eating breakfast slowly, thinking up a plan for the rest of the day, when Jutte suddenly rushed into my room.

"Good morning, Myne. How are you feeling?" said Jutte, her tone sounding far too on-edge for someone merely asking a simple question. She seemed like the kind of person to only say what she found necessary, so I answered her question up front, having nearly dropped my bread in surprise.

"Not great, but I don't have a fever."

"Could you help us prepare Freida for her baptism? I do not know how to put on the hairpins."

I had made the hairpins, so one could consider it customer service to explain how to put them on. *That should be simple enough that I won't draw any more unwanted attention.*

I finished my breakfast relatively quickly then followed Jutte to Freida's room. Hers was on the third floor. According to Jutte, the guildmaster's generation lived on the second floor, and their children plus grandchildren lived on the third floor. But the floors were connected by a central staircase and they all ate meals together, so it didn't feel particularly like living apart.

"Mistress Freida, I have brought Myne."

Freida's room had a partition by the door. Going around the partition revealed a room similar to the guest room with a canopied bed in the corner, only with what looked like a writing desk on the opposite end of the room. There was also a small table in the center of the room with several chairs around it. The curtains and canopy were red and pink, fitting for a girl, but it was otherwise a simple room lacking any dolls or toys.

There were several brushes and hairpins lined up on the table and Freida was sitting in a chair, getting her hair brushed. She looked like a life-sized doll as the brush went delicately through her flowing, lush pink hair.

"Good morning, Myne. Feeling better?"

"Morning, Freida. I don't have a fever, but I'm not doing great either." I stated my health in clear terms so that she wouldn't ask too much of me.

Her expression clouded a little and she lowered her eyes. "I see. Sorry for calling you, then. I assumed that since you had made your elder sister's hairpin, you were also the one that did her hair."

"That's right, I did."

"Could you do my hair the same way?"

I had braided Tuuli's hair half-up from both sides leading inwards. That wouldn't look bad on Freida, but that would kinda be a waste of her two hairpins, and I thought she looked cute with twintails anyway.

"Mmm, since you have two hairpins, I don't think the exact same hairstyle would be best here. I'll make you two braids. Does that sound okay?"

"I would appreciate it if you taught me how to braid like that as well," added Jutte with sparkling eyes.

We split Freida's hair into halves and I explained what I was doing while braiding the hair next to her right ear. "You slide this under here, combine it here, and twist like this."

Jutte watched from the left and began braiding as well. As expected, she did pretty well. My hands were small and while I wasn't clumsy with them, it was hard to stop hair from spilling out. Tuuli's hair was naturally a bit wavy so somewhat sloppy braids didn't stick out much, and even looked a little fancy on her, but with Freida's hair they would stand out in a bad way.

"I think it'll be for the best if you do both sides once you learn how to do this, Jutte. My hands are just too small to work with hair well."

"I imagine it is quite difficult to work with hands as small as yours. Very well, I will braid the rest of her hair."

With the technique now memorized, Jutte smoothly braided Freida's hair. I could tell she was used to touching Freida's hair since she didn't let any slip out of her hands. And since it was so well brushed, the braids were tight and not loose like the ones I had given Tuuli.

...Aww. It hurts to see my own incompetence thrown in my face like this.

"I would have liked more time to practice this technique, but..." murmured Jutte in frustration, looking at Freida's braided hair. I opened my eyes wide, surprised to see Jutte openly voicing her emotions.

Freida gave a troubled smile. "It seemed that Jutte had planned to consult you about this last night and practice all evening."

"Aaah, but I went to bed early... Sorry." I apologized for having once again burdened another with my weakness, but Jutte just shook her head.

"You have nothing to apologize for. Your ill health is no fault of your own. I merely regret that had I asked earlier, I could have dressed the mistress up even more today."

...I see. Jutte's hobby is dressing Freida up. She is cute like a life-sized doll, after all. I understand. Even I put extra effort into her hairpins, so.

Once she finished braiding above Freida's ears, Jutte inserted the hairpins past the strings she wove into the braids. Since each hairpin had four dark-red mini roses, you could see at least one from any angle. The white flowers went well with her light-pink hair and emphasized the roses further. The green leaves here and there added a nice accent too.

"Yep, these are even better than I expected! They're perfect for you, Freida."

"You look exceptionally cute, my lady."

As the other maids who had been helping Freida get ready praised how she looked, Jutte brought her today's outfit. Freida stood up and a maid pulled the chair back. She immediately held her arms out for the maids to put on her clothes, so I hurriedly fled the proximity.

When Freida lifted one arm, an open sleeve was slid over it, and when she lifted the other arm, the other sleeve was likewise slid over it. Several maids at once fastened buttons, tightened strings, and dressed Freida up as she stood in place. I let out a sigh as I saw what looked like a princess changing scene from a movie happen before my eyes. *...This definitely takes years of practice to get right. If it were me, I'd lower my arms at the wrong time and hit someone beneath me.*

"Myne, if you would be so kind, could you watch the baptism procession from this room's window? It just so happens that this window shows much of the outside, to give me a better view."

The guest bedroom I was in had wavy glass, but Freida's room had straight glass suited for looking outside. It would be accurate to say that Freida's room was like VIP seating for watching the baptism procession enter the temple.

"You don't mind?" I looked between Freida and the window. She smiled.

"Of course not. If you're afraid to be in here alone, Jutte can watch with you."

"I find that idea quite splendid," said Jutte, a bright smile on her face. She probably wanted to see Freida fully dressed up in the crowd more than anyone, even if it had to be watching long-distance from a window. And if Freida assigned her to me, she would be justified in doing so.

I would have felt awkward staying in someone's room when they weren't present, so I jumped at the idea. "Jutte staying with me would be really nice."

By the time we settled on that, they had finished putting her shoes on. The maids crouching by Freida's feet stood up in unison and each took a single step back.

Freida, completely dressed up, spun in place. Her white outfit had warm-looking fur around the neck and it was embroidered with bright red and pink colors. It suited both her hair and her hairpins.

"Does anything look strange on me?"

"Not at all, you look adorable."

"Wow, just wow! Freida, that looks so good on you."

"My lady, I have brought your family to see you." As we praised her outfit, Freida's family was informed that she was ready and came to see her. The guildmaster was the first to walk past the partition.

"Goodness gracious, you look splendid, Freida! Such magnificent bundles of flowers are so rare for this winter season that you resemble the spring-bearing Goddess of Sprouts. Truly adorable."

"The hairpins you bought look wonderful on me, do they not?" Freida smiled with a finger on one of her hairpins.

The guildmaster practically broke down where he stood. "Yes, they quite do. Your happy smile is worth all the money in the world."

Freida's family began entering her room one after the other, almost as if they had been waiting for the guildmaster to finish praising her first.

"Wow, Freida. Those look really good on you."

"You're cuter than any girl I know."

Two younger boys, both probably around ten years old with one a bit older than the other, both heaped on piles of praise onto her.

Wait... I thought Freida wasn't used to being complimented. What am I missing here? I tilted my head in confusion and Freida looked up, wearing an expression that made it clear she didn't appreciate what they'd said.

"...Dear brothers, why are you here?"

"What do you mean, why? It's Earthday and we promised to celebrate with you."

"You did, but neither of you have ever made good on a promise, and I had not expected today to be any different."

Ooof, her older brothers break promises with her all the time? Okay, that's fair. I would have a hard time believing anything they said too if they broke promises all the time like that.

The brothers, noticing Freida's lack of faith in them, paled and started making excuses. A relaxed-looking couple was looking down at the kids, and they noticed Freida's hairpins.

"Huh. Those are some nice hairpins."

"Indeed, I would like one for myself. How splendid they are."

I watched the chaotic family in a daze, awed at the sight of them focusing entirely on themselves and ignoring others, when suddenly the guildmaster crouched right in front of me.

"Oooh, Myne!"

Crap…! I forgot I was hiding in my room to avoid meeting these people! Gaaah! I let out a tiny squeak and took a step back, but the guildmaster nonetheless clasped my hands and began speaking with emotional tears forming in his eyes.

"You have done me a great favor. I thank you, Myne. I have never seen Freida this happy over anything I have ever given her. You were correct, a happy expression is infinitely more valuable than a surprised one."

"I-I'm just glad she likes it." *Gyaaaaah! Save me, Bennooooo!*

"It is rare for me to meet one who understands these finer matters. I will consult you before giving Freida gifts from now on. In particular, Myne, I would like to ask you about… ngh?!" The guildmaster was pulled back with a grunt. For a second I was relieved to be free, but that relief lasted only a moment. Several over people rushed to take the guildmaster's place.

"So you're Myne, huh? My Dad and Freida have told me all about you."

"Um, yes…" I started to properly introduce myself to Freida's father, but within the span of a blink, her mother was right in front of me.

"Thank you for spending time with Freida. She's been smiling a lot more than usual lately. As her mother, I would like to express my gratitude."

"Sh-She's been a very good friend to me, so I…"

Before I could even finish my sentence, the two brothers pushed their faces up close to mine. *Please! At least give me enough time to respond! Also, your faces are close! Too close!*

I was panicking so much I could barely speak, frozen in place and blinking rapidly, when out of nowhere the brothers began patting my head without any hesitation.

"Wow, you're real. She's said a lot about you, but I was sure you were just an imaginary friend. Didn't think I'd ever see the real thing."

"Yeah, 'cause this is the first time we've seen you at all and you've been here for days. Also, your mouth's kinda flapping open and shut."

What do you mean, wow I'm real?! Am I some kind of rare monster with a low encounter rate?!

"Brothers, it's about time for the ceremony to begin. Shall we go downstairs? Step back from Myne, please."

"Right, right. You don't want to be late, do you? The sooner you leave the better."

I clung to Freida's helping hand and backed up as much as possible. One of the brothers grabbed my right arm and the other my left.

"Come with us, Myne. Let's celebrate Freida's baptism together."

"You're our guest, so you can come with us no problem. The more the merrier!"

They held me up from both sides and I shook my head desperately, but naturally nobody from this stubborn family would take no for an answer. *Is this the power of genetics?! Does everyone in the guildmaster's family have a gene that makes them not listen to people?!*

"Brothers, even I was scolded for pushing her past her bodily limits. Please do not force her to do what she is not comfortable doing. Her family is coming to get her this afternoon and it would be unthinkable for her to fall ill before then."

As the rest of her family just watched with warm smiles, Freida alone let out a sigh and got her brothers away from me. Today, she was truly my guardian angel.

"But we don't want to miss this opportunity to spend time with her."

"Myne is unwell, so she will be watching the baptism from this room's window. She won't be going outside. I would love for her to come too, but this is out of our hands."

Her brothers suddenly let me go, looking glum. They must have remembered Freida's past as a sickly shut-in, stuck in her room and looking out of the window enviously.

"Now then, the bell is about to ring. We must go outside and show our fine mistress to the world," said Jutte, after which the ensemble of family members swarmed around Freida and went outside all at once. I could only stand there and watch the tornado of chaos recede.

It seemed that eating breakfast alone had been the right call. I would have been overwhelmed by their flurry of questioning and sent to bed unconscious in no time.

"Are you okay? They're not bad people, but they are a tad bit forceful."

What do you mean, a tad bit?! They're the definition of forceful! I shot back a quip at Jutte in my head and approached the window. Despite the lit fireplace heating the room, the area around the windowsill was cold. I wrapped myself in a shawl Jutte gave me and looked down through the window.

It was very sunny, but the tiny flutters of snow sometimes floating by and my breath clouding the window indicated how cold it really was outside. I could see Freida surrounded by her neighbors, standing out like a princess. Her family surrounded her and she looked happier than I had ever seen her before. I could easily tell from above that few kids had on hairpins, which made the ones I sold Freida stand out all the more. I could understand how Freida had noticed Tuuli's hairpin while watching from this window.

...Tuuli must have stood out a lot as well. She was so cute that I was sure she became the talk of the town afterwards. For a little bit, at least.

Despite today being Freida's baptism, all I could think about was Tuuli's baptism. Thoughts of Mom smiling in her best outfit and Dad trying to avoid his meeting flashed through my mind. Suddenly, I really wanted to see my family.

"Myne, you look unwell. Is everything okay?"

"Seeing Freida happy with her family made me miss my family. It's weird, I'm homesick even though I'm going home today."

"Did ya miss me, Myne? I sure missed you."

My family came to get me right after noon bell rang, as if they had been waiting for it exactly. Dad's love was usually a bit overwhelming for me, but now it warmed my heart.

"Just a little. I missed you just a little."

Freida's family invited us to have lunch with them, but my mother was firm about not wanting to burden them further, and I settled things by saying I wanted to eat my mom's cooking for the first time in what felt like weeks. We managed to leave and get home without them stopping us.

"I wanted to eat their food too thoooough…" said Tuuli, pouting with cheeks puffed out.

I giggled. "Sorry, Tuuli. But I wanted to eat Mom's food instead of their fancy stuff."

"Yeah, 'cause Effa's food is great."

We returned home together with Dad, who was in a good mood, carrying me on his shoulder. I had only been gone from our poverty-stricken apartment for a few days, but it was home — and returning there filled me with relief from the bottom of my heart.

Freida's home had expensive food, a lavish bathing room, fluffy beds, and basically everything you could ask for. Each of those things excited me, but at the same time, I was so anxious there that I just ended up exhausted. Life there was clean and convenient, but for some reason, I just couldn't imagine living there.

Aaah… At some point, this place became home to me. My stay at Freida's had made me notice a surprising change within myself.

Winter Begins

The day after I returned home, Lutz and I went to Benno's store together. Snow was sprinkling here and there, but if we didn't go to Benno's before the snow built up, I would lose my opportunity to report my recovery and thank him for his help.

"Benno's been super worried, Myne. He was convinced that the guildmaster was tricking you somehow or putting you in a bad spot."

"Oooh, maybe he heard me calling for his help?"

When Freida's family had me surrounded, I cried for Benno's help on the inside. Maybe I sent out some weird brain waves that he picked up or something.

Lutz frowned at my suggestion and glared at me. "You didn't ask for my help?"

Seeing Lutz's pouty face made ticklish laughter build up inside of me. I ended up giggling, and his mouth bent into a sharper frown.

"Why're you laughing?!"

"'Cause I mean, you already saved me."

Lutz blinked in surprise and looked completely stunned, which made me giggle more.

"You told Freida I was going to get sick if I kept moving 'round, right? Thanks to that I got enough rest, avoided eating dinner with them, and basically everything went a lot better."

"Heh, is that right?" Lutz gave a pleased grin, squeezed my hand a bit, and took a step forward. It felt to me like the wind had calmed down a bit too, as less snow was hitting me on the face.

"Good morning."

"Ah, hello Myne. It's good to see you healthy again."

Benno's store was warm and full of energy. We let out sighs of relief as we went inside and Mark quickly walked up to us. Despite the snow, it felt like his store had just as many customers as always. Which was strange, since the workshops had already closed for the winter. I looked around, murmuring those observations, and Mark smiled.

"Our store profits the most during winter."

With blizzards came more days where you couldn't work, so I had thought winter was a season where most people tightened their purse strings and lived as frugally as possible, but it seemed that wasn't the case.

"The nobles grow bored while snowed in, and their purses loosen to a surprising degree when presented with opportunities to kill time."

"Oh, I get it. Leisure products..." Video game consoles were slightly outside of my reach, but a bunch of card-based games I was used to like hanafuda, karuta, and Western playing cards ran through my head. It might be smart to make those when I had the chance.

For now, though, my thoughts were interrupted by Lutz pulling on my sleeve. "Did you just think of something to sell?"

"...Well, maybe if we had paper." Thin pieces of wood could function as cards, but a proper set of cards would need to be cut fairly thin with similar dimensions. That wouldn't be a problem if I could just hire a woodsmith to cut the cards, but I wanted to at least wait until my baptism before breaking the "I think things up, Lutz makes them" setup.

...Could Lutz cut thin pieces of wood? And I hadn't seen any paint in this world yet. It probably existed, given that people used dyes, but it was beyond me or anyone I knew to color playing cards properly. With some ink and wood it shouldn't be impossible to make shogi or reversi, but playing cards were ideal since there were so many games you could play with a single set.

I was apparently taken to Benno's office while I was thinking to myself, and before I knew it, he was staring right into my face.

"You back in the game, Myne?"

"Bwuh?! Y-Yes. Sorry for worrying you," I replied, blinking in surprise. Benno furrowed his brows suspiciously and didn't stop staring at me.

"Sir, Myne's fine. She's not sick, she was just thinking about something."

Benno was finally convinced by Lutz's assurance, and he stood up straight. He sat us at the table near the fireplace and let out a heavy sigh. "It took a lot of prying for that old geezer to give up one of those magic tools he got for his grandaughter. To be honest, I had to gamble on him using it on you at all."

"Oh, it turns out that the guildmaster wanted to trick me into working for him. If I didn't have the money to pay for it, he would have had me switch to his store to pay off the debt."

"Yeah, figures. That's why I paid you all those golds earlier." Benno grinned confidently.

I nodded, then revealed how he had been tricked. "Right. But it looks like he told you they were worth one gold and two large silvers, when in reality they were worth two golds and eight large silvers."

"That freakin' geezer!"

"I was really relieved when my savings just barely managed to cover it. Both Freida and the guildmaster hadn't expected that at all. They were really surprised when I managed to pay," I added after Benno scratched his head with frustration and groaned.

For a second he froze in surprise, then grinned to himself. "Oh yeah, I upped the price. Good. Their suffering is good enough for me. But don't let your guard down around that family. They'll eat a dimwit with no sense of danger like you alive."

I figured it was best that I report to Benno what this little dimwit with no sense of danger had done. However, I wanted to put off him yelling at me, so I kind of worded it in a long-winded way. "Um, Mr. Benno. I have a question. How developed is the sweets culture in this area?"

"What're you talking about?" Benno glared at me with his dark-red eyes and I explained, adding excuses as I went.

"Where I live, people don't really eat many sweet things. We have honey, fruits, and parues in the winter, but that's about it. So, um. Mr. Benno. This may be a silly question for me to ask, but Freida had sugar in her home. Is that rare?"

Despite the fact that my family didn't have sugar, it was very possible that wealthy people generally did. Still, though, I wanted a hard answer from someone more informed than me, and if possible, I would like for him to tell me that the better part of the city had sugar even if we poor people couldn't afford it.

Of course, there was no chance that he would give me that answer that I wanted.

"It's still rare around these parts. It's only just recently that we've started importing it from foreign countries, but it's growing in popularity around the royal capital and among nobles... Wait. Did you do something again?!"

I was building things up so deliberately that Benno almost immediately noticed what I was getting at. His brows shot up in anger.

To sum up what he was saying: Sugar itself was starting to be popular among nobles, but not many sweets had been developed from it. One could say that sweets culture was still in its infancy. Pound cakes were simple and orthodox, but I had without a doubt gone too far.

"Um, I made some (pound cake) for them, and they really loved it."

"Oh, right, that stuff. It tasted so good. It was moist and like melted in my mouth. I've never had anything as sweet and... Wait, Myne!" Lutz, who had eaten some of the pound cake himself, glared at me too. I instinctively knew I had done something I really shouldn't have.

"Why do you always gotta stick your neck out for carnivores like them?! Do you wanna get eaten alive?!"

If simple pound cake was getting him this furious, I was glad I hadn't made short cake for them. My decision had been motivated purely by my inexperience with the scales and wood oven, but still. All's well that end's well.

"I promised to make sweets with Freida, and that was the only way I could think to thank her, so..."

"THANK her?! You paid her, that's enough!" Benno was basically saying the same thing Freida had. Merchants expected their price to be paid and nothing beyond that was necessary.

"Awww. Freida said the same thing."

"AGAIN?! How are you gonna survive when your enemies have to teach you? Didn't I tell you to pick your battles and be more careful about what will happen if you lose?! You thoughtless idiot!"

...Noooo! I never learn. But still, isn't it normal to want to thank the person that saved your life?

"I mean, she did save my life, so..."

"So basically, you're forgetting that the geezer lied to screw you over."

"Ngh..." I had no argument against that. In the end, he was thinking purely in terms of how money had saved my life and nothing else. I didn't feel the same, but if I had been forced to leave Benno's store and join the guildmaster's store due to debt, my feelings would probably be a lot more conflicted.

"Sheesh. They're only letting you get away here 'cause you have the Devouring and will probably die before you can do anything special. If they were serious about you, they'd have you on their side before you realized what happened. Don't jump into the fire yourself."

I see. That seemed about accurate. I had indeed been thinking that for all their traps, they were a bit loose on the execution. In the end they were probably just playing around with me a little, figuring that I would either die of the Devouring or get snatched up by the nobility.

"Ummm, when you say they'd have me on their side before I realized what happened, what exactly are you talking about?"

"The simplest thing would be going straight to your parents and forcing the issue. They wouldn't be able to turn him down after he saved your life. He could bribe you by promising to look after you following your baptism, and it wouldn't be surprising if you ended up betrothed to one of Freida's brothers before you knew what was happening. He's just not doing that because his effort would be wasted if you died a year later."

"Um, what?! That's terrifying!" I hugged myself and rubbed my goosebump-covered arms in fear as Benno watched with an exasperated expression on his face.

"You just figured this out? Myne, you have to learn to recognize the dangers around you. But anyway... Did you just give them the finished sweet?"

I didn't understand the point of Benno's question, so I tilted my head and explained how I made the cake with her. "No, I'm not nearly strong enough to make sweets myself, so I taught Freida's home chef how to make it while helping. They had a lot of pure white flour and sugar, even a real wood-fueled oven. Isn't that amazing?"

"Yeah, sure, just amazing. So basically, they know the whole recipe now." Benno was holding his head so hard it honestly worried me a little. I really hadn't expected that a little cake I made as a form of thanks would end up causing so many ripples.

"Ngh. Did I do something bad?"

"Only an idiot would give away something worth a lot of money for free, so yeah, you did. We could have sold those to nobles."

To be honest, I just didn't understand which products were for nobles and which were for commoners. But I did understand that my cake recipe was worth money. I would be more careful with recipes in the future.

"Aww... Can't we just have our own chefs make them to sell? They haven't started selling them yet, so..."

"Getting sugar is still difficult." When I suggested that we could sell the cakes first, Benno gave a clear grimace. But no matter how much he grimaced, I had no way of knowing how difficult it was to import sugar. Purchasing products was part of Benno's business.

"Well, we just have to give up, then. If you have sugar and a chef that can work a wood oven well, I'll teach you the (pound cake) recipe for free too."

"...That sounds like you've got more recipes," said Benno, reading between the lines and giving me a hard look, but all my sweets recipes required sugar. There was no point telling them to someone with no sugar.

With my newfound knowledge that sweets recipes were worth money, I puffed out my chest and smirked. "Those will cost you."

"Be that stubborn around them, not me."

He was right, so I replied "I'll try..." weakly. I wasn't used to putting a price on what I did out of goodwill, but I would have to adjust if I wanted to survive as a merchant.

"Is that all you've got to report?"

"No, although this is kind of a personal thing. I won't be able to leave home much during the winter, so I probably won't be coming to the store again until spring. That's normal, don't worry about me."

Really, Mark and Benno were more anxious about me collapsing than pretty much anyone else. The store could operate just fine without me, but I felt it necessary to warn them ahead of time that I wouldn't be visiting before they got worried about me.

"Yeah? What happened to helping Otto?" It seemed that Benno thought I went to the gate almost daily during the winter, but that was far from the truth. My family would never let me push myself like that.

"I only go to the gate about ten times over the whole winter since I can only leave if it's sunny, there's no blizzard, I'm feeling fine, and my dad has morning or noon shift at work."

"...Are you even gonna be healthy enough to do work after your baptism?"

"Honestly, I don't know and it kind of scares me." Benno looked pretty apprehensive, but really, I wanted to know that more than he did. Was there any job I would be capable of doing?

"Looks like you better think hard about what you want to do. So, how are you gonna sell your winter handiwork? I'd like to have some on hand as the spring baptism gets closer."

My initial plan had been to sell them all once spring came, but that wouldn't be giving him enough time before the spring baptism ceremony. The ones we had made in a rush for the winter baptism had already been sold and he barely had any left in stock.

"I'll keep an eye on the weather and bring them when the weather's good, sir," said Lutz. "But since we gather parues on sunny days, I'll probably only come on cloudy days."

"Oh yeah, parues. That's nostalgic. I loved my parue juice back in the day." Benno gave a nostalgic smile. He must have gone parue-gathering in the past as well.

I smiled a bit, imagining a young Benno splitting his spoils with Corinna. Lutz grinned himself, probably thinking about the parues he was going to eat. "I'm definitely gonna make some parue cakes again this year," he said.

"...Parue cakes? What're those?" Benno narrowed his eyes. A cold sweat ran down my back as I thought about how I had spread the parue cake recipe for free.

"Umm, Lutz? Maybe we should keep that recipe our little secret? We don't want to lose our chance to get parues for ourselves."

Parue leftovers weren't fit for human consumption. They were animal feed. Or at least, that's what people believed, and it's thanks to their misunderstanding that they traded them to Lutz for eggs. If they knew how much they were really worth, the parue leftovers would get a lot more expensive really fast. That would be a problem not just for us, but for everyone who relies on them to feed their animals in the winter.

"Oh yeah. It's a treat just for us, our little secret."

By the time we finished our discussion and left Benno's store, snow had begun to build up along the sides of the roads. I let out a tiny sigh. Snow meant I couldn't go outside.

"Looks like it's time for us to be shut-ins again." Lutz looked at the built-up snow angrily and gave a tiny nod. His home life has been so rocky that even his mother was complaining about it to me. And it was beyond a shadow of a doubt that Lutz was feeling a lot worse about it than she was. Winter forced Lutz to stay inside, and I could imagine that it was a miserable time for him.

"Hey, Lutz. Why don't you get your study tools together and come to my place every couple of days?" The best I could do to help Lutz was offer him an occasional breather. If he came every day his family would just treat him worse, and he would need a reason for visiting me so often. We could pass it off as him showing me their progress on making sticks.

Lutz's expression lit up a bit at my suggestion. "Yeah, sounds good. Thanks."

The number of snow days increased and fewer people were walking the roads. To fight back against the cold, most families stayed holed up at home and rarely went outside. Just like last year, Dad was a soldier who had to keep working at the gate year round, so he didn't get these days off. He had work on snowy days and was rarely at home.

Whenever Tuuli had spare time at home, she took the opportunity to work on hairpins. She took it more seriously than her basket-making from last year since each was worth so much more money. Mom was equally interested, but she had to prioritize making our clothes. First came my special outfit, since my baptism was this year.

"Mom, can't we just stitch up what Tuuli wore last year?" Tuuli had grown more over the past year. The special outfit she wore for her baptism last summer was doubtlessly tight on her now. As far as I could tell, it would save a lot of time to just fix up the outfit that she had barely ever worn.

"Tuuli's so much bigger than you that even just reworking it will be a hassle," said Mom with a wry smile.

Normally, a family wouldn't have to make multiple dresses for special occasions. Handing down a single outfit from sibling to sibling was standard. But Tuuli and I were just too different in size. Tuuli looked about eight or nine when she was seven, and I looked about four or five. It was honestly impossible for us to wear the same clothes. I tried putting it on by the hearth, but it hung from my arms and the dress that should stop around my knees went all the way to my ankles.

"Mmmm… But I think if we pulled up the bottom of the skirt, we could make it shorter and add some cute looking frills. Maybe we could add little flowers at the folds?"

"Myne, that's more than a little remaking. It'll end up looking super fancy." Tuuli giggled at my suggestion.

When the size had to be completely changed like this, it was considered standard to undo all the thread, cut the cloth to its new size, and then redo all the sewing. I was weird for suggesting that we pinch the cloth up and add decoration to hide the seams. This was definitely a case where I should just keep my mouth shut and not try to push my luck.

"Oh, okay. We don't want the dress to look so fancy that it sticks out. I was thinking that if we just fold the cloth, we could undo the stitches to make it longer and keep using it when I get older, but…"

Only people with money to spare used more cloth than they needed. Frilly clothes with pleats needed extra cloth, so generally only rich people wore them. The same applied to decorations on clothes, which required spare material we generally didn't have. Which was exactly why Tuuli's outfit had been made to fit her perfectly.

I fell silent, thinking that despite the convenience here frills would stick out too much. But despite my hesitation, Mom seemed oddly enthusiastic about my idea. She grabbed onto my shoulders and smiled.

"…I think that's a great idea, sweetie. If it doesn't work, we can just remake it like we normally would. Okay?"

Ah… Well. Now nothing I say will change her mind. I hope I have time to help her with this on top of me making my own hairpin, tutoring Lutz, cooking… I sure am a lot busier than I was last winter.

Naturally, there was no way I could escape Mom once she got excited about something. Despite relocating by the hearth, I was wearing nothing but Tuuli's summer outfit and thus my weak, weak body caught a cold while we discussed how to fold and tuck it. *Achoo!*

Completion of My Outfit and Hairpin

My temperature finally went down two days after I had caught a fever. Remaking the outfit would be a lot riskier than I had expected. At this rate I would catch another fever before Mom was finished.

With those thoughts in mind, I climbed out of bed and went looking for Mom. In the kitchen, I saw the table pulled up close to the hearth with Mom and Tuuli making progress on their handiwork. It seemed that she couldn't work on the outfit while I was out of commission and had shifted her focus to the handiwork instead.

"Oh hello, Myne. Has your fever gone down? That's perfect, we can get back to reworking your outfit." Mom cleaned up her handiwork somewhat regretfully and spread out the outfit.

"Where's Dad? Is he on morning shift?"

"Noon shift, but so much snow fell he left early."

The city guard was also assigned to clearing the main road of snow. They received special pay for their work, but Dad always grumbled over his beer that the pay didn't match how exhausting it was.

"Okay, Myne. Please put it on."

I flinched a little at the sight of the thin, short-sleeved outfit. If I wore it like Mom wanted I would end up with another fever, hearth or no hearth. "Mom, can I at least wear a long-sleeved shirt underneath it?"

"The clothes won't be a perfect fit if you do that, sweetie."

"That's fine. I'll get bigger by the time summer comes around."

Mom put a hand on her cheek and looked at me dubiously. She looked me over as if thinking back to how much I had grown in the past, then sighed. "I understand how you feel, Myne... But that doesn't seem likely."

A-At least say you believe in me, Mom! Still, she allowed me to wear a long-sleeved shirt beneath the outfit so that I wouldn't catch another cold.

"Your shoulders are what don't match the most. What should we do about that?"

Mom was right. When I put on Tuuli's special outfit, the most loose and unsightly part ended up being the shoulders. So I tried scrunching them up, and this transformed the outfit into an off-shoulder dress that had nice loops around the top of my arms.

"Now we just need to make shoulder straps out of string or pieces of cloth. If we have any scraps of cloth left over from when you first made this, it'll be a perfect fit. If not, blue string should work. It'll match the sash and embroidery just fine."

"I have some left over, yes. Plenty for shoulder straps."

Mom went and got some scraps of cloth from the cloth basket. After twisting it into a string shape, she sewed it onto the shoulders of my outfit. The dress that once slipped off my shoulders became an off-shoulder camisole.

"Perfect, now it won't fall off your shoulders."

Mom nodded in satisfaction, then furrowed her brows and pointed at the armpit of the outfit. Due to bundling up the cloth around the shoulders, the rippling cloth had ended up gathered by the armpit.

"Myne, the armpit looks terrible with all that cloth in it. What can we do about that?"

"Well, I'm going to be wearing a wide sash, so I don't think a little extra cloth by the armpit is a problem."

"No. It looks terrible."

"Okay, then what if we sew them into proper pleats? It'll take time, but I think it'll look really cute."

I tried taking the apparently terrible-looking cloth by the armpit and put it into three equidistant folds from the chest to the side. Sewing them into place would be annoying, but there wouldn't be any excess cloth and the chest would look fancier.

Mom thought for a minute, then nodded and held her hands out to me. "Naturally I won't be able to sew that with you wearing it."

I took off the outfit and handed it to Mom. I then immediately put on several layers of clothes and sighed in relief. It was legitimately cold. I would probably catch a fever after we finished this.

"I'm jealous, Myne. You get to wear a super fancy outfit." Tuuli looked at Mom tucking the cloth and sighed enviously. It was true that all the frills were making it look fancy already. But this was only necessary because Tuuli was so much bigger than me. Mom wouldn't have to do this if we were a normal pair of sisters, and I felt bad about that.

"You're just too much bigger than me, Tuuli. We're only doing this because it's faster and easier than taking it all apart. And this was an outfit she made for you in the first place, right? It'll still be yours, even after we change it a bit. I'm just wearing your hand-me-down."

"Oh, that's true." It was the fate of we younger siblings to never wear new clothes. Most of the clothes I wore came from either Tuuli or our neighbors, and it was very rare for me to ever wear new clothing.

"I think I'll make my own hairpin while Mom's busy sewing." I decided to work on my baptism hairpin while Mom was sewing the pleats in. I wanted to take the opportunity to make a new kind of hairpin that was different from the ones I had made before it.

"Mom, I want to make a hairpin for myself. Can I use our thread?"

"Since I don't need to make a new outfit for you anymore, you can use what you need for the hairpin."

Last year it had been a struggle to get enough thread for a hairpin since she didn't understand what I was doing, but this year we were on the same page and she gave me some without hesitation. I picked up the fresh thread while feeling a newfound appreciation for the importance of mutual understanding.

"I think it went like this…" I dug through my memories and used my thin needle to sew a small, rounded flower in the image of a lily. Tuuli finished a hairpin of her own and peered at my hands.

"Myne, what's this? That flower looks different from Freida's flowers and our handiwork flowers."

"I'm actually going to put this on the hair stick I'm planning to wear for the ceremony."

"You're not going to make one like Freida's? But it was so fancy and pretty." Tuuli pursed her lips as she rolled the lily around in her hand. She had liked the rose-shaped flowers a lot. I thought back to the lustrous, delicate roses I had made for Freida and let out a tiny sigh. Even if I tried to make those again, they wouldn't end up looking the same.

"The quality of the thread is just so different, I don't think I can make roses like that right now."

"They don't have to look the same, they'll still be pretty. Here, I'll make them for you. You made my hairpin for me and now I want to make yours for you."

I was so touched by Tuuli's words that I decided to ask her to make a rose for me. A large rose that stood out would be best left to Tuuli and her significantly superior sewing skills.

"Thanks, Tuuli. In that case, would you use this thread to make roses a little bigger than the larger ones we made for Freida? Do you remember how to make them?"

"I'm not you, Myne, of course I remember."

I-I'm sorry for having such a bad memory...

I left the rose-making to Tuuli and got to work on the little flowers. Even at my top speed I couldn't make them very fast, and by the time I finished three Mom had completed sewing the pleats.

"Myne, trying wearing the outfit again."

I took off all my shirts but the long-sleeved one and put on the outfit again. It was now an off-shoulder dress with a pleated chest area. Thanks to the curving, the sleeves looked like natural curvy drapes.

"Mom, could you get the sash? I want to try it on."

Mom got the wide blue sash for me and I tightened it around me, which made the skirt portion of my dress balloon outwards.

"I didn't think it was that special while sewing, but now I see that it looks pretty cute."

"Because I'm cute?"

"My my, because I'm a skilled seamstress." We looked at each other and laughed for a bit before Mom spun her shoulder in determination. "Just the hem left. It looks cute enough right now, but the hem's simply too long."

A dress that ended at Tuuli's knees ended at my ankles. I didn't know where this rule came from, but it was known that in these parts, girls younger than ten wore their skirts to the knees. Incidentally, miniskirts didn't seem to exist at all. At most, kids one to two years old were so short that skirts intended to reach their knees ended up looking like miniskirts.

The annoying thing was that skirts couldn't be too short *or* too long. Ten- to fifteen-year-olds wore dresses to their shins. Adults generally wanted to have even their ankles covered. But skirts that long were only worn by women who didn't have to work for a living. My mom, a fine working class citizen as she was, wore a skirt down to her ankles just like most wives around the neighborhood.

"I wonder if we could just bundle it up like we did with the shoulders?"

"I think it'll be fine if we bundle up two parts in the front and two parts in the back. Do you think that'll work, Mom?"

"Hmm. I think that might just do it."

We hefted up four parts of the hem and ended up with something that looked like a balloon curtain. Once we sewed the cloth into place, we added small flowers to hide the thread, just like we did with the hairpins. We then added a drape to make the embroidery look prettier, and that was that. The outfit was done.

"As expected, it looks like a wealthy young lady's baptism outfit now."

The chest was pleated, the sleeves were wavy, and the hem was ballooned out. The outfit used a lot of spare cloth, and from every angle it looked entirely unlike something a poor commoner would wear. By bundling up the loose parts and sewing them together to forcibly shrink the outfit, we had created a design rare for even the wealthier classes. It clearly didn't match the rest of the wardrobe, or even our home itself.

"This was a lot easier on me than what I had intended to do, but it will stand out a lot I'm afraid," said Mom, to which Tuuli shrugged and pointed at our half-finished hair stick ornament.

"Isn't it a little late for that? We're already sticking out with the hairpins and stuff." Even Tuuli stuck out enough for Freida to notice her just by wearing a hairpin unlike anybody else's. The hair stick I was making would definitely stick out just as much, so either way, eyes would be on me. And as Freida said, the hairpins sticking out would be great advertising for them. We may as well go all the way here.

"It's cute and we worked hard on it, so I won't mind the attention. I'm going to wear it!" I had sacrificed my own body to sickness and the cold to complete the outfit. I won't abandon it here. And not to mention, compared to the frilly mini-skirt maid outfit I wore for a high school culture festival back in my Urano days, it wasn't embarrassing at all. It went all the way down to my knees and had a respectable design — what more could I ask for?

"If you're fine with it, Myne, I am too. So, with that settled, what kind of hairpin are you making there?" Mom peered at the rose Tuuli was making, clearly interested.

"Tuuli's making big roses for me, so I'm making about ten more little flowers like these."

"I'll help. Consider this my thanks to you," laughed Mom as she went to get a needle out of her sewing box.

"Okay, if you want to thank me more, can I have some blue thread and light-blue thread too? I want to make about three flowers of each color."

"Well, aren't you clever. How could I say no?"

"Yay! Thanks, Mom."

We all got to work sewing together, making the hair ornament bit by bit. Three people working on it at once made things go by super fast. Three large white roses, three blue flowers, three light-blue flowers, and fifteen white flowers. We finished them all in a single day.

"How are you going to put this on? Aren't there too many small flowers?"

"That'll be a surprise for when I'm done. Don't watch me, I want it to be a secret," I said with a laugh, but since there was only one place I could make it, no secrets could be kept.

The two of them pretended not to look but I could tell they were glancing my way, mouths shut tightly to swallow the questions they wanted to ask. It was kinda funny.

"I'm back. Whew, today really took a lot out of me. Spent the whole day shoveling snow and taking care of drunks!" said Dad as he came inside. He had brushed the snow off him before entering the building, but there was still some on him. Tuuli and I brushed that off him while I asked about my hair stick.

"Dad, did you finish the hair stick I wanted for my baptism?"

"Yeah, gimme a sec." Dad gave a confident grin and took out a well-carved hair stick from the storage room. I couldn't help but smile as I saw how smooth and polished it was, which showed how much time he had spent carving it.

"It's really pretty. And it's so smooth there's not a single bump on it. Thanks, Dad!"

I sewed the three white roses onto a piece of cloth, which I then sewed onto the hole in the stick. I then pushed the needle through the cloth and worked my way down, attaching flowers to it like a hanging wisteria flower. First was the blue flowers, then the light-blue flowers, and finally, five white flowers. I ended up with three columns and seven rows of flowers, making a gradient of colors. I had mimicked the design of a yukata hair ornament I had seen in my Urano days, and it looked even better than expected.

"Wow, it flutters! This is so cute! Myne, try it on!"

"Put on the baptism outfit while you're at it. I wanna see it too," added Dad.

"Yes, please do. I want to see what it looks like when you're not wearing the long-sleeved shirt beneath it."

Overwhelmed by my family's pressure, I changed into the outfit. I then slid the baptism hair stick in next to my usual hair stick. I could feel the fluttering small flowers hitting my hair.

"Woah, Myne! That's incredible! Everyone's gonna think you're the daughter of some wealthy family for sure. It looks a lot cuter and special than what I saw Freida wearing back then. You really can't tell it's a hand-me-down." Dad deftly complimented both me and his wife's sewing ability while looking at the outfit in awe.

Mom shook her head with a wry smile and tossed some sharp words at him. "Now now, the materials used to make Freida's clothes are so much higher quality than what I used here that you're just being rude. But still, this looks a lot cuter and fancier than what you'd expect from a little reworking. You can just do so much more when you have extra cloth to work with."

"I'm saying that with the same materials, your clothes would be better."

"Goodness, Gunther, you always have a comeback."

Well, my parents were going off into their own world. It was honestly kind of hard to watch them flirt in a manner which could only be described as "lovey dovey." I would rather they not show romantic fulfillment in front of me, the girl who never had a single boyfriend in her life on Earth.

What returned me to reality and ended my angry internal rant was a surprise comment from Tuuli, who had slipped behind me to look at my hair stick.

"Uh huh, it's cute! Super cute, Myne! Your fancy clothes are cute too, but the flowers are doubly cute. It's fun to watch since it sways around, and your hair is really dark like the night sky, so the white flowers stand out a lot. I was thinking I might be making the roses too big, but now that they're on you I see they're just the right size."

Well... What can I say. Tuuli truly is my guardian angel. I obeyed the call of her voice and turned my back to my parents. Merely removing them from my vision as they flirted was enough to make me feel better.

"My hair's a lot heavier than your wavy hair, so without a flashy ornament it'll have trouble standing out with this outfit," I said, already shivering from how thin the outfit was. Goosebumps covered my body and I was starting to feel an ominous chill running up my spine.

"Ngh... Achoo!" My sneeze surprised my parents and had them leaning toward me.

"Myne, that's enough of that outfit. Hurry and change so you can get in bed. At this rate, you'll catch another fever."

"Oka— Achoo! I-I think it's a little late for that, Mom. My back's shivering, but my neck's heating up."

They hurriedly changed me into my pajamas and sent me to bed, but I could feel my head heating up. I sunk into the scratchy straw mattress beneath me and let out a sigh.

...Well, I expected this from the start, so this doesn't sting as much as it could have. Maybe one day my body will get stronger. One day.

Lutz's Tutor

While Tuuli and I were working on our handiwork, a knock came on the door. We exchanged glances and she went to see who it was.

"Yes, who is it?"

"It's me, Lutz. I brought some stick parts for the hairpins."

Tuuli unlocked the door and pulled it open with a creak, allowing Lutz to walk in with a gust of cold air and the snow stuck to his clothes. "Wow, it seems cold. Is it snowing a lot?"

"There's a lot of snow built up on the way to the well, but it's not as bad as it could be," said Lutz as the rest of the snow fell off of him.

"Here, the sticks. There's nine since each of my brothers made three." Lutz lined up the pins on the table. Once that was done, Tuuli stood up and brought over the finished flower parts.

"Want to go ahead and finish them up? That way, we'll know how many more sticks we need." It seemed that Tuuli had made quite a lot of flowers while I was sick and bedridden.

I looked at the flowers on the table and asked Lutz something. "We have twelve finished flower parts. You brought nine sticks. How many more sticks do we need?"

"Huh? Uuuh, three."

"That's right. Good job. I see you've been studying. Mom, Tuuli, please take care of finishing the hairpins for me. I'm going to go tutor Lutz," I said after seeing the stone slate and calculator in Lutz's bag.

Tuuli blinked several times, then tilted her head. "I heard that you were doing math stuff at the gate, but do you know enough to teach someone?"

"I'm hurt you think I don't know enough math to teach it." I pouted at her continued lack of faith in me and Lutz gave grinned.

"Tuuli, the thing about Myne is, she's crazy good with letters and math. Sure, she's crazy weak too, but still. She knows some things."

You know, I would have liked you to stop after the first line. I glared at Lutz, but Mom and Tuuli just laughed. It accomplished nothing.

Lutz took out his stone slate and pen, so I raced to the bedroom to get the bundle of usable failed paper I had shaped into a memo pad and my soot pen from the box. My plan was to use tutoring Lutz as a cover for making a book. Under normal circumstances it felt like I was being lazy and avoiding work by trying to make a book while Mom and Tuuli worked on handiwork, but I shouldn't stand out too much if I was just writing alongside Lutz while tutoring him.

…Okay. It's time to make a book. I was writing on the memo pad whenever I found the time, so it had a decent chunk of Mom's stories written on it by now, but it was far from being called a book. I hugged my memo pad, soot pen, stone slate, and slate pen close to me and excitedly headed back to the kitchen when I suddenly heard Mom say something.

"You know, Lutz, Karla and your family are against you becoming a merchant, aren't they? Are you fine with that?"

I gasped at the sudden serious topic and slowed down, silently tip-toeing to the kitchen. Tuuli had frozen in place after hearing Mom's question. Lutz was sitting in front of her, looking at Mom with a stony expression. I sat next to Lutz and Mom looked between us before continuing.

"I'm wondering if you said you want to become a merchant because of Myne. Are you following along just because you're a nice kid and want to take care of her?"

"No way! I asked Myne to introduce me to Otto 'cause I wanna be a merchant. I'm the one who wrapped Myne into this, Mrs. Effa," Lutz corrected her immediately. Lutz had wanted to become a traveling merchant, talked to a former one, learned about city citizenship, and decided to instead become a normal merchant. I honestly had nothing to do with that series of decisions.

Mom gave a small nod and looked at Lutz quietly. "Okay. I understand that you want to become a merchant yourself. But you'll try to keep looking after Myne even once you've become apprentices, right? Apprenticeships aren't so easy that you can survive like that. You'll be so distracted by her that your work will suffer."

I was right next to Lutz and thus heard him gasp in surprise. He hadn't considered that. Mom's words also pierced my heart. She wasn't wrong. I bit my lip and Lutz shot his head up.

"...I wanna become a merchant no matter what. It's happening right now thanks to Myne. That's why I want to help her as much as I can. But that doesn't mean I want to become a merchant for her sake."

"So, if Myne were to theoretically quit due to her weakness, would you continue your apprenticeship? Would you keep being a merchant?"

Lutz, clenching his fists tightly on the table, looked Mom in the eyes and nodded slowly. "I would. Definitely. My mom and dad just keep telling me to be a craftsman, but I've worked to get where I am without them and I don't want to quit now. Even if Myne told me to give up, I would still keep working."

Lutz had his own dreams. His decision to be a merchant rather than a craftsman had only strengthened as he spent more time with Benno and Mark. Working with me was the best way for him to become a merchant, but he wasn't becoming a merchant for my sake.

"I see. In that case... I think you're doing the right thing. I've only ever heard Karla's side of the story and never yours, so I wanted to clear things up here. Thank you for being honest with me."

To Karla, it probably looked like I was just dragging Lutz everywhere. That wasn't completely wrong, since my health was putting him through a lot. Which is probably why she only listened to half of what Lutz ever said, and why she thought that Lutz might change his mind if she was harsh enough. It wasn't too long ago that she asked me to stop him, but I turned her down, so...

"Mrs. Effa, there's something I want to ask you too."

"And what might that be?" Mom tilted her head a little. Her quiet eyes made it clear that she would answer honestly.

Relieved, Lutz sucked in air and continued. "Mrs. Effa, why aren't you opposed to Myne becoming a merchant? If merchants really are hated by everyone like my dad and mom say, why don't you mind?"

I knew that craftsmen didn't like merchants since they took handling fees and were always stingy about profit, but still. Saying merchants in general were hated by people was just going too far.

As if she had heard my thoughts, Mom looked at me and raised an eyebrow. "Different people have different opinions of merchants, so I don't have anything to say about that. But, well... I suppose I'm not opposed to it because Myne's been sick and weak for so long."

Lutz blinked in confusion, which made Mom laugh. "To be honest, I never thought that Myne would ever be able to work a job at all. I never even considered that someone would rely on Myne for anything. So if she's found something she's good at, something that benefits others, something that she's willing to put her all into... I couldn't imagine opposing it."

Mom's words squeezed my heart. I felt her motherly love for me so much that my eyes teared up.

"Alright... Maybe if I put my all into this, they'll accept me too," murmured Lutz with such an uncharacteristically bitter tone that I squeezed his hand.

"I hope they do."

"Yeah."

"Which means it's time to study." Lutz smiled and the room lit up instantly. The serious atmosphere vanished and Tuuli finally breathed out in relief. She had been holding her breath.

Mom took her sewing box and worked on sewing the flower parts of the hairpins onto the pin parts. I watched that from the corner of my eyes and tapped my stone slate with a finger.

"First up, we're going to practice the alphabet. Try writing them all out so we can see if you have them memorized."

"Alright." After giving Lutz an assignment, I got to work writing down Mom's stories onto the memo pad. The soot pencil resulted in pitch-black lines, which was problematic in some ways, but unlike ink they didn't cost money to use.

I glanced at Lutz's stone slate from time to time while writing the stories. I could see him writing letter after letter without pausing whatsoever. His studying was going so well it was almost unbelievable. He knew that the other apprentices would have an advantage over him due to his limited opportunities to study and thus devoured as much knowledge as he could. Not to mention that in the worst-case scenario, he was even preparing to leave his home if his family remained opposed to him becoming a merchant. I knew that was exactly why he was hurrying to learn as much as he possibly could before it was too late.

"Looks like you already know the alphabet. The letters are neat, too. Very nice, Lutz."

"It's just 'cause you wrote your example ones so good."

It was hard to write neat letters without drawing the lines over and over to implant the movements into your muscle memory. He didn't have memories of a past life like me helping him. I really had to respect the amount of hard work he was putting into this.

"Let's start working on your spelling now that you have the alphabet down. We can practice with how to write supply orders, since you'll probably be writing a lot of those."

I wrote a supply order for lumber on my stone slate. It didn't take long at all since I had written so many supply orders when making paper. While I wrote, I taught Lutz the names of workshops and foremen that Benno worked with often.

"This is the name of the lumber yard foreman. Here is where we put the name of the person ordering the materials. In our case, Benno bought the materials and sent them to us, so we put his name. This is the name of the lumber, and…"

Lutz looked at my stone slate and copied what was written with utter seriousness.

"Try and practice these so that when spring comes, you can order what we need to make paper."

"Huh?! Me? A-Alright. I'll give it a shot."

It was easier for him to work hard if he had a goal in mind, so once I gave him one he immediately started poring over his slate to make sure he hadn't made any mistakes, then started practicing writing them. I watched him for a bit, then opened up my memo pad again and resumed writing. At this rate it would be a long time before I finished writing all the stories.

"Let's practice math next," I said to Lutz after finishing a story and stretching. Lutz looked up from his slate, now covered edge to edge with words he was practicing, and nodded before wiping it clean and taking out his calculator.

I wrote math problems on his slate. Today we were going over three-digit addition and subtraction. After writing eight problems in total, I stepped back and watched him work the calculator. Unlike before, his fingers glided across it with no hesitation.

"You're faster at using the calculator now."

"I memorized how to do one-digit math 'cause you told me to learn how to use this thing, and that's really all you gotta know to work fast."

"Mhm, I think you're learning faster than I am..." With simple problems like the ones I was giving Lutz, I subconsciously did mental math despite my best efforts and thus my fingers didn't move like they should. Which meant that as always, I was faster at doing written math than using the calculator.

But well, I'm lending the calculator to Lutz most of the time, so there's really no way I could be faster than him. I was making excuses to myself. It was true that with little opportunity to use the calculator, it was hard for me to get better at it. But at the same time, if you asked me if I would actually bother to practice if it were at home with me all the time, well, that would be a hard question to answer.

"Looks like you have addition and subtraction down pat. The method doesn't change even with more digits, so that should be it for them."

"It's easy to get mixed up with a ton of digits, though," said Lutz while scratching his cheek. He had improved an impressive amount considering he started using the calculator just a month ago.

"I don't know how to multiply or divide on this thing, so we're kind of stuck here for now."

Since neither of us knew how to use the calculator in full, I decided to just teach him the theory behind multiplication and division, along with multiplication tables. I wasn't being particularly elegant about it and just introduced them in a "one times one equals one" structure without any fancy mnemonics for them like the ones I knew in Japanese. That made it harder for him to memorize them, but as long as he could shoot back an answer as soon as I lined up two numbers, everything was fine.

Lutz could now read large numbers and make change from larger units of money without error. With his learning speed, he had the knowledge necessary to get through his apprenticeship with some hard work.

...But what should I do myself? Lutz had his own work and I would definitely be dead weight to him. I was weak, got tired fast, and was basically useless. I would hold him back no matter what. I could contribute by thinking up ideas for products, but since I knew so little about the culture of this world, I needed Lutz around to guide me.

...*Speaking of which, Benno was worried about whether I could work or not too.* I remembered Benno once asking me if I could even work at all with a sickly body like mine and fell into thought. Winter afforded one plenty of time to think, so I wanted to really work this through while I had the chance. Could I work as a merchant without being dead weight to Lutz and the other employees working there?

Otto's Counseling Room

I couldn't think up a good answer by the next day. I was sitting at the table, sewing and still thinking about it, when Dad called out to me.

"Myne, if you're feeling up to it, want to go to the gate? The snowing stopped last night."

I looked up with an enthusiastic "Yes!" and immediately started getting ready to go. I put my slate and stone pencil into the tote bag and put on a bunch of layers to ward off the cold.

Otto was at the gate today. I could count on him giving me a harsh reality check if need be given his experience as a merchant and status as a third party. I wanted to ask him if I would survive an apprenticeship with Benno.

Naturally, there was a bunch of snow piled up outside. I spent most of the winter stuck inside and rarely left. The sight of snow piled up higher than I was tall made my jaw drop. The snow in the narrow alleyway leading to the main street had been mostly pushed aside, but the walls looked like they could collapse at any time and that was terrifying.

"Here you go, Myne." Dad knelt down and held out his arms, so I went ahead and let him pick me up with my arms around his neck. He wouldn't make it to work in time if I had to walk through this snow.

My head got above the snow once I was in Dad's arms. When a gust of cold wind went by, I saw a field of glittering white rising and falling in front of me. I thought that with this much snow there wouldn't be many people walking along the main road, but there was a surprising amount of them hurrying along to their destination.

"There's a lot more people out in this snow than I thought there would be."

"Not often the snow stops like this, yeah? There's a lot less people when it's snowing," said Dad, speeding up because a bit of snow had started falling here and there while we talked. "Here it comes again. Hold on tight, Myne. We're gonna run!"

"Gyaaaah! I'm gonna fall!"

We reached the gate in no time. After brushing the snow off ourselves, we went straight to the night watch room. Dad opened it with a light knock, and inside we saw Otto at the desk near the furnace working on a huge pile of paperwork.

"Otto, I've brought the helper you wanted. Move away from the furnace."

"Thank you, Captain! It's good to see you, Myne." He cleared some space on the desk and moved to the side so that I could work alongside him. Judging by the overjoyed smile on his face, I could imagine that he had a lot of work stacked up. I took my slate and pen from my tote bag and climbed up onto the chair.

"Okay, Myne. Could you check to see if the calculations in this section are correct for me?"

I wouldn't be able to ask him for advice with this much work piled up. I looked at the mountain of paperwork and readied my slate pen. For a while, we worked in silence with only the sounds of Otto flicking the calculator and my slate pen accompanying us.

A rough knock sounded on the door and a young soldier came inside. "Excuse me. I have a question for you, Otto."

"Hear that, Myne? He's got a question." Otto pointed at me without looking up from his work.

"What? Me? Um, hold on a second. At least let me finish this problem…" I finished the math and stamped the seal of confirmation on it before raising my head. The young soldier looked between me and Otto, who was blasting through his work at a furious pace, and sighed. He then took out a piece of parchment.

"What is this? Oooh, a letter of introduction from a noble. Is the commander here?"

"No, I think he's on night shift today."

"In that case, get his seal and direct him to the inner wall as soon as possible. It's likely that even a normally good-spirited noble would be in a bad mood right now due to journeying through the snow, so go as fast as you can. If he has to wait, bring him to a waiting room with a fireplace as soon as possible and give him a cup of warm tea if you can."

"Understood." The young soldier saluted and rushed out of the room. I returned the salute and got back to work.

"You've gotten pretty good at that," said Otto without stopping his work.

"It's mostly the same thing each time, so…" I replied while moving my slate pen too. Work at the gate was basically bureaucracy in a nutshell. Once you memorized the manual, you could deal with just about anything, barring extreme exceptions.

I got a little tired after doing math for a while. I gathered up the sheets I had completed and stretched my back. Otto must have reached a stopping point as well since he did the same.

"Yeah, that's enough work to get tired. Want to take a break for a bit?"

Otto brought me some warm tea. I sipped it and began telling Otto about my work troubles.

"...And then Mom said this to Lutz: 'But you'll try to keep looking after Myne even once you've become apprentices, right? Apprenticeships aren't so easy that you can survive like that. You'll be so distracted by her that your work will suffer,'" I said, to which Otto nodded as if it was obvious.

"I mean, yeah. An apprentice that's already half as competent as an adult trying to help another apprentice will just end up hurting themselves. If Lutz actually wants to become a merchant, I can't see him helping you much at all."

"...I knew it." As it stood, we weren't apprentices and we weren't working in the store. We were just bringing in products to sell, and that gave Lutz more than enough leeway to stick around me and keep an eye on my health. But once we became apprentices and had work to do, he wouldn't have that kind of leeway. I didn't want to put more weight on his back and potentially break him.

I started to worry about what to do and Otto looked at me with quiet eyes. "Hey, Myne. Do you actually intend to become a merchant?"

"That's the plan right now. I know a lot of things that could be good products to sell, so..." One had to belong to the Merchant's Guild to sell things, so I was pretty much locked into the merchant life to some degree.

"That's fine, but you should probably not join the Gilberta Company."

"Why not?" Benno had more or less confirmed that he would take me as his apprentice. I was feeling uneasy about working there, but didn't know why Otto would warn me off it entirely.

"That store's growing fast. Everyone's working hard each and every day. I don't think you have the stamina to keep up with their pace," explained Otto with a shrug. His reasoning lined up exactly with what Benno had implied earlier, which was the source of all my unease in the first place.

"...Benno actually said something like that to me earlier. He asked if I was healthy enough to do any work at all."

"There are some jobs that just involve sitting around and doing math or checking paperwork, but a merchant's work is always on a tight time limit. It'd be hard to trust a kid who collapses at the drop of a hat with important jobs like those."

I knew that Benno was focused on earning as much profit as possible from my ideas and didn't want to let another store get their hands on me. But when it came to actually working in his store, my stamina and strength were just fatally lacking. I don't think he would want to hire an employee so unhealthy they would be constantly missing work at random intervals. If I were in Benno's shoes, I wouldn't want an employee like that either.

"I have some thoughts that would normally be too harsh to tell a kid, but I can say them anyway if you want me to." Otto eyed me calmly, waiting for my reaction. I consulted with Otto specifically because I wanted a harsh, objective viewpoint that my closer friends and family would be unable to give me.

I clenched my fist beneath the table to ready myself for whatever he might say and slowly nodded. "Please do."

"The main reason I think you shouldn't enter the store is the effect you'd have on the other workers. It wouldn't take long for the delicate balance of human relationships to fall completely apart. Think about it. A new apprentice that just joined the store is constantly taking days off, getting all the easy work, and basically having an easier time than anyone else."

Despite my health problems, others wouldn't be amused by the favoritism shown to me, and within weeks there would be problems boiling beneath the surface. I had been so focused on securing Lutz's employment that I hadn't considered what would happen after I became an apprentice myself.

"Not to mention… Don't you think that there will be problems with your pay, too?"

"Bwuh? My pay?" I had never thought about my pay at all, so I let out a goofy "bwuh" in surprise after he brought it up. Otto sighed as he saw me tilt my head in confusion.

"You're bringing such enormous profit to the store that Benno could never hire you with the same pay as a normal apprentice."

"I would think that my pay and my percentage of the profits would be separate."

We had contractually agreed to not receive percentage-based profits on the paper to secure our future jobs, but I fully intended to take a cut from products I introduced in the future. Far be it from me to hand over all my information for free.

"Even if he paid you separately for that, I can easily see your pay as a new apprentice shooting over that of a veteran employee with decades of loyal service. Honestly, that's just not going to end up well."

"Gaaaaah…" Few things could twist human relationships as easily as money. Otto was completely correct. And if things started breaking down there, the store itself would, like, cease to function.

Ultimately all employees were important to the store's continued operation.

"You're right. No matter how I think about it, things would just be better if I didn't work in the store." Everything Otto said was right and left me with no room for argument. I now felt that joining Benno's store as an apprentice would just breed more problems than it solved by far.

"And y'know, there's something else I'm worried about here." At this point he had dunked on me so hard I was ready for anything. I nodded at him to continue. He leaned forward, lowered his voice, and slowly continued. "So it turns out you're sick with the Devouring after all, right?"

"You knew, Mr. Otto?" I widened my eyes in surprise and Otto shook his head.

"Nah, I didn't know, but Benno brought it up as a possibility. I only confirmed it when Corinna asked me if I knew a disease called the Devouring."

"Mrs. Corinna?"

"She was talking about how she saw Benno acting pretty panicked, which is rare for him. Apparently someone with the Devouring collapsed in his store and nearly died. For days after that the captain was barely thinking about work, it was hard to look at him. Put two and two together and I can guess you're the one who collapsed from the Devouring."

It seemed that Otto's information network was larger than I had imagined. Though a lot of people had probably seen me passing out in Benno's store and getting carried to the guildmaster's house.

"The captain seems to think you're all better now, but according to Benno the Devouring is incurable, yeah?"

The guildmaster had sold me a magic tool to drain some of the Devouring heat from me, but the heat would be building back up. Freida said that I had a year left at best before it overflowed again. I silently nodded.

"Did you tell your father it's incurable?"

"No, not yet. It'd be hard to tell my family when they're so happy that I'm better now..."

Right now I really, really didn't want to talk about the price of magic tools and the time limit on my life. I was avoiding talking about the Devouring every time the conversation moved in that direction. Though it was also true that it was hard to go into too much detail when I only really knew that the heat inside of me was growing on its own and that I would die when there was too much of it for me to contain.

Otto shook his head slowly with a firm expression on his face. "You should tell him. The captain thinks you're cured and that you'll be fine working when you're old enough. You should get everyone on the same page and have a serious conversation about your future. If you just wing it, you'll be making things harder on a lot of people in a lot of different ways."

I had indeed been winging everything I did and making life harder for everyone around me, so I had no choice but to take Otto's advice seriously.

"The fact of the matter is, you need magic tools to survive. You should go work for the guildmaster if you want to negotiate with nobles for better terms. The Gilberta Company is large, but still relatively new. No matter how hard Benno works, history and tradition hold weight. He won't be able to change the status quo so easily."

"That's true, but..." I faltered and Otto raised an eyebrow.

"Is there some reason you have to work at Benno's?"

"No, it's just that… I don't really like the guildmaster too much. It's hard for me to deal with how forceful he is." Being forceful was definitely an important trait for a merchant, but I couldn't bring myself to like someone who lied about the price of the magic tools my life was riding on in an attempt to force me onto his side. I appreciated what he did for me, but I didn't want to be anywhere near him.

"Isn't Benno the same way?"

"Mmm, Benno's forceful too, and he's greedy, and he also tricks people, but I can tell that he's just noticing my flaws and trying to help me grow as a person."

"Oh?" Otto grinned a nasty smile and I gulped. It would be safe to assume that everything I said here would be leaked straight to Benno.

"Also, I still haven't decided if I want to live the rest of my life as a noble's slave."

I had finally come to consider my family here as true family. I was finally used to living life in this world and I was looking forward to spending a lifetime with everyone here. It was hard for me to even consider signing my life away to a noble who could very well treat me poorly. If I had to choose between wasting away with my family or slaving away for a noble, well, at the moment I would rather choose the former.

"Well, in that case, you've gotta decide on your future before you can do anything else. If you don't want to join the Gilberta Company for their connections to nobles, you should think about joining another store. To be honest, if you think of products and Lutz makes them, you might not even need to join a store if you keep your rights and cuts of the profit straight," said Otto.

I gave him a big nod. Up until now I had been focusing on joining a store with Lutz and working with him, but as Otto said, I didn't have to join a store considering what I was capable of doing.

I gave another nod, smaller this time, and Otto smiled so warmly that he actually ended up looking suspicious. "I have an idea. Why don't you act as a professional writer of sorts, writing letters and dealing with paperwork on others' behalf while keeping your business contributions to just thinking up new products? You can sell things to Benno and help out here when you're feeling up to it just like you have been. I think that'll be best for your health."

Otto was right in that living life as I have been would be best for maintaining my health, but... his smile was so suspicious I wanted to disagree.

"Well, in either case, talk about this with your family. For now we've rested enough. Let's get back to work." Otto cleaned up our cups and I took out my slate to get back to checking the math on the paperwork.

...Talk with my family, hm? I feel like Dad will go crazy if he learns I only have a year left to live.

"Let's go home, Myne."

"Well, there he is. Thanks for your help today. I owe you my life, Myne." By the time Dad's shift ended and he came to get me, I had done so much math that I felt dizzy. Numbers appeared in my head when I shut my eyes. But Otto looked fine despite using the calculator constantly, so maybe it was just impossible for me to do a job that involved so much constant math.

"Dad, won't you be cold?" Dad was carrying me home along the somewhat snowy road with his coat over me. I was warm thanks to the coat, but he was opening it up so much that I could imagine how cold he was.

But he just shook his head with a grin. "I'm not cold with you this close to me. Never felt this warm in my life."

Dad loved his family to a fault. We were his everything. How would he react when I told him about my Devouring? His smile made my heart freeze up. I was scared, but I couldn't avoid the topic any longer.

"Something wrong, Myne? You're looking down. Did Otto yell at you?"

"...No, he didn't. I have something to talk to you about, Dad. It's about my sickness," I said, and that alone made him freeze in place. His smile hardened into a thin line and he looked at me with the most serious expression I had ever seen on him.

He lowered his eyes for a moment, then sped up his pace as if running from something. "Let's talk about it once we get home. Don't want to leave out Tuuli and your mother." Dad hugged me tighter, protectively, as if he had a bad feeling about this and wanted to keep me safe.

Family Meeting

"Welcome back!" Tuuli opened the door for us with a smile, blinked a few times at us, then furrowed her brows with worry. "What's wrong, Dad...? You look kind of upset. Was it cold outside? Or was Myne too heavy?"

"Tuuli, that's mean," I pouted, and Dad forced a laugh.

"Myne's too light. She needs to get a little bigger," he said while setting me down and patting my head. Tuuli giggled, relieved at the sight of Dad relaxing a bit. She then said "Sorry, sorry" while brushing off the snow still stuck on me.

"The snow started turning into a blizzard on the way back, it was suuuper cold." Clapping for Tuuli on the inside for lightening the mood, I pursed my lips and complained about the cold.

Tuuli copied me and pursed her lips too. "Dad was carrying you and put you in his coat, so I bet it wasn't cold at all. He couldn't do that for me."

"I sure could," Dad replied before scooping Tuuli up.

"You probably couldn't take her all the way to the gate, though," I shot back before heading to the bedroom to put away my bag and coat.

Mom was making dinner in the kitchen. "Welcome back. Let's eat before we do anything else." She had guessed from Dad's tense demeanor and expression that something was up. She furrowed her brows for a moment, then got to work setting the table with a slight smile. "Okay, eat up."

At Mom's urging we began eating a much, much more quiet meal than normal. I hadn't said anything yet, but Dad's brows were furrowed hard. Mom was keeping her eyes on the table. Tuuli was watching us, worried. The atmosphere was already dark. I spooned the hot soup into my mouth while glancing at my family.

…Should I really tell them about this? Won't Dad go on a rampage if he learns I have a year left to live? How should I tell them about it? I want to hide how much I spent on the magic tool, if possible… I could only think of the conversation we would have after dinner and my heart was pounding the whole time.

"Thank you, it was very good." We put our utensils down and Mom set cups of tea made from calming herbs onto the table.

"I suppose now it's time for the talk?" said Mom as she sat next to Dad, who slowly shook his head. His light-brown eyes were locked onto me. His normal grin was nowhere to be seen and his eyes were scarily serious, so much so that I gulped.

"Myne's the one who has something to say, not me," revealed Dad, leading everyone else to lock their eyes onto me as well.

I was just talking with my family, but I was so nervous that my throat felt bone dry. What should I start with? What kind of explanation would help them understand the best? Hesitant thoughts stirred through my mind and the actual explanation just wasn't coming out. Sweat beaded on my brow and the more I panicked, the blanker my mind became.

"Ummm, about it's about my sickness, but, um…" My mouth flapped as I searched for words.

Dad narrowed his eyes. "You stayed at the guildmaster's house for a few days and came back cured. Am I missing something?"

"Um, well basically, I can't be cured." My head was so empty that I forgot the preamble and just jumped straight to the point. That was a bombshell for my family and after a moment of stunned silence, everyone's eyes widened and somebody gasped.

Dad immediately stood up so hard his chair fell back and he pounded the table with his fist. "What do you mean, it can't be cured?! The guildmaster said you were better! Did he lie to us?!"

"You're not cured, Myne?!"

Dad and Tuuli leaned toward me from the side. I waved my hands desperately to try and calm them down and get them back in their seats. "Please, um, stay calm and sit down. There's not much I really know, and I'm not sure where to start my explanation, so I'll just be saying the first things that come to mind, so…"

Dad sat down, grinding his teeth so hard I could hear it. Mom picked up her cup with a shaking hand, maybe trying to calm herself down somehow. She took a small sip and urged me onwards. "Well, please do your best."

I saw Tuuli reaching for her cup, so I did the same and took a sip before continuing. "The thing is, I'm sick with something called the Devouring. It's really rare."

"Yeah, I've never heard of it," Dad said with a nod.

Tuuli murmured quietly with her cup in hand, "…Myne told me about it. She said it takes a ton of money to cure."

This time Mom's the one who stood up with her eyes wide. She looked horrified. I could guess that she realized we hadn't paid the guildmaster for what he did to cure me. I had wanted to hide how much I spent on the magic tool, but I guessed that wouldn't be possible.

"Mom, I'll explain, so just listen for now."

She sat down slowly, her eyes making it clear that she had a lot to say. With everyone's focus back on me, I started explaining what the Devouring was.

"The Devouring is a heat that lives in my body, basically, and it grows over time. When I get really mad, or so disappointed I want to die, it rampages inside of me on its own and basically eats me alive from within."

"Eats you alive…?" Tuuli stared at me, looking ghostly pale. She looked at my hair and fingertips, checking to see if any parts of me had already been eaten.

"I can usually control the Devouring heat myself. I can, like, squeeze it into a box inside of me, which works, but then it just keeps growing."

"Wh-What happens when it grows too big?" asked Tuuli, squeezing my hand while shaking.

"I can't keep it in the box anymore, and it bursts out and starts to kind of overflow from my body. I'll get swallowed by it before it overflows, and that's what happened last time. It burst out, started leaking out of me, and I was almost eaten alive. The guildmaster used a magic tool to suck the heat out of me. It really did suck out a lot, but since it grows back, I'll never be completely cured."

Tuuli groaned a little and glared at me with wet eyes, on the verge of tears. Or maybe I should say she was trying so hard to hold the tears in that it just looked like she was glaring at me. Looking at her made me tear up a little too, so I looked away and took another sip.

"Um, Freida said that I'm not growing much bigger because the heat is eating me bit by bit. To 'cure' the Devouring we need magic tools to keep sucking the heat out, but only nobles have them, which means they're super expensive and you can only buy them if you have a lot of connections to the nobility like the guildmaster's family does."

"So that means... the guildmaster did save you, then...?" Dad collapsed into his chair and spoke in a raspy voice, having lost the one target he could have blamed for this.

"Mhm. He gave me one of the magic tools he had gathered for Freida. But he doesn't have any more to give me, and he said I'll have to decide on my future for myself."

"Your future?! There's some way to cure it?!" Dad leaned forward again, hope in his eyes. Tuuli's eyes were shining with hopes as well behind the built-up tears. Their hope hurt me as I informed them that I had an option to potentially save my life at the cost of everything else.

"They said I have two choices. Sign a contract with a noble and become their slave, or live with my family and rot away."

"Their slave? I don't understand." Dad's expression twisted with bewilderment. Tuuli also tilted her head in confusion, not really understanding what I meant. Mom alone paled and tightened her grip on her cup. She was squeezing so hard that her fingertips went white.

"Freida's healthy because she signed a contract with a noble who gave her magic tools. She said she managed to get good terms because she belongs to a powerful and rich merchant family. We don't have any connections to the nobles, so they'll have full control over the contract and we have no idea how they'll treat me."

"...Can't really call that living," whispered Dad weakly. I nodded solemnly. It was precisely because I had lived my life as Urano once before that I couldn't bear to live a life as a noble's slave.

"Myne, what about the money? The magic tool they used on you couldn't have been free, right?" Mom finally spoke, unable to wait a moment longer.

I nodded, disappointed on the inside that I hadn't been able to avoid this subject. "I paid for it, don't worry."

"How much was it?"

"Well, a lot, but when you consider it saved my life…"

"I'm asking how much it cost. You'll tell us, won't you? No secrets."

I meandered around the subject and Mom's brows shot up with anger. I groaned to myself and answered while looking away. "…Two small golds and eight large silvers." That was the equivalent to two and a half years of Dad's salaries.

Everyone's eyes widened and their jaws dropped.

"Two small golds and eight large silvers?! How did you earn that much money…?"

"…Benno bought the rights to my simple all-in-one shampoo. I traded him the rights to make, sell, and price it. In return, he…"

"Whaaaat?! The all-in-one shampoo was that expensive?!" Tuuli cried out in shock, which made sense given how she been squeezing the oil herself for so long. It took time and effort to make the shampoo, but cost nothing since all the materials could be gathered in the forest. Tuuli hadn't expected at all for it to be worth so much money.

"Mhm, it turns out that nobles will buy it for a lot of money. He already has a workshop making it, and…" I started talking to Tuuli about the rinsham workshop when Dad shook his head and looked at me with a grim expression.

"That's in the past. What we want to hear about is the future. You're going to get real sick again no matter what, yeah?"

"Mhm."

"…How long until then? It sounds like you already know. I'm guessing you changed the subject because you didn't want to tell us."

"I can't hide anything from you, can I…?" I let out a sigh at Dad's unexpected sharpness. He had kicked his chair back and pounded the table just from hearing that my sickness was incurable. How could I tell him how long I had left to live? I couldn't, but I didn't have a choice.

"I'm your father, it's the least I can do. C'mon. Don't look away." He glared at me with his light-brown eyes. It was clear he wouldn't be fooled by anything and wouldn't let me leave until I answered, so I nodded in defeat and spoke.

"…A year at best. They said I'd be lucky to live for another year, so I should figure out what to do before then."

The uncomfortable silence turned into a painful silence. I thought Dad would go berserk, but he just shut his eyes, brows furrowed and head lowered.

The silence was broken by Tuuli choking up. "Ngh… Myne, you're going to die?! In just a year?! That's not fair!" She gave up on holding back her tears and started sobbing loudly, jumping off her chair to cling to me. I wrapped my arms around her and patted her back gently to calm her.

"It'll be okay, Tuuli. I honestly should be dead already. Think of this as me getting an extra year of life thanks to the guildmaster selling me a magic tool." I said that to calm her down, but it was just oil on the fire. Tuuli shook her head as tears streamed down her face.

"Nnn! Don't say you should be dead! It's only a year! I hate that! *Sniff*… You were finally getting better! You were finally going to the forest with me! I don't want you to die!"

As Urano I had died to a sudden earthquake, so I never saw my family's grieving. I wondered if they cried for me like Tuuli was now. I definitely made them cry. And now, I was making my second family cry as well. I was a bad daughter no matter when or where I was born.

"Don't cry, Tuuli. Please. I'll try to see if I can find something other than magic tools that can do something about the Devouring heat."

"What'll happen if you can't?! You'll die, Myne! I don't want you to die!" She clung to me and cried so hard it hurt my heart. My eyes heated up and even though I was trying to hold the tears in, they started flowing out.

"Tuuli... Don't cry. I'm the one who wants to cry..."

"Sniff... Sorry, Myne. I'll look too. I'll try to find some way to cure you... Nnn... But...! I want to stop crying, but I can't...!"

I was crying and patting Tuuli's back as she worked hard to stop crying herself when Dad quietly asked a question. "What do you think, Myne?"

"*Sniff...* I don't want to live apart from my family with nobles who could treat me like a slave. F-Freida said she only gets to live with her family until adulthood because the noble she signed with is allowing it. Maybe the one I sign with won't. When, then?" I already knew the answer to that. "They'll immediately take me away. I don't think many nobles will wait."

"...Yeah."

I had no idea how nobles intended to use children with the Devouring. But I could imagine that it was rare for time to be given. If I was taken away right after signing the contract, I would have had even less time with my family before I die.

"That's why I think I would rather just stay with you guys until I die. *Sniff...* I don't wanna live without my family."

"Myne..." Tears were forming in Mom's eyes too. She looked away and rubbed her eyes so we wouldn't see. Dad was looking at me with a blank look on his face that could barely be called an expression.

"I have another year left. I want to live the rest of my life to its fullest so I can die without regrets. Can... Can I stay here? Or should I go live with a noble?"

"Stay with me, Myne! I don't want you to go away!" cried Tuuli, and my parents both nodded without saying anything. I was so happy that they would let me stay that I wiped my tears away and smiled.

"Okay, so, I have something else I need to talk about too."

"There's more?" said Mom, looking at me with surprise.

Me telling them about my disease had partly been preparation for what came next. I wanted to discuss my future after they understood my disease as well as they could. "It's about my job," I said.

"You're gonna be a merchant, aren't you?" Dad furrowed his brows in puzzlement. I continued, feeling relieved that Dad was calmly listening to me and not going on a berserk rampage.

"That was the plan, but I realized I wasn't thinking far enough ahead, or really enough at all. I'm really just not strong enough to work a job. Otto told me I wouldn't be able to handle life as a merchant. He said I'd just be dead weight that drags Benno's store down."

"Friggin' Otto..." murmured Dad with clear anger. That was bad — I didn't want Otto to get punished for telling me the truth. I hurriedly explained the suggestion Otto had given me.

"But the thing is, he said it would be best for my health if I worked at home as a writer or something and continued selling things to Benno and helping out at the gate when I can."

"Yeah. Otto's right, you should stay at home. No need to push yourself." Dad grinned, looking a little more happy now. Tuuli, still clinging to me, and Mom both nodded in agreement repeatedly.

"I promised Benno I would be his apprentice. That won't cause any problems, right?" I asked the question that was the point of this entire discussion. My parents knew how jobs worked and I didn't. Maybe breaking that kind of promise would be harder than I thought.

"You're not officially his apprentice yet, and he doesn't want you collapsing during work either, so you'll be fine if you tell him what you told us."

"Okay. I hate to lose the job I worked so hard to get, but I'll try looking for one that suits my health better." It might be smart to consult with Benno over what kind of jobs I could do at home. That can wait until spring.

"Fwaaaah…" We had been talking for so long that the moment the conversation died, I let out a huge yawn. Seeing that, Mom clapped her hands together.

"If that's all you have to discuss, I think we should head to bed. It's late."

"Okay, goodnight."

"Ngggh… *Sniff…* Good, night…"

I headed to the bedroom with Tuuli, who was still crying, and got into bed with her. "Don't cry, Tuuli. I like it when you smile. We'll have lots of fun tomorrow, okay?"

"Uh huh. Definitely. We'll play together a lot. I'll stay with you," I consoled Tuuli as I got the covers over me. Tuuli wiggled beneath my blankets and clung to me before sleeping, as if saying she wouldn't let me go anywhere. I closed my eyes too, not bothered at all if it meant calming her down.

I had thought that Dad would have gone more berserk and made more of a fuss, but contrary to my expectations, he listened to what I had to say very seriously. I gently fell asleep too, while sighing in relief that I had finally talked to my family about this.

I had let Tuuli sleep with me to help calm her down, but I woke up to her hugging my neck a little too tightly. It was so hard to breathe that I hurriedly unwrapped her arms and wiggled away to escape. *Th-That would kill me. Devouring or not, I need air to live.*

I blinked while rubbing my neck. Normally it was pitch black when I woke up at night, but light was streaming into the bedroom. I rubbed my sleepy eyes several times, but it seemed I wasn't dreaming. The door was half open and the hearth still had its fire lit. Since I didn't hear anyone talking, it wasn't likely that both my parents were awake. I looked at the dark bed next to mine and saw a bump in the covers, indicating that Mom had already gone to sleep.

…Maybe she forgot to turn off the fire? I climbed off the bed, carefully so as to not wake up Tuuli, and walked to the kitchen.

There I saw Dad alone, drinking beer with only the fire lighting up the dim room. He wasn't drinking cheerily the way he normally did. He was crying quietly as he drank. It was like hearing the wordless agony he had kept hidden before. I quickly looked away and returned to bed.

Report to Lutz

Everything was awkward the day after the family meeting. Dad's smile had a tinge of sadness to it, Mom hugged me out of nowhere multiple times, and Tuuli would randomly start crying. But as the days passed we slowly returned to the lifestyle we had before the meeting.

"You don't have to do that, Myne. I'll do it."

"Bwuh? But I can do it just fine. Weren't you the one who said I had to learn how to do this, Tuuli?"

Things were definitely the same as they used to be, except that Tuuli had become even more overprotective of me at the expense of encouraging my independence.

"Wow, it's so bright! We need to get some parues!"

I was awakened by Tuuli's voice. The sky was still murky and dark, but there weren't any clouds. The dim light sneaking its way into our roomed hinted at the good weather and Tuuli threw the window open, allowing a burst of cold outside air to flood in.

"Tuuli, it's cold."

"Ah, whoopsies." She closed the window and hurriedly got to work eating breakfast. I also went and nommed away at my food while everyone else rushed through theirs.

Mom and Dad finished quickly and began preparing the hearth and firewood. As Dad lined up wood next to the door, he turned to look at me chewing my bread. "What're you gonna do, Myne? Want to wait at the gate?"

"Mmm, maybe I should go gather parues too?"

According to what Tuuli had told me, parue trees were weird fantasy plants but in a good, not-terrifying way. Her explanation of a spinny, shining tree or whatever didn't exactly give me a clear mental image of it, so I wanted to see one for myself. But my innocent suggestion was met with angry glares from my whole family.

"No! You're either staying at home or helping at the gate."

"Gathering parues is very difficult, too much for you to handle. You'll definitely get sick."

"Yeah! You're not good at climbing trees and you can't walk through the snow, so you won't be able to do anything."

Everyone shot down the idea of me coming along to help them. They were right that I couldn't even walk to the gate through all the snow and would basically be dead weight in a snowy forest.

"Okay. Parue-gathering ends at noon, right? I'll help at the gate until then."

I grabbed my tote bag and started packing for the gate. I thought that since Dad had today off that Otto might not be at work either, but it seemed that around this time of year Otto went to the gate basically every day.

We left once both I and the parue-gathering tools were on our slightly large sled. Dad pulled the sled in the direction of the southern gate where a crowd of other city goers were also heading, doubtlessly to gather parues as well. The air was so cold it felt like needles on my skin, but everyone was so excited to gather parues that I got excited too. It was like a festival.

"Sorry, but take care of Myne for me. She's helping Otto out until noon."

"Yes sir!"

Dad set me down gently by the gate. I waved goodbye to everyone and greeted the guard, who I now knew on sight, before heading to the night watch room like always with him.

"Good morning, Mr. Otto."

"Huh? Myne? I thought the captain had today off." Otto blinked in surprise and I nodded with a small smile.

"It's sunny today, so everyone's going to gather parues. I can help while waiting for them to get back."

"Ah, I get it. Guess we've got until noon then." Otto grinned, figuring out the situation right away, and started piling up paperwork that needed its math checked. Once he scooted aside to give me some space, I thanked him for giving me advice earlier.

"Mr. Otto, thank you for the other day. I talked to my family about my Devouring and we decided to search for a job I can do at home. I'm thinking about telling Mr. Benno when spring comes."

"Makes sense, your health's the most important thing here. I can assign you some work to do at home if Benno can't think of any jobs for you, so just ask whenever you're ready."

"Okay! Thank you." His pitch-black grin made me as nervous as always, but I felt so relieved in general that I got right to work with a smile on my face.

My family returned from the forest after noon passed, and I once again got on the sled as we returned home. Since all three of them had gone gathering, we got six whole parues this time. That was thanks in part to Mom working extra hard now that she knew even the wrung-out parue leftovers were useful for something.

We juiced the parues while Mom got lunch ready. Tuuli took the thinnest twig from the firewood pile and poked it into a parue. That was all it took for the parue peel to tear.

"Myne, here it comes!"

I caught the thick white fruit juice with a cup, making sure not to spill any. I waited for the juice to stop flowing out with my heart dancing at the sweet smell, upon which Tuuli handed over the fruit to Dad.

Dad crushed the fruit and got out the oil. It didn't take long at all since he could use the pressure weights. We saved the leftovers of the first four fruits for ourselves and decided to bring the rest to Lutz's to trade for eggs.

After eating, I brought both the parue leftovers and a new recipe to Lutz's. If they at least had an oven I could make gratin or even pizza, but my options were limited by the fact they only had a pot and a metal pan.

"Hi, Lutz. Could you trade us some eggs for these? I thought up a new recipe we could try out."

"Sounds good, but my brothers aren't home. You're gonna have to come inside and wait."

"Where'd everybody go? Are they playing 'cause it's bright out?"

"They're shoveling snow to earn some pocket money." I didn't know how it worked since I had never participated, but apparently shoveling snow was a good way for kids to earn pocket money. Such was the value of hard labor.

"Why'd you stay behind, Lutz?"

"Parues just melt if you don't squeeze'm dry, remember?"

It was true that parues were a high priority, but it felt like Lutz's brothers had just pushed chores onto him so they could go make money. It was frustrating. But if Lutz himself wasn't saying anything, it wasn't my place to butt in where I didn't belong.

I would have liked to at least help him juice and drain the parues, but that took strength, which I lacked. All I could do was watch Lutz swing the hammer and Karla collect the juices.

I watched them work in a daze and then remembered I hadn't told Lutz how my family meeting went. I needed to tell him that I had decided not to join Benno's store.

"Um, Lutz. I decided not to become Benno's apprentice."

"Huh?! Why?!" Lutz looked my way with his eyes open wide and the hammer still in the air. Karla looked at me with wide eyes of her own.

"Remember what Mom said? I would just be dead weight to you. There's no way I can work there when I'm this weak and sickly. I talked about it with Otto and he pointed out that there were plenty of other problems with me working for Benno."

"Like what?" Lutz urged me on with a glance as he got back to swinging the hammer.

"What would our coworkers think of a new apprentice who gets sick all the time and barely ever works?"

"Aaah," replied Lutz as he swung the hammer.

Karla closed her eyes as she pressed weights against a parue. "You'd make things harder on them, plus yourself since you'd miss lessons and the like."

"That's right. And on top of that, I plan to make a lot of new products. Can you imagine how much money I'll make from them? An apprentice that barely works and makes a ton of money would just make everyone mad."

"...You've got a point." Lutz nodded, but Karla's eyes widened.

"Well," I continued, "The high pay goes for you too, but I think you won't have the same problem if you work hard enough and take your job seriously. It might be smart to talk to Benno about this."

"Yeah, I'll bring it up to him once spring comes." At the very least, Benno could split his wages from his cut of the profit and mostly keep it a secret. He could pay us just by tapping his guild card against ours, for instance.

Then Lutz asked, "If you're not gonna join Benno's store, what'll you do after your baptism?"

"I'm not sure what's going to happen with my sickness, so for now I'm going to stick to doing paperwork and stuff at home, thinking up new products, helping at the gate... Basically, the same things I've been doing up until now."

"Alright. That's probably the best for keeping you healthy," Lutz agreed, which made me sigh in relief.

Karla looked relieved too. "If Myne's not going, that means you don't have to either, Lutz. Now you can be a craftsman."

Why did she think that Lutz would stop being a merchant because I had? I tilted my head in confusion and Lutz's eyebrows shot up in anger at the thorough relief in his mother's voice.

"What're you talking about, Mom?!"

"What do you mean, what?" Karla sincerely didn't understand and Lutz clicked his tongue before shouting.

"I want to be a merchant! Myne's got nothing to do it! I've been dragging her into this, not the other way around!" said Lutz, surprising Karla so much that she stared at him in shock.

"You what?! Does that mean you're still planning to be a merchant?"

"Duh! I really want to be a traveling merchant, but I heard about city citizenship from a former traveling merchant and decided to just be a merchant here in this city."

"You never said anything about that before!"

"I did! You just didn't listen or you didn't care!"

It seemed that they really hadn't understood each other. Karla looked shocked, like she had never heard any of this before. I kept silent, figuring that this was a conversation between family that I had no place in.

"...I remember you saying you wanted to be a traveling merchant, sure. But that's just nonsense all kids say. It's like telling someone what dream you had last night. I never thought for a second you were serious about it. I was just waiting for you to wake up and see reality," said Karla, weakly shaking her head while looking nervously at Lutz and me. I could tell that she was thrown off by the fact that, contrary to her expectations, Lutz had been completely serious.

And I could understand that. Most people who lived in this city never left it, aside from going to the forest or some nearby farming villages. Traveling merchants were foreigners who came and went like the wind, they weren't a goal to live one's life working toward. Karla expecting Lutz to "wake up and see reality" was completely normal here.

"...I wanted to be a traveling merchant for real. I wanted to leave this town and go to places I've never been before. I wanted to see with my own eyes the places I've only ever heard about in stories before. And I still want all those things."

"Lutz, you..." Karla started to stand up and say something. I could tell from her expression that it was going to be a harsh scolding. However, Lutz continued before she could say anything.

"But I talked to someone who used to be a traveling merchant. He said only an idiot would give up their city citizenship. He said traveling merchants don't take apprentices and I wouldn't get anywhere with them."

"Well, he's right." Karla let out a tiny sigh of relief and sat back down. People really did hate the idea of their children becoming traveling merchants. I hadn't taken it too seriously, considering it a fun job where you travel the world, but it seemed I still lacked knowledge of how this world worked.

"I was thinking of just becoming a traveling merchant on my own without any help, but Myne gave me a better idea. She said I could just become a normal city merchant. Normal merchants could probably go to other towns to buy things and stuff. I wouldn't have to risk everything on somehow becoming a traveling merchant. She said it'd be much more realistic and likely for me to succeed as a city merchant."

"Well, that'd definitely be better..."

"So I asked a merchant to make me his apprentice. He turned me down at first since I'm just the friend of a friend of a friend, though."

"...Yeah, figures," replied Karla with a tired voice and a shrug. It was clear she was in a state of disbelief. She hadn't expected her son to be completely serious about becoming a traveling merchant.

Considering how apprenticeships worked in this city, there was an almost zero chance of Lutz becoming a merchant apprentice. Perhaps that was why Karla hadn't taken him seriously when he mentioned wanting to become a merchant. It was even possible that she hadn't entirely believed him when he said he could become a merchant apprentice.

"But he gave us a job and said he'd take us as his apprentices if we did it. Me and Myne already finished it and he's promised to take us as apprentices. I'll become one even if Myne doesn't. I can and I will."

Karla finally realized that Lutz had paved his own way through life with his own two hands. She looked at him with somewhat hard eyes, having listened to him seriously for the first time.

"...Lutz, are you really gonna ignore your parents and become a merchant against our will? You think that'll work out?"

"I'll be a merchant even if it means being a live-in apprentice. I worked hard with Myne to make this dream a reality. I'm not going to give up now."

"A live-in apprentice...?"

Live-in apprentices lived in the worst conditions possible. First of all, apprentices only worked for half of the week, so they didn't get paid much. To make matters worse, they didn't have any family they could rely on. It was both physically taxing and time consuming for a single child to live all on their own, handling all the chores themselves. They tended to live in the attic, which meant hot summers and cold winters. Only the lucky ones had proper roofs that didn't leak. Carrying their stuff around and getting water up the stairs were both physically draining. It may even stink something awful since it wasn't unheard of for people to raise livestock like chickens in their attics.

There was no place to cook food, unlike a home rented to a whole family, so they would have to borrow a kitchen from their employer or eat out. Naturally, a lifestyle like that led to empty purses and most could only survive by getting advance pay at the cost of growing debt. The employer would look after them, but only to the extent of keeping them alive. Live-in apprentices were fated to live a life of constant work and suffering until adulthood.

"Lutz, think for just a second! You couldn't survive a life like that!" No reasonable parent in the world would want such a hard life for their children. Karla basically screamed in fear at the idea. But Lutz just shrugged.

"I could survive. I'm already preparing for it." Lutz was a special case in that he could save money this spring by selling paper. He could have a hefty sum ready by his baptism if we used the bark we saved in the storage building. The plan was for him to have money left over even after buying the clothes and whatnot he needed to become a merchant apprentice.

Not to mention that due to him having every other day off as an apprentice, he'd be able to keep helping me make and sell products. He'd profit from their sales and doubtlessly end up with much more money than an average apprentice. I could imagine that he still wouldn't have a comfortable life per se, but at least he wouldn't be experiencing crushing poverty. The main thing was that he probably wouldn't be able to afford to rent a whole room, which meant living in a terrible location for some time.

"…You're preparing for it? That means you're serious, doesn't it?"

"I'm serious."

After a long moment of silence, Karla let out a heavy sigh. She shrugged with a complicated expression that looked both like she had and hadn't given up after learning about how serious Lutz was.

"I still think it'd be safer and better for you to just have a stable craftsman job. Merchants have big highs but really hard lows."

"…If I become a craftsman like Dad says, I'll end up stuck like this forever. No thanks," pouted Lutz with clear frustration.

Karla frowned. He had basically said he wasn't happy with his current life, which upset her. "What do you mean, stuck like this?"

"My brothers do whatever they want and push chores onto me, they take stuff from me when they feel like it and I'm left with nothing."

"Well… they're your brothers. They take stuff from you, but they give you some stuff too, right?" Karla furrowed her brows, troubled. And Lutz shot her right down.

"What're you talking about? The food they take never comes back, and the only things they ever give me are messed up hand-me-downs. Sometimes their hand-me-downs are so awful you guys buy me something new, but they steal those too."

Just like me, everything Lutz had was a hand-me-down. But unlike how Tuuli always helped me out, Lutz's brothers ruled him with iron fists. That made a big difference.

"I learned from working hard with Myne on our merchant work that stuff I do on my own sticks with me. I want to see how far I can keep going with my own strength. A craftsman? I'm not even thinking about becoming one at this point."

Lutz had been held underwater by his family for his whole life and had broken free. He had secured a path to his dreams and escaped their rule.

Karla hung her head and whispered, "I didn't know you were that serious about this. I thought she was just dragging you around..."

"I'll be doing this job for my whole life. I wouldn't take it if I didn't want to."

"I've been opposed to you being a merchant 'cause I thought you were just messing around, y'know." Karla let out a heavy sigh and lowered her eyes. She thought for a while, then slowly raised her head and gave a resigned smile. "If you've thought it through this much and are even prepared to run away from home, well, I think you should do what you want. You should do your best and see how it goes. Your dad won't like it, but I'll be on your side."

"Really?! Thanks, Mom!" Lutz's expression lit up. He had given up on his family ever understanding him. After his eyes widened in disbelief, he jumped with joy. I couldn't help but smile at Lutz finally acting like a kid his age instead of just worrying about work and his future. Having even just a single family member on your side meant a lot.

Lutz's good mood didn't falter, even after his brothers came home. We all worked together to make a new recipe.

"Warm up the metal pan, Zasha," I instructed. "Lutz, you put lots of the grated cheese onto the parue leftovers. And Ralph, would you chop up the lage leaves for me?"

I doled out work while adding parue oil and salt to the bowl of leftovers that Lutz was putting the cheese into. After putting in the basil-esque herbs that Ralph chopped up for me, all we had to do was mix it well and cook it.

"The pan's all heated up."

"Okay, time for cooking. We can make it just like a parue cake."

We cooked it all together and ate it after the melted cheese ended up crunchy. It looked like okonomiyaki, a popular kind of Japanese savory pancake, but the cheese made it taste like western food. This recipe had been inspired by all the times I'd chopped up leftover noodles after boiling what I needed for soumen or spaghetti.

"These're simple to make, but they're really filling."

"They're even better if you add super chopped-up ham and vegetables."

"That would make this a real meal instead of just a snack like parue cakes are."

Everyone smiled, enjoying the food as they ate. At some point Ralph reached out to steal one of Lutz's extra pancakes, but Karla smacked his hand away.

"Don't steal other people's food. It's greedy. If you want more, make it yourself."

Ralph and Lutz were both shocked by Karla's smack. She smiled warmly as she saw Ralph get to work cooking a new one for himself and Lutz eating his food peacefully. It seemed that Lutz's home problems wouldn't be so bad now that he had a powerful ally in his mother.

Meanwhile, I cycled through tutoring Lutz, helping at the gate, and getting stuck in bed with fever. Lutz brought the pin parts for hairpins over, studied here, and sometimes went to the Gilberta Company to sell the finished hairpins.

Over time, the blizzards weakened and foretold the end of both winter and my shut-in lifestyle.

Back to Paper-Making

The snow began to melt and sunny days came in sequence rather than once in a blue moon. It was still cold, but my family permitted me to go the Gilberta Company, so I went there with Lutz to get our pay. We set out with bags we could use to carry the money our winter handiwork had earned.

There was no snow in the middle of the main street, but there were mountains of half-melted snow in the alleys reaching up to my neck that kept the feeling of winter alive. Everyone looked excited for spring, and the people walking along the street all had a skip to their step. There were more carriages and wagons passing along the main street than I could remember seeing for a long time. More people were going to the Gilberta company, too, and despite us aiming for the relatively non-busy afternoon, they were still swamped when we arrived.

Lutz and I began discussing whether we should come back later when we saw Mark walking our way. An employee had recognized us and called for him.

"Hi. Long time no see, Mr. Mark."

"Indeed. Blessed be the melting of the snow. May the Goddess of Spring's boundless magnanimity grace you both." Mark clenched his right hand into a fist in front of his chest and placed it against his left hand, fingers pressed together and stretched out. I had no idea what he was doing and could only blink rapidly in confusion.

"Um? What?"

"…I merely said the traditional spring greeting." Mark looked confused about why we were confused, which told me that his greeting was commonplace in these parts.

"I've never heard it before. Have you, Lutz?"

"Nope, first time I'm hearing it too."

"…Is it maybe a greeting only merchants say?"

"I have never thought much about it, given that it is so commonplace in my family, but given that my job leads to me primarily associating with merchants, that could be the case. Melting snow means more trade, so it is blessed. The greeting in general is one to bless each other with the good graces of the Goddess of Spring," said Mark, teaching us how merchants greet each other. Or at least, how they greeted each other specifically the first time they meet after spring. I interpreted it as the equivalent of saying "Happy New Year."

I pressed my right fist against my left palm in front of my chest as Mark had done and practiced the greeting. "Blessed be the melting of the snow?"

"That's correct."

"And then, um, may the Goddess of Spring's boundless magnanimity grace you," I murmured the greeting to myself several times, but I was confident I would forget it by tomorrow. Once again, I wished I had a notepad. I had my stone slate in my bag, but it wouldn't work as a notepad.

"The master is in a business meeting right now. Might I ask in his stead what brings you here today?" asked Mark, to which I replied while counting everything I had to talk about on my fingers.

"Ummm, first is the money for our winter handiwork. Second, I want to confirm if the large suketa has been finished, since I want to start making paper again soon. Third, I need to talk to Mr. Benno about my apprenticeship, but I guess I can't if he's in a meeting."

"Understood. Let us begin with the handiwork payment. His meeting will end before long." Mark guided us to a table within the store. Lutz and I sat next to each other, and Mark sat in front.

"Um, I present the last of the hairpins. P-Please assess them, sir," stumbled Lutz as he held out the bag of hairpins, not used to being so polite. Mark took them out and counted.

"There are twenty-four here. Including those you delivered, you have brought us a total of one hundred and eighty-six hairpins. Is that correct?"

"Mhm, perfect." We had the exact same number written on our slates. Each hairpin was worth five middle coppers. From that Lutz and I put our one copper share directly into our guild savings. We then put the rest into a separate bag we had brought with us, to make it easier to distribute.

Lutz's three brothers had been making an equal amount of them to prevent fighting, so we owed each of them six large coppers and two middle coppers. Very simple. On the other hand, Mom had made eighty-three hairpins, Tuuli sixty-six, and me thirty-seven, which made things kind of annoying. Mom had earned one small silver, six large coppers, and six middle coppers. Tuuli had earned one small silver, three large coppers, and two middle coppers. I had earned seven large coppers and four middle coppers.

"With this many hairpins, our stock should last until next winter. They are selling fairly well. Our customers enjoy browsing the different colors and selecting their favorites."

I smiled, imagining a mother and daughter browsing hairpins together. "Really? That's great. I made a hairpin too, for my own baptism."

"What kind is it?"

"That's a secret for now." I giggled and Mark raised an eyebrow.

"Oh? In that case, I will look forward to its grand reveal. Moving on, then. You wish to resume making paper?"

"Yes. We can't be sure until Lutz goes to the forest and checks out the river, but now that it's spring, I want to start making paper again." Benno would only give us free financial support until the beginning of this summer. The sooner we started, the better.

"Understood. I will speak to the craftsman. You ordered two of these suketa the size of contract paper, yes?"

"Mhm. Thank you."

Just as we finished the first two topics, Benno's business meeting ended and several merchants left his room.

"I will report this to the master. Please wait just a moment." Mark entered the room, then popped back out to gesture us inside.

It was the first time I was seeing Benno this spring, so I put my right fist against my left palm to immediately say the spring greeting I had just learned.

"Hi Mr. Benno, nice to see you. Blessed be the melting of the snow. Ummm, may the Goddess of Spring's... boundless magnanimity, um... Um? H-How does it go again?"

Lutz, seeing that I couldn't remember something I learned five minutes ago without a notepad, shook his head and stepped forward. "Blessed be the melting of the snow. May the Goddess of Spring's boundless magnanimity grace you."

"Right, that! Blessed be the melting of the snow. May the Goddess of Spring's boundless magnanimity grace you both."

Thanks to Lutz, I remembered the greeting and corrected myself. Benno returned the greeting while clearly holding back laughter.

"Yeah, blessed be the melting of the snow. May the Goddess of Spring's boundless magnanimity grace you. Anyway... you sure messed that up, huh? Do better next time," said Benno with a grin as he tapped his table. Lutz and I sat down on the other side and began our discussion.

"Mr. Mark just taught me that today. I've never heard it before, so at least compliment me for getting most of it right on my first try."

"...Yeah? In that case, good job, Lutz. Anyway, what's all this about your apprenticeship?" Benno complimented only Lutz, who had given the entire greeting correctly.

I puffed my cheeks out, pouting, and got to the main point of why I was here. "I've decided not to become your apprentice after my baptism."

"Huh...? Hold up. Where's this coming from? 'Cause I didn't compliment you just now? You didn't say it right, but I appreciate that you tried your best, y'know." Benno rubbed his temples and tossed out a lukewarm compliment for my greeting.

"No! That's not it! The greeting has nothing to do with this."

"Then why?"

"Umm, you know how weak I am, right?"

"Obviously. You're so weak I can hardly believe it." Benno's immediate reply pierced my chest.

"Ngh... You were worried about whether or not I would even be able to work, weren't you? I think that if a new apprentice takes a lot of days off work and is given all the easiest jobs, the other employees will get upset and everything will start collapsing."

"Is that all? Why else are you saying this?" Benno glared at me with his dark-red eyes and I thought back to all the important points Otto had talked to me about.

"Ummm, also, isn't it likely that the profit from my products will lead to me earning a lot more than a veteran that's been working here for decades? Money can break apart human relationships faster than anything."

"Who told you that? Don't try and say you thought of that yourself." Benno narrowed his eyes and peered at me, so I replied with a big nod. I had a very narrow perspective due to my entire life up until this point being built around reading books. Even now, I was mainly just thinking about my own health. I hadn't thought about human relationships and all that abstract stuff until Otto pointed it out to me.

"Mr. Otto told me all this."

"Is that right? Otto, huh...?"

Wait... Is it just me, or did his voice just drop an octave? And is that a violent look in his eyes? I must be imagining things. I tilted my head in confusion at Benno's sudden shift into predator mode and asked the biggest question on my mind.

"Also, you know that I'm sick with the Devouring, right? I don't think you should hire an employee that could die before the year is up." It was very likely that the resources he put into training me would all be wasted. A merchant wouldn't be willing to do that.

Benno rubbed his temples hard and stared at me with eyes that had sharpened drastically. "So, what'll you do instead of joining my store?"

"I'll do paperwork and stuff at home, make new products with Lutz on my days off, sometimes go to the gate to help... Basically, the same things I have been doing. I talked with my family over the winter and we decided that the less work we put on my body the better."

"Alright. I'll take you off the future apprentice list." The strength drained from Benno's eyes and shoulders. He rubbed his temples and murmured "What am I gonna do about this...?" while deep in thought. I called out to him after he started whispering to himself.

"Um, Mr. Benno. Is there any work you could give me that I can do at home?"

Benno's eyes immediately flashed with a sharp light. His expression looked calm, but his lips were curved into the grin of a carnivore. "Your handwriting is pretty nice. You could find good work as a stand-in writer for others. So, come to the store with Lutz every once in a while. Alright?"

Um... Why do I feel like a predator has just captured me? I decided not to think about it since he was offering me a job and instead asked another question.

"Um, in that case, what will happen to my guild card? I was planning on selling things through Lutz, but my card is assigned to your store right now, isn't it? Will it need to switch over to a merchant stand?"

My plan had been to register as an apprentice at the Gilberta Company once my baptism was over, so I had no idea what would happen to it if I didn't do that. A temporary registration wouldn't fly after the baptism ceremony, I imagined. But I didn't belong to any store and I couldn't do trade without being registered.

"I don't know how many products you intend to think up, but how about we turn your storage building into the Myne Workshop and make your card into a forewoman's card? If you sign a contract making it a branch of the Gilberta Company, not much will change from right now."

"Forewoman?! Wow, that sounds cool. If doing that will keep things the same, it's what I want. Thank you." I clapped my hands with joy and Benno nodded with a happy grin.

Then I continued, "Okay, with that settled, I'll tell you what I told Mark. I want to start making paper again after checking the river. We'll keep making paper until our baptism, but after that Lutz has his apprentice work and I'll stop being an apprentice at all, so I think it would be best if you left the paper-making to another workshop. Does that work?"

"If I left it to another workshop? You're supposed to be the one to pick it, remember? But I mean, whatever works for you."

The magic contract Lutz and I had signed was meant to ensure us stable, safe work with Benno's store. Wood paper-making would be a new business, and I could imagine that Benno wanted to select the workshop and workers carefully to maximize his profit. Meanwhile, given that I wasn't getting a cut of the overall profits, I honestly didn't care who made it as long as paper ended up mass produced and common throughout the world.

"Well, I don't know anything about workshops, and I don't know anybody who wants to make paper. Though since a step involves dunking wood in a river, you'll maybe want a workshop near the river."

"Near the river, huh...? That won't be easy. How are you two managing it?"

Lutz shrugged. "We carry our tools to the river and do our work there, but I'm thinkin'... I believe that carrying the tools there each day would be, er, not good."

"Mass production will involve larger tools, which would make carrying them close to impossible. But thinking about that is your job and the workshop people's job."

"...It sure is." Benno nodded, signaling that he would deal with choosing the workshop, buying tools, and so on himself.

"Please make these decisions before the baptism ceremony. Lutz will come teach you how to make paper once the baptism is over."

"Me?!" Lutz's eyes widened and his mouth flapped.

I smiled and nodded. "Well, there's a lot of steps I can't do myself. You teaching him would be for the best. We'll make so much paper in the spring that you'll end up memorizing the process whether you want to or not."

"You're really abandoning all responsibility here, huh?" laughed Benno in amusement.

I looked away. I knew that I was burdening others by abandoning responsibility. But now that I had mostly ironed out the paper-making process and found a way to mass produce paper, I wanted to advance to the next step. Just paper wasn't enough to make a book. I needed to make paper for myself over the winter and start getting to work on printing.

I left Benno's store with my time-limited dream held closely in my heart. Mark was a fast worker and our new suketa would be in our storage building by tomorrow. Hearing that, Lutz went to the thawed-out forest to investigate the river for us.

"How was it, Lutz? Warm enough to make paper?"

"The river's bigger thanks to all the melted snow, but unless there's some heavy rain, I don't think the bark will get washed away," concluded Lutz, which meant it was time to make paper again.

The next day Lutz left in the early morning to get the storage building key, then we headed there together. We walked along the alleys and I thought about what we needed to do today as still-chilly air pushed against my coat.

We would go to the storage building first and check to see if the black bark and trombe wood we'd left there was safe. Once that was done, we could get to work turning it into white bark while simultaneously using the saved white bark from the volrin wood to start making actual paper.

"Well, considering my health, it would be better for us to wait for the water to warm a bit."

"Aaah, yeah. But we need to start saving money, so the sooner we start the better." Benno would only fund our paper-making until our baptism. We wanted to earn as much money as possible before then.

"I wonder if the trombe black bark is doing okay..." I murmured.

"It's been drying since we left it here. It should all be dried out by now."

"I'm worried that it grew mold since there's no sun here!"

"Y'know, I don't think mold really grows on trombe wood." Lutz shrugged, but we had completely skipped the sun-drying process, so I couldn't help but feel worried. It had definitely dried out given how we left it here for the entirety of winter, but who knew if it would be dried the way I wanted it.

We reached the storage building and unlocked it. The door creaked as it opened. A ton of what looked like ivy was hanging off the shelves of the dim storage building. Add that on the dust everywhere and it looked pretty horrible in there.

"Is this really gonna be okay?"

"Alright, I gotta say I'm a little worried now too." He poked the black bark with a finger and it was completely crusty, showing that it had finished drying. But since it was black, it was hard to tell by color whether or not mold was growing on it.

"Let's go ahead and take it to the forest and put it in the river."

"What else are we bringing?" asked Lutz while dusting off the carrying basket he had left here.

"Ummm, you should take the pot and the ashes, I think? We don't need something as big as a tub, but a bucket would be nice. And we'll be in trouble if we can't find any firewood in the forest, so maybe we should bring some of that too. I'll carry the black bark and our saved volrin white bark, plus my (chopsticks)."

"I dunno about the bucket, but if you say so." I prepared the dried-up trombe black bark and volrin white bark, grabbed the chopsticks Lutz had made for me to stir the pot, and put them into my basket alongside several rags. We put our stuff on our backs and hurried to the meeting place where the other kids were.

We arrived at the forest with everyone and scattered to do our own things. Lutz and I went to the riverbed. Once there, Lutz prepared the pot near the river. He placed the pot on top of the hearth of stones and began drawing water with his bucket.

"I get it now. We can get water from the river without going inside of it like this. Good thinking, Myne."

To get water into the pot directly one had to enter the river, but it seemed Lutz hadn't thought of a workaround for that. He put the water into the pot and ignited the firewood we had brought with us. As the water boiled, we put the black bark into the water to clean it as much as possible.

Lutz glared at the river flowing with melted snow and murmured about how cold it looked. He had to position the rocks into a circle to keep the black bark from washing away, but only half of the rocks from autumn were still here. Which meant he needed to enter the river and get to work placing the rocks.

"Gaaah! So cooold!" Lutz yelled miserably as he walked into the ice-cold river.

"I believe in you, Lutz!" I would definitely get a fever if I went in there, and if I got a fever my family wouldn't allow me to go outside for a bit. All I could do here was support him from the sidelines.

I walked around the riverbed and collected firewood for Lutz until eventually he called out to me from the river. "Myne, get the black bark!"

"Okaaay."

Once he got the black bark into place, Lutz dashed out of the river and squatted in front of the burning hearth. He held out his bright-red hands and feet to the fire and rubbed them together. I scooped up a bucket of warm water from the pot and held it out to Lutz.

"Put this on your hands and feet. If you don't rub it in enough, you might get frostbite."

"...Now this is warm. Feels great." Lutz let out a sigh of relief after getting the warm water on his hands and feet. The water cooled almost immediately, but that had been enough to heat his body up.

We put the ashes and white bark into the now-boiling water, then once it was finished we put it into the river to wash away the ashes. Thanks to Lutz's tearful yet noble efforts within the cold river, we safely finished the day's work.

Vested Interests

The next day came and it was time to peel the black bark to turn it into white bark, so we brought a pan, a tub, and a bucket with us. We peeled the bark with knives while occasionally holding our hands up to the fire and dipping them into hot water to warm up.

"You know, I really don't want to do this outside of summer. It's so cold my fingers are all tingly," I said.

"Yeah. Going into the river is real killer."

We complained to one another while continuing our work and getting white bark from all the trombe wood. I didn't see any moldy spots on the white bark, which made me sigh in relief.

"...Looks like it didn't get moldy. Whew."

"Didn't I tell you that? Maybe the volrin wood, but the trombe wood's definitely fine."

"Trombes sure are dangerous plants, aren't they?"

Once the bark was peeled, it was time to gather in the forest. There were some herbs that could only be foraged in this season, and I picked them up with Lutz while he taught me what to look for. Along the way, I noticed that Lutz was actively avoiding red fruits about the size of an adult's thumb. Maybe they were poisonous. I pointed at one, making sure not to touch it, and asked Lutz.

"Hey Lutz, why don't you pick up these red fruits? Are they poisonous?"

"Ah, yeah, you don't need to bother with tau fruit. They're basically just water inside. Can't eat'm and the water dries up eventually if you take them home. Nothing you can do with them right now."

The phrase "right now" implied they would be useful later, so I gave Lutz an inquisitive look. So he explained, "Once summer comes, they end up about as big as your fist. They'll explode if you throw them at someone, so we can have fun tossing'm at each other."

I concluded that they were nature's water balloons. They would just dry out at home and they wouldn't get bigger if not left on the ground. Weird.

"Kids and adults end up having big wars in town. I mean, you remember the Star Festival, right?"

I had lived in this world for over a year, but I didn't remember any festival like that. "Um, Lutz. I've never heard of the Star Festival. Has there always been a festival in the summer?"

"Last year you were close to dying when the festival came around. I went to your place so we could go together and your mom told me your fever wasn't going down at all. I went to get the bamboo after the festival was over," said Lutz, establishing that I had been on the verge of death back then. That had been the first time I fully understood that the Devouring heat was actually trying to swallow me up. I was unconscious for days in a row and ended up in bed for a while afterward, so going to a festival was the last thing on my mind.

"Tuuli must have wanted to go and play too. Did I make her stay home to look after me?" It was possible that I had stolen away nice childhood memories from Tuuli. The thought of that made my shoulders droop, but Lutz just shrugged and shook his head.

"Nope, Effa was looking after you and let Tuuli go to the Star Festival. She and Ralph fought to see who could gather the most taus in the forest."

"Oh, okay. That's a relief."

"Hope you can go too this year, Myne."

I promised Lutz I would watch my health this year so I could go to the festival, and before long, we had finished our gathering. But well, promise or not, I didn't know if my parents would let me go to a festival that involved getting pelted with water.

Starting from the next day, we had to work in front of the storage building. The water was so cold that we had to repeatedly dip our hands into hot water while we worked, but nonetheless, we swished around volrin pulp in the contract paper-sized suketa. While the pulp dried over several days, we started making paper from the trombe bark.

"Looks like the volrin paper is dry now. Good thing it was so sunny today."

"We're gonna have to dry the trombe wood for a full day tomorrow, yeah?" confirmed Lutz as we split the twenty-six completed pages of volrin paper. Lutz looked at his thirteen sheets of paper and furrowed his brows. "Wait, why are we splitting them? Shouldn't we just split the money?"

"Well, I want some paper for myself. I couldn't keep paper made from wood Benno bought for us, but since we got this wood ourselves, it should be okay." If I were to buy the paper back after selling it to Benno, I would eat the cost of the thirty-percent handling fee, if not more. It would be better not to sell him the paper in the first place.

"So you're not selling yours?"

"I'll sell half of mine. I want to collect paper and make a book." Now that we had the process ironed out and we were both fairly used to it, there were fewer failures in each batch of paper. That was problematic for my book-making. I honestly cared more about paper than money, especially since Mom had started telling me a ton of stories I wanted to write down.

Once our work was done, we went to Benno's store to both sell the paper and return the key.

"Oh, all done?" Benno took the volrin paper from the both of us and counted the sheets. Thirteen from Lutz, six from me. He frowned at the clear difference.

"Not many from you, Myne. Why's that?"

"I wanted the paper for myself. There's no problem with that since we used wood we got ourselves, right?"

"...Yeah. I don't mind that for wood you got yourselves, but what do you even want that paper for?" asked Benno, looking somewhat on guard.

"I want to make a book. You need paper to make a book."

"A book...? Why would you want one of those? They don't sell."

"Bwuh? I wouldn't sell it. I just want to read it by myself."

Lutz looked between us. He and I were both confused. Benno couldn't understand why I would use valuable paper to make something that couldn't be sold, and I just wanted to read a book regardless of profit. There was no way we could understand each other.

"I don't know what's going on in that head of yours, but I get the feeling it'd just be a waste of time to think about it. Here's your pay. Paper this big has a market value of one large silver each. My handling fee is a thirty-percent cut. How much do you earn?"

Lutz still wasn't great at percentages. He hurriedly glanced at me and I gave an immediate answer. "Seven small silvers."

"Huh?! Seven small silvers?! I, uuuh, what?! Isn't that a little too much?!" Lutz hadn't expected that at all and his jaw just dropped at the value of paper.

"...Calm down, Lutz. It may seem like we're earning too much, but we're only going to be earning money from paper for this season. Compared to how much Benno's going to make as he sells paper for decades and decades after this, we're basically earning peanuts. Don't worry about it."

"Seriously...? Don't worry about it?" I was trying to calm Lutz down, but he just blinked rapidly at me in stunned disbelief.

"You sold thirteen sheets of paper today, Lutz, so you get nine large silvers and a small silver. I sold six, so I get four large silvers and two small silvers."

"I mean, no matter how I think about it, nine large silvers isn't peanuts."

"Oh? Should we sell them for less, then?" I saw how frightened Lutz was and suggested that we lower the prices, but Benno shook his head with a frown.

"You can't lower the price. That'd cause unnecessary conflict with the vested interests. We have to keep the price up. Once your wood paper's solidly in the market, I'll think about how to handle the price. But if you're scared of earning that much money, I can boost my handling fee. Sound good?" Benno said to Lutz with a grin.

"We don't have the right to change the paper's price, so I'll leave all that to you, but I won't let you increase the handling fee. In which case, Lutz, I can take your money if you don't want it."

"I'm not giving it to either of you! It's just so much money it's kinda spooking me!" roared Lutz, clutching his guild card. Guild cards confirmed identities through blood, so only the owner of a card could use it. A very safe place to store your money.

"Don't worry. You won't have to see the money yourself if you store it all in the guild."

"Grrr. I dunno how you're so calm about this, Myne. Wish I had your guts."

Putting aside how I had saved most of my money back in my Urano days, I had already gained and lost several small golds worth of money in this world, so I was used to dealing with large quantities of cash. I wanted to shout that I wasn't gutsy at all.

I puffed my cheeks out, pouting, and Benno laughed hard while paying us through our guild cards. I took five large coppers to give to my family and saved the rest. Lutz also split his pay into savings and hard cash to give to his family.

Several days after that, Lutz went to get the storage building key and came back with a large bundle and a letter. Or to be more precise, it was a letter of invitation written on a board. The bundle contained ponchos with hoods.

Lutz held up the differently colored ponchos and blinked in confusion, not recognizing what they were. I read the letter, which neatly and concisely described the meetup location and why we were being invited.

"It says we're going to go clothes shopping, so meet up in the central plaza at fourth bell."

"Huh. Clothes?"

"...Benno says that there are people coming to his store who are angry about the paper we made. He wants to work things out with them but in such a way that they don't learn that you and I exist. Our current clothes will stand out where we're going, so he wants us to come wearing these."

"Huh? Wait, what? Is something dangerous happening here?!"

We both tried the ponchos on. They were warm and hid most of our clothes, which was ideal. We could hide our faces and hair too with the hoods, so we would wear them when going outside. My hair stick would especially stand out.

"I'm not sure how dangerous it is yet, but since we're meeting Mark there, maybe we should finish up the trombe paper soon so we can sell it to him there? Oh, but if he's trying to keep us a secret, maybe we shouldn't walk around with it. What do you think?" I said while checking how the trombe paper looked, and for some reason Lutz got mad.

"Why are you so calm, Myne?!"

"Bwuh? I mean, I expected that there would be some conflict with the vested interests. That's just what happens when you introduce something new. They acted faster than I thought they would, but still."

"Wait, vested interests? What's that?" Lutz blinked in utter confusion and repeated the phrase that didn't flow off his tongue very well.

"'Vested interests' refers to an organization or people who already have rights related to earning profit in a certain market or product. That is to say, they have a vested interest in the product or market. Remember what Benno said? Lowering the price would cause conflict with the vested interests. He's probably talking about the people who make parchment."

"What've they got to do with anything? We're making paper from wood, not animal skin."

They seemed completely unrelated due to how they were made, but paper and parchment overlapped in usage and market — they were used the same way and by the same customers. No other product had been competing with their parchment and therefore threatening their profits, so I could imagine that they had fallen into a complete panic over the appearance of a new kind of paper.

"Up until now, they were the only ones who could make paper, and people had no choice but to buy that paper to make contracts, right? They had control over the price. But now there's a new kind of paper and their customers could move over to buying it instead."

Lutz nodded, getting what I was driving at. If both products were used the same way, it just made sense that some customers would be drawn away.

"If that happens, they won't earn as much money, right? They don't want that. Not to mention, prices tend to fall once there's a lot of something in the market."

"Huh? Really?"

I took out my stone slate and drew a graph. I started with two perpendicular straight lines for the X and Y axes, then two simple curves representing supply and demand.

"This graph shows the relationship between supply and demand. This is the supply curve and this is the demand curve. Think of supply as products that exist and demand as the people who want those products."

"Right."

"When a lot of people want a product but there's not much of that product, the price of the product rises." I pointed at the leftmost part of the graph and Lutz understood my point, recognizing that things got more expensive when there wasn't much there.

I nodded and traced my finger along the supply curve. "So it follows that when more of the product enters the market, more of the people wanting the product will get it, which means demand will decrease. That lowers the price."

Then I poked the point where the two curves made contact. "Once there's more of a product than there are people wanting it, it'll stop selling no matter how many more you make and put on the market. That means its value will steadily drop, right?"

I moved my finger to the right and showed that the supply and demand curves had completely switched over with demand now above supply. "Understand? The more paper we make, the more its value will drop. The people making parchment don't want its value to drop. They want to keep their profit secure, so they're protesting Benno's new paper."

"Uh, isn't this kinda bad?" said Lutz nervously.

I smiled and shook my head. "Benno's trying to hide us, which means that he'll take care of them himself. It's not something we have to worry about. Though I can't say anything for sure until I hear the details."

We finished twenty-four sheets of trombe paper before the meeting time described in the letter of invitation, but left them in the storage room for safety's sake.

"You should put your hood on too, Lutz, so nobody can see your hair or face too well." Benno being this guarded meant that it was indeed possible that we could get wrapped up in something dangerous. Better safe than sorry.

We waited in the central plaza somewhat anxiously, and after fourth bell, Mark finally came. "Sorry to keep you waiting. Shall we go buy your apprentice clothes, as promised?"

"Yes, thank you." I didn't need apprentice clothes since I wasn't becoming one, but it would probably be smart to buy clothes that wouldn't stand out when I went to Benno's store. Or maybe it would be a waste of money.

I started to debate internally over the best course of action when Mark suddenly picked me up. He must have interpreted my hesitation as a sign of poor health.

"Um, Mr. Mark, I can walk on my own!"

"I became uneasy due to your hesitation. Please allow me to do this, for the sake of my own health."

"I was just thinking about something. I'm perfectly healthy right now!"

Mark sped up his walking pace, smile not faltering for a moment. "Feel free to think as much as you like," he said, solidifying that he had no intention of setting me down.

"LUUUTZ!"

"This is faster, just suck it up for a bit." Lutz immediately shot down my cry for help, so having no other choice I gave up and accepted my fate. *Grrr! Traitor!*

The three of us entered the clothes store and were greeted by the pleasant shopkeeper. Both the workers and the customers here were wearing fine clothes. Lutz and I definitely would have been kicked out if we had come alone.

"Oh, hello there Mark. Good to see you again. New apprentices?"

"Yes, that's right. I would like to order Gilberta Company apprentice clothes for these two." Benno must have bought all his apprentice clothes here, as the storekeeper nodded immediately to Mark's request.

"Wait, what? An apprentice outfit for me too?" Lutz was becoming an apprentice, but I wasn't.

Mark just nodded with his unfaltering smile. "You will simply stand out too much wearing what you are now. My apologies, but we will be ordering clothes for you as well. It will be convenient for when you enter our store on business."

I wasn't becoming an official apprentice, but I would be inventing new products in the Myne Workshop and visiting Benno's store to discuss profit details and the like, so it was likely that I would be going there about as much as I had been for the past few seasons. It would just be sad if I went with Lutz in my patchwork hand-me-downs while he wore fancy new clothes. Maybe it would be a good idea to buy new clothes now that I had spare money.

Lutz was taken to the back of the store first and stripped down to his underwear for measurements. I was taken to another room where the same was done to me. It was exhausting to get measured all over.

"We request an advance payment of one small silver." After ordering a full set of apprentice clothes — jacket, shirt, pants or a skirt, and even shoes — we tapped our guild cards against the storekeeper's to pay one small silver. Benno had been right when he said that the final price would be around ten small silvers. That was the cost of one Gilberta Company apprentice outfit. Given my ignorance of the world, I had no idea if that was expensive or cheap.

After finishing our order, Mark brought us to Benno's store. Benno was glaring at a piece of paper with a somewhat grim expression on his face, but it softened after he saw us.

"Oh, there you are. My bad for being so sudden with all this. Things got bad faster than I thought they would. Maybe I went too fast. But either way, I'm on guard now. You two should stay on guard too. Keep your eyes open. There are people who will do anything to keep their power safe, and those people are everywhere."

Benno was aware that he was potentially being overprotective, but when product rights and the power they granted got involved, no amount of caution was too much. We were kids too young to have been baptized, but if we wore apprentice outfits we wouldn't stick out in the store like we did before.

"When you mentioned the vested interests in the letter, were you talking about the people who make parchment?" I asked.

"Yeah. Some members of the Parchment Guild sent an official complaint to the Merchant's Guild."

"To the Merchant's Guild, really?" I tilted my head, not knowing what connection the Parchment Guild had with the Merchant's Guild.

Benno explained that part of the Merchant's Guild's job was to protect vested interests, minimize the friction caused by new products entering the market, and arbitrate between different Guilds and parties.

"They sent a complaint to the Merchant's Guild last evening, saying I started selling paper without joining their guild or paying them anything. According to a contact of mine, they asked the Guild to 'get this lawbreaking ruffian under control.'"

"Uh huh... So, what'd you do?" No way would Benno just sit quietly and let them order him around. He must have found a good compromise they could settle on before making his move.

I urged Benno on, not feeling worried in the slightest. His lips curved into the confident grin of a successful carnivore. "I gave a hard objection. My paper's made of plants, not animal skin, so the Parchment Guild's got nothing to do with it. Basically, I told'm to back off."

I felt the blood drain from my face at Benno's bloodthirsty attitude. He hadn't found a compromise or anything, he was just picking a fight with the vested interests head-on. If things got violent, it would be all Benno's fault.

"Um? So like, you didn't think of a compromise, or something?"

"Idiot. They'd just look down on me if I tried to compromise. The fact of the matter is, I didn't steal any of their manufacturing secrets and I don't owe them anything for their manufacturing fee. Plant paper and animal paper aren't made the same way and they aren't the same things. One's not derived from the other. They're just trying to monopolize the paper market for themselves, and if possible, suck up the profit my new product is going to make."

This was just how Benno operated and it wasn't my place to complain about how he ran his business, but I wished he could have handled things a little more peacefully.

"Mmm, parchment is made from animal skin, so I don't think they'll be able to increase production no matter what they do. What if you work with the Merchant's Guild and agree that official contract paper will always be made from parchment so that you can guarantee that at least some of their profit will be preserved?"

"You're as soft as ever." Benno snorted. I thought that the Parchment Guild would be more cooperative if we guaranteed some of their profit and parchment's relevance in the future, but Benno apparently didn't think that was a good idea.

"I just don't like unnecessary fighting. Plus, I really just want paper to spread throughout the world and be used for all sorts of things. Contract paper isn't my end goal. I want it to be used for books, memo pads, painting, origami... I want paper to be something even kids can use without worrying about the price."

"Thaaat's a bigger dream than I expected," murmured Benno, eyes opened a little wide in surprise and exasperation.

"Hm? Is it really that big of a dream? I think it'll happen no matter what once paper gets mass produced. So really, the best thing to do here might be to go ahead and make volrin paper a lot cheaper than parchment while using it for everything but contracts. For example, these written reports on your desk. They'd be easier to carry with plant paper and easier to store. They'd be easier to write on than wood boards, too."

"I see, using different paper for different purposes... I'll have to think about it." This time, Benno's eyes narrowed in thought and he didn't say I was being soft. Something I had said must have tickled both the profit-seeking part of his brain and his heartstrings.

"If we use different paper for different things, then you can treat trombe paper as specialty paper for high-class purposes. It's better than parchment even, right?"

"Yeah. I've been planning to make trombe paper a lot more expensive than parchment."

"Wait, come again? A lot more?" I blinked in surprise, which made Benno narrow his eyes a bit more and look between Lutz and me.

"...Don't tell me you two haven't realized it."

"Huh? Realized what?"

"Lutz. What's special about Trombe wood?" asked Benno.

Lutz bounced a little in his chair in surprise at the unexpected question, then began to list off his answers. "Huh? Eeer, trombe wood grows super fast, and it's hard to burn."

"Oh, I get it...! Is trombe paper hard to burn too?" Speaking of which, Dad had said that furniture made of Trombe wood was so hard to burn that it sometimes survived fires. Young and soft wood couldn't be made into furniture, but it could be made into paper.

"That's right. Compared to normal paper, it's extremely hard to burn. That's not to say it can't burn at all, but it's exactly the kind of paper nobles will want for recording classified government information and preserving official documents. I'd be stupid not to give it a high price."

It certainly was a special kind of paper deserving a higher price. Even back on Earth, different kinds of paper had different prices. Unique or otherwise difficult to make paper was always fairly expensive.

"Okay, I understand now. So... how much will each sheet of trombe paper be?"

"For a contract-sized sheet, five large silvers."

"Bwuuuh..." The price was so overwhelming that I actually felt a little headache come on. Lutz was so shocked he couldn't speak.

Meanwhile, Benno just flatly repeated that it was rare paper made from materials that could not be consistently obtained. The price was obvious to him. Apparently, he wouldn't put it on the market until he had built up a large enough stock of it.

"With that out of the way, don't come to this store again until this business with the Parchment Guild is finished. There's a reason I want to keep you two hidden. If the method for making plant paper leaks out and others start selling it, people could die."

"Wait, what? People could die?" I blinked in surprise at the sudden escalation and Benno brought up the magic contract I had completely forgotten about.

"Our magic contract states that you will decide who makes the paper and Lutz will sell it. If someone starts making and selling the paper without knowing about that contract, anything could happen."

"Bwuh?! Contract magic is that dangerous?! It involves people who didn't have anything to do with the contract too?!" I held my head in my hands, stunned by this unexpected development. I had never thought for a moment that the magic contract I had made to secure our employment would end up being so dangerous.

"Contract magic exists to keep nobles under control. Whether you know about the contract or not, breaking it will give you some kind of punishment. I'm going to hide your identities and tell the Merchant's Guild that I have a magic contract stating that only I can make and sell this plant paper. That should shut the Parchment Guild up."

The contract might have brought us more danger than safety. Since only I had the right to decide who makes paper, and only Lutz had the right to sell that paper, we were actually in a pretty risky position.

"I want to hide that you two have the rights to the paper. You can keep the key to the storage building for a bit, so don't come back here. I'll contact you through Otto once the dust has settled."

Lutz and I both nodded, assured by Benno's confidence. ...*I just hope that the contract magic I asked for doesn't kill anyone.*

Result of the Meeting with the Vested Interests

I felt terrified of the danger that magic contracts had introduced. Lutz and I just wanted job security, we didn't want to hurt anyone. I went home with Lutz, trembling in fear. My stomach was churning, as if I had swallowed a whole boat that was floating around.

"You don't gotta worry so much. Benno'll do something."

I nodded at Lutz, but I just couldn't stop thinking about how someone I didn't know might soon be hurt or worse because of me. I was so, so worried. My stomach ached. What was I afraid of? Forcing people I didn't know to get involved in my business and hurting them as a result.

I really wanted to just shut myself inside my home, but Lutz basically forced me outside each day, saying that he had no idea what I would do if left alone. I hated that we could only wait for Benno's contact while going to the forest and making paper.

But in the end, even after several days passed, Benno didn't say anything to us. He never mentioned anyone dying a suspicious death. Everything was normal. Too normal.

Several more days passed and my fear turned into distrust toward Benno. Would the contract magic really kill someone? Maybe he was just exaggerating. I thought back to exactly what Benno had said to find any clues. Even his tone and expression might have hinted at something.

"…You know, isn't it a little weird?"

"What is?" Lutz frowned at me while angling the suketa to make volrin paper. I turned to look at him after putting fresh paper onto the draining bed.

"That contract magic would affect people who don't know the contract in question exists."

"That's not weird. It's magic, what do you expect?" replied Lutz casually as he put his finished paper on the draining bed on top of mine.

I pursed my lips while scooping up water and shaking it. "I expect it to make sense somehow. It'd be weird if it didn't. I mean, think about it. What if someone signed a magic contract about a product that's already on the market? People all over would break it. And what if someone signs a magic contract in a city far away from ours? We'd have no idea."

I kept pondering this while shaking the suketa. If contract magic was used to enforce the equivalent of patent rights, there was probably a patent office or something that managed them. Someone had to inform the public what magic contracts were in effect. It'd be too dangerous otherwise.

"I think contract magic has a bunch of conditions and a limited range that we don't know about. And anyway, don't you think magic this dangerous would be restricted a little more?"

"Alright, I can tell you're building up to something. What're you nervous about?" said Lutz, which made me reflexively stop shaking the suketa. He picked it up from the side and continued for me. "You always talk faster when you're trying to hide how you feel." Lutz jerked his head, urging me to spit it out. I couldn't hide anything from him.

"...I'm scared of hurting people we don't know with our magic contract. I want to think that Benno was joking or lying. Nobody's been hurt yet, right? Maybe he was just trying to scare us. I want to think he was just trying to scare us."

"It'd be nice if he was just joking, but why would he do that? What would he gain from tricking us?"

"Ngh... I-I mean, he's tricked us a lot already. I get the feeling that he's hiding something from us again to test us or something." I was about to say that he probably had some secret reason for distancing us from him when suddenly I heard a familiar voice from behind us.

"Wow. I didn't know you had so little trust in Benno, Myne."

Lutz and I, surprised that someone else was in the storage building, spun around. There we saw a grinning Otto in his normal clothes, raising both a hand and an eyebrow.

"Mr. Otto?! Why are you here?!"

"Why else would I be here but to deliver a message from Benno?"

Benno had indeed said that he would contact us through Otto, but I had expected him to wave us down on our way through the gate. I never thought for a second he would come visit us in the storage building.

"Seems like everything's over."

His short message didn't tell me anything. I lurched toward Otto, desperate for any information that would calm my aching stomach. "What's over?! How did it go?!"

"Well, it sure sounded like a big deal. He really broke his back making things work."

"What do you mean by that?! What happened?!"

Otto just shrugged, not giving me any hard answers. I had no idea if he actually didn't know or if he was just pretending not to know. "Benno didn't tell you anything?"

"He told us some stuff, but not much. He said that it would be really bad if people who didn't know about our magic contract started making paper on their own. Then he said that we shouldn't go to his store until he was finished dealing with the Parchment Guild, partially to keep the manufacturing process for paper safe." I summarized what Benno had said and Otto stroked his chin.

"Hmm. Sounds like he told you the bare minimum, at least."

"Did anyone get hurt from the contract magic? That's what I'm really worried about…"

"You two hid so the process wouldn't get out, right? Nobody's been hurt. Everything else you should hear from Benno. Want to go together once you've finished your work here?"

"Okay!" The weight on my chest was lifted by his confirmation that nobody had been hurt. Feeling lighter than I had in days, I got back to rocking the suketa.

"Shaking that thing makes paper? What even is it?"

"That's a secret."

"Looks like there's some gooey stuff inside. What's it made of?"

"That's a secret."

Otto watched us, full of curiosity and questions, but I just kept working without giving any answers.

"We're on the same side here, Myne, you can tell me."

"Benno will get mad if I tell anyone. Right, Lutz?" I direction the question to Lutz and he shrugged with a grin.

"He gets mad at Myne for not thinking before she talks all the time. Keeping quiet is the best call for her."

"Hahaha… You tell people this kinda thing without thinking? I can picture Benno now, so mad his veins are bulging."

"It's less that he gets so mad his veins bulge and more that he just gets really exasperated."

We cleaned up our tools and headed to Benno's with Otto. By the time we got out of the alleyway and onto the main road, Otto was looking down at me while rubbing his temples.

"Hey, Myne. Do you always walk this slow?"

"...Um, yes?"

"I've gotta hand it to you, Lutz. You're a better man than me. I couldn't take this. Which meeeans... up you go."

"Hyaaah!"

Otto, saying he couldn't take my slow speed, hefted me up with his arms. He then power-walked forward. I got the feeling that lately Benno and Mark had been carrying me around everywhere too. It seemed that my walking speed was so slow that adults felt compelled to pick me up.

We arrived at Benno's store and Mark came out to greet us. "Hello, Myne and Lutz. Thank you for your help, Otto," said Mark, lowering his head in thanks.

"No biggie. This was pretty fun. Is Benno there?" replied Otto casually as he walked inside. He held me up with one arm and used his other hand to open the door to Benno's office.

"Benno, your Goddess of Water has arrived."

The moment Otto walked into the room and said whatever that weird comment was, Benno glared at him with such a forceful gaze that I could feel murderous intent radiating from him. Since he was looking in my general direction, I got hit with the gaze myself and jerked in fear.

"Shut it, Otto. Want me to force Corinna to divorce you?"

It seemed that Benno had the authority to make Corinna divorce Otto, since he was the patriarch of the family. He had said that Otto was basically his son-in-law, so Benno was indeed the family head. The force of Benno's glare and the low tone of his voice made it clear he was serious, and I wasn't the only one who noticed that. Otto hurriedly covered for himself, not wanting to lose the pillar of support that kept him going in life.

"Woah! I'm just kidding! It was just a little joke!"

"Jokes that aren't funny aren't jokes." Benno grabbed Otto's head and squeezed with a grim expression that made it hard to tell whether he was playing around or not. I wished he would stop; Otto was about to drop me.

"Mr. Benno, are you in a bad mood right now?" I ventured to ask.

"Yeah, 'cause of this guy," Benno replied with a glare, but Otto just casually set me down.

"Y'know, Benno, these kids don't trust you too much. I heard Myne complaining a lot about you. 'He's tricking us again! I think he's hiding something! Maybe this is another test!'"

I felt like I understood why Benno was so mad. Otto had definitely said something he shouldn't have. There was no doubt that he was intentionally trying to get us mad.

"Otto, you didn't have to say that!" Thinking that Otto's comment would make Benno's mood worse, I peered up at him. But Benno didn't look mad at all. He just looked at me and sighed with what felt like exhaustion.

"Haaah... Myne, do you have a sharp mind? Or are you just distrustful? Do you have a bad personality? I went out of my way to help you avoid this mess, and you just couldn't be happy about it...?"

"But hey," interjected Otto, "a good merchant never takes someone's word up front, yeah? She was right to doubt you and try to figure out the truth by reading between the lines of what you said and did." He gave me a thumbs-up with a grin.

"Well, whatever. I'll answer your questions. Sit."

I sat at the usual table, and the first thing I asked was what had been bothering me this whole time. "Does contract magic really affect people uninvolved with the contract?"

"Yeah, depending on the contents of the contract. Our contract could potentially affect other people. Didn't I explain that to you?" He had indeed. But not in a way that convinced me.

"But couldn't you hurt a lot of people by making a magic contract about a really common product or manufacturing technique? We have no idea what kind of contracts are being signed in far away cities, so... Is there some kind of condition for the contract to activate, or maybe they have a limited range of effect? Also, is there like a building that manages magic contracts...?"

Benno's eyes widened as I listed out my thoughts. Then, he nodded. "Yeah. Generally, magic contracts only work in the city they were signed in. Small-time magic used inside cities doesn't penetrate the magic barrier built into the outer walls surrounding them."

"Magic barrier?! Ummm, what?!" My heart thumped at the fantasy-sounding term and I instinctively leaned forward, but Benno just glared at me.

"A city's magic barrier is built into its foundation, but that doesn't matter right now. Unless you don't have any more questions about what happened, that is."

"Wait, no, I do! If contract magic actually can affect people who don't know about the contracts, isn't it super dangerous? I think it's weird that it's used so frivolously."

Benno, displeased, raised an eyebrow and glared at me. "Contract magic isn't used frivolously. The magic tools necessary to perform it are given only to certain recognized merchants, and they're so expensive your jaw would drop if you heard the price. Not to mention that, just like you thought, magic contracts that could have an effect on others must be reported to the lord of the region, the Archduke. I'm the one who'd be punished if I didn't report it and people got hurt."

"Wait, does that mean..." The second I started to wonder if Benno had forgotten to report our contract and began panicking because people might have gotten hurt because of that, he thumped me on the forehead. "Kyah!"

"Don't get any stupid ideas. I already reported it to him." He guessed my thoughts before I said them. I held my forehead and groaned. Benno let out a *hmph* and his lips curved into a triumphant grin.

"When I reported it to him, I was told to report to the Merchant's Guild since it was magic contract pertaining to a new product."

"...Which means, you actually reported to the Merchant's Guild too?"

"Naturally. I reported the contract to the guild and recorded it. While I was at it, I got permission to start a new guild."

Permission... to start a new guild? What's he planning? Is he trying to do something he really shouldn't do, just to get more money? His unexpected revelation made my eyes open wide and my head tilt. Seeing that, Benno puffed out his chest with pride and an annoyingly smug look on his face.

"Plant paper's gonna turn into a massive industry, y'know? So, I decided to make a Plant Paper Guild in the image of the Parchment Guild and spread the business to other cities too."

"...That's the first I'm hearing of this." I flinched and Benno nodded like I had just said something obvious.

"That's 'cause this is the first time I'm mentioning it."

"H-Hold on a second. Doesn't this mean you're picking a head-on fight with the vested interests?! I thought you were going to have a talk and end this peacefully!" I had no idea why he was being so forceful about this. Benno's methods involved nothing even resembling compromise or consideration for others.

"It's not my fault things ended up like this. Blame the geezer."

"Aren't you avoiding responsibility here?" I said, which made Benno glare at me and Otto burst into laughter next to him. I didn't know why it was funny, so we just glanced at him and waited for Benno to answer.

"I'm not avoiding responsibility. I went to the Merchant's Guild to register the magic contract and start the Guild, but got rejected since we signed the contract before there was a real-life prototype. I had to go back after you finished the first ones."

"Aaah."

"But the guildmaster didn't like the idea of me starting a new guild, so he dragged things out and ultimately didn't finish processing my request by the end of the whole season."

Speaking of which, the guildmaster had blocked our temporary registrations too. He eventually caved in and reluctantly approved it for the hairpins, but I remembered how stubborn he had been.

"I remember how he did something like that with our temporary registrations. Can he just reject applications for personal reasons...?"

"Naturally, he comes up with an excuse for what he does. He blocked your temporary registrations 'cause we weren't related, and this time he blocked the Plant Paper Guild because there already existed a guild for paper and he didn't see the need for a second one," said Benno, looking extremely displeased.

I thought back to how he and the guildmaster had acted in the meeting back then. It was clear they basically hated one another and were doing everything they could to one-up each other. "I can imagine how things went down."

"I submitted my registration in autumn and sold paper in the spring without even thinking he wouldn't have processed it by then. I should have been more careful, but can you really say I'm avoiding responsibility here?" Benno glared at me and I hurriedly shook my head.

"Umm, I think it's the Merchant's Guild's fault for being slow."

"Right. The Parchment Guild complained because I sold paper that hadn't been registered. That geezer ignored what he had done and gave them all his support like the scum he is." It seemed that Benno's true foe hadn't been the vested interests — it had been the guildmaster.

Benno went on, "Archduke Ehrenfest told me to register with the Merchant's Guild. What do you think would happen if people got hurt because the magic contract's registration hadn't been completed?"

Being told to do something and then not doing it would look pretty bad, so I would guess Benno would get punished pretty severely. "I think the Archduke would get really mad at you."

"Yeah. He'd take the tools needed for magic contracts away from me, limit what trade I can do with nobles, and punish all those involved with the contract. That would be giving that geezer the perfect chance to hit me where it hurts. I couldn't let the method of producing paper get out until the registration was processed, no matter what."

Considering his opponent was the guildmaster, I could understand why he was being so cautious.

"You can see why I didn't want to involve you two in this struggle between adults. And really, you know the guildmaster and he saved your life, so you would probably blabber about all sorts of secrets without thinking before you spoke."

"Bwuuuh?! Do you really trust me that little?!"

"History repeats itself. Think about what you've done."

"Guuuh…" I remembered all the mistakes I had made in the guildmaster's home and faltered. It was true that from Benno's perspective, I was a rogue element he couldn't predict. Distancing me from the problem was the safest bet.

"I understand what happened now. So, was your meeting with the Parchment Guild a struggle?"

"They weren't a big deal after a little prep work. The problem is just that dang geezer."

The guildmaster is the final boss, huh? I didn't expect that the vested interests would just be small fry to Benno. Back when I was making paper with an aching stomach, I hadn't expected any of this.

As I thought about what I had learned, Otto, who had been listening up to this point without saying something, spoke with a grin. "He dragged me to that meeting too. The Parchment Guild ended up agreeing to a compromise."

"A compromise?"

"They agreed to allow different kinds of paper to be used for different things," said Benno, reminding me what I had suggested to him.

I clapped my hands together. By cooperating, we would protect the parchment market to some degree while mass-producing paper for all sorts of other purposes. It was a massive step toward my dream of making books. If paper spread enough and lowered in price, it would be that much easier to make books. Once Benno had workshops mass-producing paper, I could get all I needed for cheap. *Now I need to think about ink and printing,* I thought, but before I could get too far off track, Otto continued with an amused expression.

"So we were all like, who managed to change Benno's mind for the first time?! Who made the unmovable rock budge? Rumor is, Benno's finally found his own Goddess of Water."

The tone of the conversation shifted from complex politics and into a more casual joking mood, so Lutz joined. "What's the Goddess of Water...? I mean, uh, may I ask who the Goddess of Water is...?"

"Melting snow is a sign of spring. She's the goddess who brings an end to long winters," said Otto, which made me snap back to reality.

Right. I don't know any of the religious myths here, but they're so popular that the names of gods pop up in spring greetings. It's likely that religion is deeply intertwined with the lives of people here.

"...The Goddess of Water is different from the Goddess of Spring in the spring greeting, right?"

"Different? Well, it's more like... The Goddess of Water, the Goddess of Sprouts, and all goddesses that have to do with spring are lumped into the Goddess of Spring. It's more accurately Goddesses of Spring, but people just say Goddess most of the time."

"Neat." Maybe it was just me, but I was glad the world was polytheistic like I was used to. It would have been a lot harder for me to adjust to a world that demanded you worship one single god, given my Japanese background in Shintoism. I was a little less nervous about the baptism now.

"'Neat'…? Is that it?" said Otto, surprised. Maybe it had been rude of me to just say "neat" in response to his explanation.

"Umm… I'm glad I know more about goddesses now. Thank you very much and please tell me more if you can later."

"That's not what I meant. I called you Benno's—"

"Want to get kicked out, Otto?" said Benno in a low voice, making Otto fidget.

I felt like I had caused an issue by not reading between the lines enough, but judging by the angry expression on Benno's face, maybe not understanding was the smarter choice here. When ignorance is bliss, 'tis folly to be wise.

"Um, speaking of which, why did Mr. Otto go to the meeting anyway?" I threw out a helping hand to Otto before Benno could start talking about divorce again. I successfully managed to shift Benno's attention — he turned to face me and Otto signaled his thanks with a grateful look.

"I'm going to have him help run this store once the Plant Paper Guild gets going."

"Bwuh? Does that mean Mr. Otto's going to be a merchant again?!" Otto had given up his life as a merchant to marry Corinna, but perhaps now he had a chance to return to doing what he loved. I thought that was great, but Benno lightly shook his head.

"Nah, Otto's still a soldier. I'm just gonna work him to the bone on his time off."

"Whaaat?! Isn't that like, super mean?!" I raised my voice in shock and saw Lutz nodding. The idea of Otto finishing a grueling day at the gate and then working as a merchant without any rest was just sad. But Benno just snorted and grinned at Otto.

"He's just working to cover his rent, for Corinna's sake. Nothing odd about it at all. Right, Otto?"

"Pretty sure you're working me harder than the rent's worth." The two of them glared at each other with dark smiles. Lutz and I didn't fit in at all.

Eventually I got bored of their endless staring contest and tapped the table. "Mr. Benno, could you continue please? What happened with the guildmaster in the end?"

Benno looked away from Otto and faced me, then shrugged and gave a triumphant grin. "The Parchment Guild agreed to the creation of the Plant Paper Guild thanks to the compromise, so he sadly had no choice but to approve my application. You should have seen the petulant look on his face."

"And who's the one who made sure he had no choice?" Otto butted in with a joke, but he was right. Benno had played the political game and forced the guildmaster's hand.

I looked at Lutz and Benno clicked his tongue. "I got all the right paperwork ready, made peace with the Parchment Guild, and prevented anyone from getting hurt. The application was only delayed this long because the Merchant's Guild was being negligent."

"Yeah, you're not wrong. But y'know, you didn't have to ask 'If you're getting too old to read properly, maybe you should retire already?' And honestly, saying 'Hey, I'll do you a favor and take your place' was going a bit too far," revealed Otto, making me gasp in shock.

"He dragged this out because you said those things! That's why he has it out for you! I bet he got really mad!"

"He got so mad his face went red. Never knew faces could get that red, actually," said Otto casually, but that was information I didn't need to hear. Benno nodding and saying that it was indeed an impressive sight didn't help.

"Who cares how mad that geezer gets? I had to work twice as hard to get this finished 'cause of him being a jerk." The divide between Benno and the guildmaster had become deeper and wider because of all this.

"Anyway, this time I made sure he finished the registration. Now I'm gonna make a ton of paper and sell all of it. But first comes settling on a workshop." Benno began talking about setting up a workshop to mass-produce paper now that the bureaucratic issues had been solved. "I'll start mass production once the summer baptism's over."

"Why's that?" asked Otto curiously.

"I did a detailed profit calculation and figured out that I'd earn more if I waited for the baptism to end and for Lutz to become my apprentice. I won't have to fund them anymore, and anyway, it'll take that long to settle on a workshop, make the tools, get the raw materials ready, and learn the manufacturing process."

Lutz and I had struggled a lot to secure our tools. Benno was definitely right when he said that preparing large tools for mass production would be very time consuming.

"Alright, with all that said, it's time for you to spit out how to make paper so I can make informed decisions here."

It seemed that Benno's real purpose in calling us here was to learn how to make paper. Lutz and I exchanged looks, then sighed.

Tools and Selecting a Workshop

Benno had been all like "spit it out" with total self-assurance, but I figured that this was a good opportunity to ask for an information fee, just like with the rinsham.

Observing him carefully, I began to speak. "Since we won't be seeing any of the profits earned by the Plant Paper Guild, I would like to receive an information fee for teaching you the manufacturing process of paper."

"…Alright, sure. How much do you want?" Benno grinned and tapped the table. To be honest, I had no idea what the proper price for this kind of information would be.

"Ummm, how much are you willing to pay, Mr. Benno?"

"Name a price and I'll pay it. How much?" Benno, knowing exactly how I was feeling, grinned and threw the ball in my court.

The only frame of reference I had for information fees was the three small golds he paid for the rinsham information. The fact that Benno went out of his way to make a guild for this paper made it clear he expected it to sell extraordinarily well for a very long time.

"Ngh, I… I want twice as much as you paid me for the rinsham information."

"Sure. C'mere." Benno took out his guild card and waved it in the air. He accepted my price with his grin not faltering for a moment. Maybe I should have asked for more money? I just didn't understand how much the information was worth. Still uncertain, I took out my guild card and tapped it against Benno's.

I fell into thought, groaning a little, when Otto crossed his arms and looked at Benno. "Even supposing you decide on how many tools to get, how big to make them, and so on after asking Myne for details, shouldn't you still take the tools in the storage building and start making paper now, as soon as possible?" said Otto.

I gasped at the idea. "Those are property of the Myne Workshop! We won't be able to make our own paper if he takes them! No!"

"...I mean, the storage building itself belongs to Benno, so..." butted in Lutz. I pursed my lips, pouting, and looked at Benno. We would be in trouble if he took our tools away to use himself. And in any case, those tools weren't fit for mass-producing paper.

"Still, it's not right. The Myne Workshop's tools aren't made for mass production." Benno raised an eyebrow, confused, so I started to explain. "Our tools were built with completing prototypes in mind, and they're smaller, lighter, and simplified so that we kids can use them. They aren't fit for mass production. There's also a lot of alternative tools we're using to avoid making you pay too much."

"Huh? Why are you holding back when he signed a contract to fund you? Shouldn't you take advantage of that and get all the best tools you can?" said Otto, his tone making it clear he thought we were being stupid. But I hadn't even considered exploiting someone else's money for my own benefit. At the time, it was hard for me to get my hands on a single nail. My mind was focused entirely on minimizing expenses.

"I'm not that kind of person. Or maybe I am now, a little, but I didn't used to be."

"Hey, you don't need to be greedy with me. But anyway, why aren't your tools fit for mass production? Just 'cause they're smaller?" asked Benno, so I tried thinking of the simplest example.

"The smaller the tools get, the less efficient they are. For example, we're using a suketa that makes one contract sized piece of paper, but an adult would be able to use a larger suketa. It would just be a waste of time to make one piece of paper at a time when you could be using larger tools and making four pieces of paper in the same time frame."

"Yeah, sounds like using the same tools as you would be a waste."

"Also, Lutz and I are just using a tub, but you'll want something called a 'sukibune' to hold more water. And we're using chopsticks Lutz made in place of a rake, but I can't recommend that you do the same."

"Those sure are a lot of tools I don't recognize." Naturally, since I hadn't ordered any of them. Benno tapped his temples while glaring at me. But no matter how hard he glared, I wouldn't hand over my current tools.

"Mmm, I think it will be hard for you to understand what our tools are and how we're using makeshift tools to compensate for what we don't have unless I physically show you what we're doing while explaining."

"Alright, I can make time tomorrow. I'll come watch. This'll be a good opportunity since I've never seen what you two have done with the place." He settled on that instantly, but I hurriedly tried to remember what part of the paper-making process we were in.

"The thing is, we just finished making the paper today. Tomorrow we're just drying the paper and don't have anything in particular to do, so I was planning to go to the forest to get more materials."

"Oh? So in other words, you're starting with step one?"

"That's right. We're going to chop wood, steam it, and peel the bark off. Then we dry it in our workshop."

Benno nodded as he listened. "Alright, I'll send Mark with you," he said, so I tried visualizing Mark going with us to the forest.

...Mr. Mark, chopping wood and peeling bark in the river? That doesn't suit him at all. Rejected.

"Mr. Mark is a gentleman too pure for rugged nature. He wouldn't look right at all cutting wood and peeling bark. But... you would be fine working with us, Mr. Benno."

"What's that supposed to mean?!"

"You're the one who wants to know what we're doing, so I think you should come with us."

"That's not what you just said." Benno frowned, but since he really did want to see the whole paper-making process for himself, he decided to go with us. Before I knew it, we had agreed to go to the forest and work together tomorrow.

The next day, when Lutz went to get the storage building key from the store, he found Benno there waiting in a work outfit. Lutz stealthily told me that Mark came out to say goodbye and was very worried that Benno would go on a rampage or something of the sort.

"Surprised you two can work in a cramped place like this," said Benno after entering the Myne Workshop and looking around. He was used to working in a large store with plenty of space, so a storage building just barely big enough for two kids to walk around must have seemed tiny to him.

"It's fine when it's just us, but it does feel cramped when you're in here too. Well, we do most of our work outside, so that's not a big deal."

As usual, we prepared the tools we needed to harvest raw materials and whatnot before heading to the forest. We had a pot, the steamer, a bucket, and some firewood. This time my basket had nothing but the chopsticks, a board to use as a plate, potatoffels, and butter.

Benno offered to carry some of Lutz's stuff, but Lutz shook his head. "I'm used to it, uh... sir. It'd be a bigger help if you carried Myne."

"You carry all of this stuff each time, Lutz? That must be rough," said Benno, impressed, as he picked me up, basket and all, to put on his shoulder.

"Hyaaah?!"

"Hold on tight. And at least give me that wooden frame thing. You look like you're about to get crushed, it's hard to watch." Benno took the steamer in one hand and started walking. I bounced on his shoulder as he took wide strides forward. Shaking in fear, I clung to his head for dear life.

"Um, we settled on a pot this small so Lutz could carry it, but smaller pots means less wood steamed per trip. You should consider whether you want a much bigger pot, or if you want to set up a bunch of tiny pots. A workshop near the river would be best so you don't have to carry the pots to it."

"Hmmm..."

We had an adult with us today, so we didn't have to leave with the group of pre-baptism kids like usual. We skipped by the meeting place and went directly to the south gate from the storage building. There we saw Dad and Otto talking about something.

"Hi Dad, Otto. Be back soon." I waved at them as we passed and they both looked at me with surprised eyes, then came jogging over.

Dad narrowed his eyes at Benno. "Myne, who's this?"

"It's Mr. Benno, the merchant who's been helping me a lot. This is my dad, Mr. Benno."

Otto's shoulders trembled as I introduced my dad to Benno.

"What's wrong, Mr. Otto?"

"Nothing, it's just… Benno totally looks like he's your dad right now…"

"Shut it, Otto. I'm a bachelor." Benno dropped a fist of anger on Otto's head and resumed walking, a little faster than before.

…*Wow, Benno's single? That's surprising, he's kinda old. Definitely close to thirty.* People married young here and even my dad was thirty-two years old. It was odd that Benno was close to thirty and still hadn't married.

"Mr. Benno, are you not going to marry anyone?"

"…Yeah, probably not."

"Would you mind if I asked why? I'm just curious, you don't have to answer if you don't want to."

"Well, not like I'm keeping it a secret," replied Benno with a forced smile. "When I wanted to get married, I had my hands full supporting my family. By the time my mother died and Corinna was married, the girl I wanted to marry was dead and gone. There's not a girl in the world better than her, so I won't get married. It's that simple."

…He said it was simple, but that sounded like a heavy and complicated story to me. I slowly let out a sigh. Benno's reason involved a person close to him dying. I couldn't dig further or joke about it. I just silently patted his head, which made him force another smile.

"What's with you all of a sudden?"

"Nothing really. I just thought a lot of people must be bothering you about marriage and successors since you run a large business."

"Yeah, pretty much. But things have calmed down a lot now. I'll train Corinna's child to be my successor. That was my condition for letting those two marry." *Oof... Good luck, Otto.*

As I prayed for Otto in my heart, we exited the dark tunnel passing through the gate, and the paved road turned into a bumpy dirt road. The air became fresh, the landscape spread before my eyes, and overall I felt like a bird being set free from its cage.

"Mm. Been a while since I've gone to the forest."

"That reminds me, you mentioned going parue-gathering before. I thought that merchant children didn't go to the forest. Freida was suggesting she only even went there on picnics, or something like that..." I still hadn't forgotten the shock of her saying us going to the forest every day was like having a picnic every day.

Benno let out a laugh and gave a nostalgic smile. "It was back when I was an apprentice. I snuck out of my house on my days off, y'know, all secret-like."

"You snuck out...?"

"All the kids my age who came to the store as apprentices talked about going foraging in the forest. How could I not be interested? And aren't there still kids like that sneaking out?"

"...Aaah, now that you mention it, when apprentices come with us there are some new faces now and then."

Even baptized apprentices sometimes went to the forest on their days off to gather or hunt. Unlike pre-baptism kids, they could go to the forest and back on their own, so many of them left without joining the group. Some apprentices brought their friends to the meeting place. That was how Benno had gone to the forest, it seemed.

"How do merchant kids pass the time?"

"At my place, I basically just studied. Studying how to interact with customers. Going to the market, looking at the prices, and calculating expenses. Learning to tell who was from the city and who wasn't. Judging the quality of the products, from good to bad…"

His entire lifestyle had been built around trade and business, so I couldn't understand it from a brief explanation. All I knew was that his childhood had been entirely different from ours. "That's is pretty different from how we live."

"I'm guessing the children of smaller stores have different lives too."

We carried everything to the riverbed. Lutz checked the hearth, then placed the pot on top of it. He drew water from the river and poured it into the pot, then set the steamer on top. Today I was throwing in some potatoffels, too.

"I'm gonna go cut some wood. Benno, maybe you can…"

"Lutz, you're gonna be my apprentice. Call me Master Benno. Also, keep yourself clean, using rinsham or whatever. Don't come into my store dirty."

"Alright. What are you going to do, Mr. Benno? Wait here with Myne or come chop wood with me…?"

"I want to see what kind of wood you gather, so I'll go with you."

Lutz and Benno went looking for wood, so I gathered up sticks near the pot to add to the fire and waited. Soon they returned with arms full of branches. Benno raised an eyebrow at the sight of me just sitting next to the pot.

"You're not gonna do anything, Myne?"

"What do you think I can do, Mr. Benno? My job is to sit here and rest. If I collapse here, there won't be anyone who can carry me all the way back." I had been told to do the bare minimum of movement when Lutz wasn't around. Me acting solo caused more problems than not most of the time.

"…Lutz, you're surprisingly patient with her."

"That's right. Lutz is amazing."

"Quit it, Myne. I'm gonna go gather some more wood." Embarrassed, Lutz glared at me and fled the area.

After we watched him go with smiles on our faces, I took out my knife. I separated the wood they got into volrin wood and firewood, then chopped up the volrin wood to fit in the steamer while talking to Benno about Lutz.

"I'm telling you, Lutz really is amazing. I wouldn't have survived this long without him. He saved me the first time the Devouring almost swallowed me up. And he even looked after me before all this stuff ended up being worth money. He's been making things with me for a while."

"...Yeah, so I've heard. Is that why you're backing him up?" For both the winter handwork and paper-making, I could have monopolized all the profits for myself. Benno, as a merchant, couldn't understand why I was splitting the rights and profits with Lutz.

"Mhm. Lutz helps me out, so I want to help him out too, however I can. All I can do is think up new products, and that's just turning into money because you buy them for us."

"...I see. Looks like I've really gotta make sure Lutz joins my store."

"Thank you."

Benno put a hand on my head. That felt like a subtle way for him to say to trust him, which was relieving.

Lutz came back once I was finished chopping the volrin wood into equal length parts. I added water to the pot and took the potatoffels out of the steamer while putting the volrin wood inside.

"Lutz, I need butter! Right now!"

"I know!"

Lutz put butter in the potatoffels. Benno looked at the potatoffels lined up on the board we were using as a plate and frowned, just like Lutz had.

"Mr. Benno, Myne's cooking tastes great. Even 'buttered potatoes' are something else." Lutz grinned and bit into a potatoffel, so Benno shrugged and grabbed one himself.

"...Not bad."

"Eheheh. The steaming packs them full of flavor and they taste even better when you eat them hot while you're outside in the cold weather."

Benno was taking a look at the pot after eating the potatoffel, so Lutz and I went foraging. We found some herbs and wild vegetables. Lately it was much more rare for me to pick poisoned food. Things were looking up.

Once the wood was steamed, we dunked them in the water and started peeling the bark. Benno helped with the bark-peeling, but since he wasn't used to working with his hands, he was surprisingly inept and the bark ended up all crumbled. At this rate, his help would make us run out of our black bark.

"Mr. Benno, that's enough bark-peeling. Could you please help Lutz clean up?"

Once I finished peeling the black bark, we returned to the workshop and set it up to dry. Benno scrunched his nose as he helped us put the bark onto the nails to dry. Unlike us, he was tall and didn't need to use a stool to reach the shelves. I was jealous.

"The bark won't dry like this if there's too much. You're normally supposed to dry them on drying rack like this." I drew examples on my stone slate to explain what tools we lacked. Benno nodded, asked questions, and examined our tools.

"We let the black bark dry until it's all crackly. If you don't dry it properly, mold will start growing. Then we dunk the dried bark in the river. We leave it there for a whole day."

"Sounds easy to steal."

"It would be. That's my biggest concern with it. As long as you know how to make paper, the bark is a good source of money. That's another reason why I think the workshop would best be located by the river," I explained while tapping the bag of ashes in the corner of the storage building.

"We peel off the black part of the bark after dunking it in the river, then boil it with ashes, then dunk it in the river again for another full day. Boiling it with ashes softens the fibers."

"Oh hoh."

"After that, we pick off all the dirt and broken fibers in the wood and beat it with this wooden club thing until it gets all fluffy. We also bought this one to match Lutz's size, so an adult could use a larger and heavier one to be more efficient." I pointed at the stand and the square lumber used as a club. Benno picked it up and swung it around experimentally.

"Yeah, you'd definitely want a heavier one to crush stuff."

"Then, you take the fluffy fibers and mix them with a sticky substance called 'tororo' and water to make pulp water. Right now we're using a tub with this suketa, but an adult will want a bigger suketa and a bigger tub called a 'sukibune' to make more pieces of paper at once. Right now we can mix the pulpy water around using the chopsticks Lutz made for me, but with a larger tub you'll want basically a large rake or comb to mix it all together."

I drew examples on my slate as I explained and Benno stroked his chin, nodding.

"Then, we shake and angle the suketa to get paper of equal thickness and size. Once that's done, we pile them onto the draining bed. They dry naturally, like you can see over there. Tomorrow we'll put a weighted stone on them to dry them further. That gets rid of the sticky tororo. Once that's done, we'll stick each individual piece of paper on that board and dry them in the sun. Then we peel the dry paper off the board and that's that." I finished explaining the process and Benno let out an impressed sigh.

"Gotta say, this is more complicated and time consuming than I expected."

"Since you can do other work while the paper is drying, it doesn't feel like it takes that much time. And you'll be busier than us since you'll be mass-producing it. Also, it's really hard to go into the river this season."

Benno, who had gone into the river to help get water in the bucket, nodded firmly. "This is gonna be one workshop that closes during the winter." The river froze during the winter and wood became too hard to be useful for paper-making.

"You can't make paper without a river, so think carefully about where you want to set up the workshop."

"Yeah, I got it. Seems like things are gonna get busy for me." Despite talking about being busy, Benno looked more than excited. I smiled and wished him good luck.

At the time I was thinking that would be all Benno's problem, but in reality, it was Lutz and I who ended up busy after Benno used his newfound knowledge to seek out a workshop.

Mark visited us while we were making paper to accompany us to craftsmen all over so we could give them details on the tools. We had no choice but to follow after he mentioned that the information fee included our help here.

By the time the tools were made, the people were gathered, Benno had the process down pat, and a workshop was more or less ready, spring had started turning into summer.

Preparing for Lutz's Apprenticeship

"Myne, what's your plans for today?" asked Lutz. "The weather's bad."

I looked out the window and saw thick, dark clouds that signaled a bad day for paper-making. I had the option to go to the forest just to gather, but if rain fell along the way, I'd be the only one who would struggle to get home. It would be smarter for me to just sit today out.

My spring had been spent making paper on sunny days and walking around the city with Mark on cloudy days to help get the workshop ready. But the workshop was mostly finished and they knew how to make paper themselves now. The other day they had made a prototype that I checked and confirmed to be a success, so there was really nothing left for us to do.

"Benno said our baptism is next Fireday, so I wanted to finish making our last batch of paper. But it looks like the weather's not cooperating."

"Hey, even without a last batch of paper, I'm so rich right now I can hardly believe it."

Each sheet of paper was worth a small silver, and whenever we sold paper, we brought some of the money back for our families. We bought enough to improve our food situation and not much else, but we both had a stunning amount of money saved in the Merchant's

Guild. That was thanks to the high price of trombe paper and the overall good weather that helped us make a lot of batches.

After the last batch we sold, my savings had surpassed two large golds. Lutz was just about to hit two large golds himself. No matter how you thought about it, that was too much money for pre-baptism kids to have. *But well, once our baptism's over, I won't be earning much money for a while.*

I started to think about if I had forgotten anything we needed to do before our baptism ceremony, when suddenly I realized something. "Lutz, let's go to Benno's today. We totally forgot something."

"Huh? We didn't promise to go there today."

"Our baptism is next Fireday, right? We should check now to see what you need to be an apprentice. Your parents aren't merchants, so they won't have any tools to give you."

"...Ah!"

Apprentice work began after the baptism, so it was customary for parents to give them work clothes and tools as a baptismal gift. It was to encourage their children and give them a head start on their journey down the same career path that their parents once traveled themselves. Tuuli, for example, had been given work clothes and a sewing set after her baptism since she was becoming a seamstress.

But in Lutz's case, his parents wouldn't prepare anything for him. In part since his father was still against him becoming a merchant and in part because his parents didn't know what tools to get him, since they weren't merchants themselves.

On top of that, we didn't know how much money it would cost to prepare Lutz for his merchant apprenticeship. Benno had said clothes were important and ordered us outfits, but that alone probably wouldn't be enough. It was likely that Lutz would need tools and other things beyond clothes to be a merchant. Luckily, he had enough savings that he could buy what he needed on his own. All we had to do was ask Benno or Mark what we needed.

"I don't know what tools you would need, really. Maybe a calculator and a stone slate, since you'll have your apprentice lessons, but what else?"

"I can buy pretty much anything right now. You were right, Myne. Saving up money was the right idea."

Karla was on Lutz's side now, but she still didn't know what one needed to be a merchant. She didn't have any connections with merchants, and his dad was as unsupportive as ever. Though Lutz said that he was more comfortable at home now that his mom was telling his brothers off.

"Benno's going to be your guardian more or less once you become an apprentice, so I think it would be best to ask him."

I picked up my tote bag and we headed to Benno's store beneath the heavy clouds.

"Oh, was it not several days until the next batch of paper would be ready?" Mark blinked in surprise after seeing us, having now grasped the schedule our paper-making followed.

"We realized we need to talk to Mr. Benno about something. But maybe we can just ask you first." If I remembered correctly, Mark was in charge of teaching the apprentices here. "We want to know what tools apprentices need. Lutz's parents aren't apprentices and won't know what to get him after his baptism, so he needs to buy his stuff himself."

"Oh, that is true. I did not consider that." Mark shook his head at himself and placed a finger on his temple.

"The baptism is really soon, do we still have time? And maybe we should talk to Mr. Benno about this, since he'll be Lutz's guardian?"

"Hmm. I believe it would be best to act after discussing things with the master."

Mark took us to Benno's office as always. Inside we saw Benno writing furiously on something with stacks of boards and paper surrounding him on his desk. He looked busy.

"Sir, Myne and Lutz are here to see you."

"Why?" asked Benno without looking up or stopping writing. I pushed Lutz's back to encourage him to ask on his own.

"Master Benno, we have arrived to discuss the tools I require to be a merchant apprentice," said Lutz shakily, having probably rehearsed the smart-sounding line in his head on the way here.

Benno, having probably just found a good stopping point, put his pen down and looked up. He looked confused, so I added on an explanation.

"I think parents normally provide these tools, but Lutz's parents aren't merchants, so they don't know what to get him. What does Lutz need to be an apprentice? He doesn't just need the clothes, right?"

"Yeah, now that you mention it. You can go shopping with Mark. I just got notice that your apprentice outfits are done. Order some changes of clothes on your way to pick them up."

"Okay." I nodded, but Lutz blinked in confusion beside me.

"Changes of clothes? Multiple?"

"Obviously. You think you can work in the same outfit all week? It'd get dirty, stretched out, and you'd stink. That's not happening here."

Benno ran a shop that also catered to nobles, so appearances were fairly important. An employee couldn't be presented to customers with dirty, stretched-out clothes with wrinkles. This was reflected by the fact that all the employees I could see working in Benno's store looked neat and clean.

"I have to change clothes every day...? Really...?"

Tuuli only washed her clothes once a week, on the day Mom had off work. I could imagine the same for Lutz's brothers. Nobody changed their work clothes every day. Generally a worker only had a couple outfits at best, and they'd wear the spare while the other dried. Washing clothes damaged them, so most avoided doing so for as long as possible, outside of underwear.

Unlike Benno who had servants working for him, Lutz was at the bottom of his family hierarchy. It would be hard for him to ask his mother to wash his clothes frequently enough that he could have a daily change of clothes. But it was necessary for him to do his job.

"If you can't ask Karla to do that for you, maybe you should wash your own clothes? Apprentices have days off, so..."

"Ngh..."

"I mean, you'll have to wash your own clothes no matter what if you end up as a live-in apprentice."

"I know that this different way of life is surprising for you, but you have to get used to it. If you don't do this, you'll gross out customers and get fired. Merchants and craftsmen just aren't the same."

Lutz nodded, and I saw that Benno was experiencing some culture shock too. He blinked slowly and murmured, "Wow. Our lives really are fundamentally different."

"Uh huh, which is why I'd like you to point it out if we ever do anything weird. We just don't know any better."

"Yeah, I'll keep an eye out. Mark... they're in your hands."

"Yes, sir." We waited for Mark to finish up work and then left to get the clothes together. It was customary by this point for Mark to pick me up on our way to the workshops, and I had completely given up fighting it.

"Welcome." An employee greeted us and realized why we were here the second she saw Mark and us. She took Lutz and me to a room inside.

"Please, try them on."

The employee gave me a simple blouse and skirt with a vest just like Mark's. I had been measured closely enough that the clothes naturally fit like a glove. The mere fact that I was getting new clothes that weren't hand-me-downs was enough for me to get pumped. I wiggled my arms around, squatted and stood up, and did all sorts of things to get a feel for the clothes. Not once did they squeeze me or feel uncomfortable.

"Wow! I like this outfit. It's comfy and easy to wear."

"I'm glad to hear that. Mark said that you'll be wearing those clothes out today, so we will wrap your old clothes."

While I was testing out my clothes, Lutz had apparently gone to order two more outfits with the same design and size. Once I walked out, Mark and Lutz headed my way.

"Very cute. A simple change of clothes, and now you look like the daughter of a wealthy family."

"Yeah, you look super rich now."

Their compliments made me feel even more pumped. I tried lifting up the hem of my skirt in a fancy bow. "Really?! I'm cute? I look like a rich girl? And not just because of the clothes?"

"When you're quiet and not being a dork, yeah."

"Hmph. But... you know, now that you're trying to keep yourself clean, you look kind of like a rich boy yourself, Lutz."

Since Benno had lectured Lutz about looking clean, he had started semi-regularly using rinsham on himself. His blonde hair was silky and sparkly. Ever since I'd mentioned using Mark as an example for dignified behavior, Lutz had started paying attention to his posture and general body language. The change of clothes was all it took to complete his transformation into a rich boy. It didn't feel like the clothes were wearing him at all.

"We can go shopping in other stores now, huh?" It wasn't rare for stores to turn people away based on their clothes. After we paid with our guild cards, Mark took us in our new fancy clothes to the next store.

It was a stationery store. Mark opened the wooden door with a pen mark on the front and inside was a counter with a pleasant-looking old man polishing something on top of it. The walls had shelves with products on them, but not many. There was one example per product on the shelves and nothing else. Which was, in fact, normal in this city. There was only a small space for customers and most of the actual store was the storage rooms containing the products. Although I knew it was necessary to ward off thievery, the fact that I couldn't browse through the products made me sad.

"What do we need here, Mark?"

"A few things. Ink, a pen, and parchment to sign the employment contract. He already owns a stone slate, slate pens, and a calculator, yes? Other than that, he will need several wooden boards," said Mark, which made me sigh. All that was too expensive for Lutz's parents to buy. We now had enough money to buy it ourselves, but ink and parchment were too expensive for those in our class to easily afford.

"I want some ink too." I took the opportunity to buy ink and a pen for myself. Buying my own ink was an emotional experience for me, since in the past it had been too expensive for me to even consider getting on my own.

The older man put my ink and pen on the counter. I paid with my guild card and took them.

"Yaaay! My own ink and pen!" I spun around in circles with a grin on my face, overjoyed to hold the ink and wooden pen in my hands, but Lutz looked less happy.

"The money I saved up is just slipping away. Didn't know being a merchant would be this expensive."

Had Benno's store been smaller, it would have been less expensive to join. A lesser store wouldn't sign its employment contracts on parchment. They would just use wooden boards.

"It's only expensive because Benno's store is so big. And you still have lots of money to spare, right?"

"Yeah, but I lost this much in a single day. I'm getting kinda nervous. I can't ask my parents for anything. Let's try and make more paper before the baptism."

"There's not much time left, but we can try if it's sunny out."

We returned to the store and informed Benno that we had bought what we needed. He told us to always come to the store wearing the apprentice clothes from now on. I took that as a stamp of approval from him. We looked just like proper apprentices.

"So, Lutz. Where should we put your stuff? In our workshop?"

"That'd be safest..."

It would be a bit annoying, but we started discussing whether we should borrow the key and put his apprentice stuff in the workshop, when all of a sudden Benno shrugged.

"Why not just put it in your room? Why bother with the storage building?"

"We don't have our own rooms. We only have boxes to put our stuff in."

Benno's eyes widened at that revelation. Judging from what I had seen of Corinna's house, they had plenty of spare rooms. It seemed that since he had been raised as the successor to a large store, Benno hadn't known anyone who didn't have their own room.

"My place is kinda worse than Myne's. I've got a box for my stuff, but everyone just goes through it and takes what they want."

"Wait, seriously?" Shock washed over Benno's face. He blinked, unable to comprehend that, so I explained to him what Lutz's life was like.

"Lutz is the youngest of four brothers. So he's basically at the mercy of his three siblings. He has it really rough."

"But still, they would steal their brother's stuff?"

"They're fine with it, since he's their little brother. What he owns, they own. What they own, they own."

Benno rubbed his temples as he learned about how Lutz lived. It was likely that things were so different from his own life that he could hardly imagine it. Benno had spent years working hard to support his family after his father's death, but he had never gone through their stuff and he had never worried about where to put his things. He couldn't believe what he was hearing.

"Why not put your stuff in one of the upper rooms? I'll rent you a live-in apprentice room for cheap. Things will get a lot harder for you if anyone steals your work stuff or you lose it before your baptism, and the storage building is too far for you to go to regularly before work."

"...Thank you." Thanks to Benno's good graces, Lutz could now rent out an apprentice room for cheap to use as a storage room. As long as he remembered to lock the door, he wouldn't have to worry about his stuff getting stolen.

"You can change there before entering the store from now on."

Lutz, having gained his own personal space for the first time in his life, nodded with a broad smile. I decided to put my stuff there too before going home. We couldn't go home right away since Benno was planning to take us to the Merchant's Guild.

"If you don't learn about the Merchant's Guild first, you won't even be able to do errand work."

The children of merchants visited the Merchant's Guild frequently while helping their parents, so dropping by to deliver paperwork was normal for them. The first work that merchant apprentices usually did was running errands at the Merchant's Guild. Which brings us to the fact that Lutz hadn't gone to the Merchant's Guild since the time we sold Freida's hairpins. He naturally couldn't run errand work there, since he had never done it before.

"Wonder what else you could do." Benno thought about what other basic jobs any merchant's child would do while putting a bunch of request forms in Lutz's hands and heading to the Merchant's Guild. I went with them so I could read the boards on the Guild's bookshelf.

"Oof..."

"This is pretty bad."

There were tons of carriages lined up in front of the Merchant's Guild by the plaza, with some passengers getting off to deliver their own forms to the guild while others got back in their carriages. It was a mess of people.

"It looks like the second floor will be crowded."

"Yeah, since market day and the baptism ceremony are both so close."

Judging by the number of carriages, I could only imagine how many people were on the second floor. Lutz struggled to the inner staircase, keeping close behind Benno as the crowd crushed him. Benno was carrying me like usual, so I avoided the crowd crush.

Benno showed his guild card to the guard, and the moment we started climbing stairs, all the loud noise vanished. The fence probably had some magical properties that blocked sound.

"Seems like running errands will be a pretty rough job." When on errands, Lutz would have to push through the crowd without Benno taking the lead. He sighed hard.

"Sometimes people try to steal your paperwork or you lose it in the rush, so be careful. Anyway. First of all, this form is about…" Benno set me down and headed to the counter while explaining to Lutz what the paperwork was. I turned around and tried to go to the bookshelf, but a hand grabbed my head and pulled me back.

"Where do you think you're going, huh?"

"…The bookshelf is calling for me."

"It's not. You're imagining things. After your baptism you'll be a forewoman, so you need to listen too."

It would be smart to have Benno teach me how the Guild worked. So he proceeded to teach us both how the counters worked and where to deliver certain paperwork.

"If you deliver a request here, you can browse what magic contracts have been registered. You're going to be making a lot of new products, Myne, so you need to learn what magic contracts are in effect."

"Oh, is really that you, Myne?" A girl with light-pink twintails came running this way from behind the counter. There was no mistaking her; it was Freida, the guildmaster's granddaughter. She was clearly wearing her apprentice outfit.

While I was in the middle of trying to process what was happening, Freida put her hands on her hips and pouted unhappily.

"Spring's almost over and you haven't come over to play once, you know."

"Oh, sorry. I've been really busy lately." I wasn't lying, either. I had been busy making paper and getting the workshop ready. I had fulfilled my promise to make sweets with her, so I had kinda just thought I didn't need to go over anymore. Her place was filled with traps and she wouldn't stop trying to get me to join her store, which wasn't exactly my idea of a fun time.

I apologized and Freida shook her head, said it was okay, and smiled. "I have tomorrow off, so you could come visit then."

"Bwuh? But if the weather's good tomorrow, I'm going to—" Benno's hand tightened around my shoulder for a second. I was about to say "make more paper," but it was still a secret that I was the one making paper for Benno, so I hurriedly closed my mouth.

Freida glanced at Benno's hand and smiled. "I will come get you if it's raining tomorrow. You may be busy if it's sunny out, but what would be better on a rainy day than visiting a friend? You promised to visit during the spring, but spring is almost over."

"Ngh..." It was hard to say no to an offer like that. It was true that I couldn't make paper on rainy days, and I would have the spare time to visit her.

As I fell into thought, Freida advanced the conversation further. "I would like to discuss more about the Devouring and whatnot with you, given the chance."

"Oh, I think there's some things I wanted to ask about too." Freida was more informed about the Devouring than anyone I knew. There was still a few things I was curious about, and an opportunity to talk with her would be welcome.

Hearing that made Freida's face light up and she clapped her hands together. "This is all if it rains, of course. I will be waiting with a pound cake ready."

"Okay. If it rains, I'll go." The allure of a pound cake made me agree and the moment I did, I felt Benno's fingers dig into my shoulders. I looked up and saw that Benno was smiling with veins bulging over his temples.

"Myne."

"Mr. Benno, we are merely discussing what we will do if it rains. Nothing is set in stone."

"That's right. I'll only go if it rains tomorrow." Freida extended a helping hand and I jumped right on it. I tapped on Benno's hand so he would let me go and I heard him murmur "this unbelievable idiot" in a low voice.

"It's raining tomorrow."

"Bwuh?"

Freida's smile deepened and Lutz let out a sigh. It seemed that even without a weather channel, everyone knew there would be rain tomorrow.

The rain started falling in the evening, and it didn't stop when the sun rose again.

Contract with Freida

...Nooo! It's raining. There's no wiggling out of this one, it's definitely raining outside.

I slumped my shoulders as I ate breakfast, listening to the rain hit the windows. Freida's smile, Benno's groan, and Lutz's sigh had all been justified. It really did rain today.

Oh well. Now that I knew for sure I was going to Freida's house, I just had to do my best to extract as much valuable information from her as possible. I'd be safe with Lutz with me.

I took my hard-to-chew bread and mopped it with last night's leftover soup before biting down. I then wiped my bowl with the last of the bread to finish breakfast and sighed as I looked around.

"I wish I could bring a gift or something, but I don't think I own a single thing she doesn't..." Freida's home was styled after the residences of nobles, and there was nothing I could bring her that she didn't already probably have.

Tuuli took a sip of water and tilted her head. "What about more simple all-in-one shampoo? She loved it when we brought some over earlier, right?"

"Mmm, Benno's started officially selling rinsham and he told me not to hand any out for free. Making some for my own use is one thing, but giving it out for free will disturb the market, or something."

"Oh, okay. It's too rainy to pick any flowers, too. This is rough," said Tuuli as she took a little bit of water from the jug to wash her bowl. Once she was done with that, she started busily preparing for work. Mom had already left and Dad was asleep since he had night shift yesterday.

I quietly used some water to clean my bowl as well. "I wish we made this promise days ago so I could have picked fruit ahead of time…"

Benno was lending a room to Lutz and helping me establish the Myne Workshop for my products, so I really really wanted to avoid upsetting him. I owed him a lot. It wasn't on purpose that I blabbed about things and often succumbed to the temptation of making food for myself to eat. I didn't *want* him to be mad at me, that's just what kept happening.

The problem was that avoiding Benno's anger meant not giving away any rinsham. Nor anything involving paper. Freida and Leise would both love it if I told them a new sweets recipe, and I personally would love to eat said sweets, but Benno would definitely get mad at me.

…Now that I'm not his apprentice, I think I'm free to spread recipes wherever I want, but that might end up biting me in the butt later.

I groaned and fell into thought, trying to think of a gift to give Freida, when suddenly there was a knock on the door. Tuuli, wearing a thick raincoat-like jacket covered in oil and wax for waterproofing since she was about to go to work, looked up and headed to the door.

"Yeees? Who is it?" I started pushing my dishes away, thinking that Lutz was just a little earlier than expected, but Tuuli's shriek of surprise wiped that thought out of my mind.

"Freida?! You're here?!" cried Tuuli.

I turned around in surprise and saw Freida standing in front of the door with a servant. She was wearing fine clothes despite the weather, as was her attendant, which meant they both stood out strongly in contrast to our poor housing. To be honest, they made us look even poorer than we actually were.

"I've been so eager to see Myne since waking up that I could bear it no longer and elected to come here myself to pick her up." She smiled and I could hear the implied "I'm not letting you get away" in her words. A shudder ran down my spine. I wanted to turn right around and flee, but I couldn't leave Tuuli behind like that.

Tuuli turned around and said, "Wow, Myne, she's so excited to play with you that she came through the rain!" with a happy smile.

...Tuuli, you're an angel. Please never lose that innocence.

"Far be it from me to make Myne walk in the rain with her ill health. My carriage is waiting on the main street." She had likely predicted that I would turn her down by claiming I didn't want to get sick by walking in the rain. I felt like shaking my head in awe at how masterfully she was weaving her web around me.

"A carriage?! Wooow! That's so nice, Myne!"

Freida, seeing Tuuli with her work equipment in hand, tilted her head. "Oh? Do you have work today?"

"Uh huh. I need to get going soon. This sucks," said Tuuli, but Freida briefly fell into thought and then clapped her hands with a meaningful smile.

"In that case, would you like to ride partway to your destination?"

"What?! I can go too?! I can ride the carriage?!" Tuuli's face lit up. Normally, poor people like us would never in our entire lives get the chance to ride a carriage. I could understand Tuuli's excitement. It seemed my only option would be to hurry up and get ready so we could leave.

"Tuuli, you have to go get Lutz."

"Oh, that's right. I'll go get him."

"Hm, but if Lutz comes, there won't be enough space for you to ride as well..." Tuuli had set her stuff down and started to run off, but Freida stopped her regretfully.

I knew I needed Lutz to watch over me whenever I went outside. If Lutz coming meant Tuuli couldn't ride, well, that was unfortunate for her.

"Huh? What? I... I don't get to ride?" Despair and disappointment feel that much worse if you once had hope. Tuuli hung her head, looking close to tears. I started to panic a little, not sure how to make her feel better, when Freida intervened. She took Tuuli's hands and smiled so, so gently.

"Dear Tuuli, I will take responsibility here and take care of Myne in Lutz's place. I promise that I will not allow Myne to fall ill. You may rest easy and ride with us."

"Myne, you won't get tired or wet thanks to the carriage, right? Will you be okay without Lutz?"

No! I won't! or so I said on the inside, but Tuuli's desperate look was too much for me to refuse. I couldn't say that I needed Lutz and that she would have to walk to work. She had been so happy to get the chance to ride in a carriage, so what else could I do? I didn't want to go to Freida's alone, but my hands were tied.

"...I'll be fine. Let's go, Tuuli."

"Thanks, Myne! I'll go tell Lutz, and you get ready." Tuuli dashed out of the house in excitement and headed to Lutz's house. Once her footsteps faded, I could hear only the rain.

Ultimately, Freida had exploited Tuuli to get rid of Lutz. I glared at her, eyes narrowed. "Freida."

"Your elder sister was happy, was she not?"

"She was. Haaah... Fine. I dug my own grave here, anyway." It was my own weakness that prevented me from cutting Tuuli off.

There was no point in attacking Freida. I got my things ready while thinking about how mad Lutz and Benno would be at me for not thinking ahead again. "Sorry, I didn't manage to find any gifts for you," I said.

"You'll be spending a day's worth of time with me, Myne. I could not ask for a greater gift than that." Her smile was that of a young girl excited to spend time with a friend, but I knew that Freida was no innocent child.

"Myne, I left a message with Karla. Let's go! We'll be late." Tuuli skipping back inside with a smile washed away the heavy atmosphere.

"Let us go."

We walked outside and locked the door behind us. In general, people of the city wore thick cloaks and wide hats to block the rain. Naturally they weren't actually waterproof, so spending a lot of time outside or under heavy rain would still get you wet with soaked clothing. That wouldn't be a problem for us, though, since we were just passing through a narrow alley on the way to the main street.

"Now then, hop inside." We hurriedly got into the carriage waiting for us and took off our rain gear. The servant sat next to the driver, so it was just us kids inside.

"Wow, so this is what a carriage looks like on the inside!"

"Please sit, we're about to leave. Will the plaza be a fine place to let you off?"

"Mhm, I work really close to the plaza, at the close end of the craftsman's alley."

Tuuli was bouncing around in excitement while looking around, so Freida told her to sit down. I went ahead and sat in the middle of the bench. The carriage was built for two adults and had just enough room for three kids to sit comfortably next to each other. It bounced around a lot once it started moving, but unlike before

I was actually sitting in my seat properly, so I wasn't flung around anywhere.

"Your baptism is coming up soon, isn't it? What kind of outfit will you wear?"

"Myne's outfit is my outfit remade, but it's so fancy now you wouldn't think that!" answered Tuuli, puffing out her chest with pride as if she were talking about herself. She and Mom had been remaking the outfit more over the past months, making it look increasingly fancy with each attempt.

"…Fancy?"

"It's not what you'd expect from remade clothes, it has a really weird design now. But Mom worked hard, so it looks super cute."

It was probably hard for Freida to imagine us having fancy clothes after seeing the poor state of our home. She looked confused, but Tuuli wasn't lying. Though it was hard to explain exactly what we had done.

"Freida, your baptism outfit was super fluffy and cute. I want to try wearing clothes like that someday."

"My my, thank you. Incidentally, does that mean you've made a new hairpin as well?" Freida smiled happily at Tuuli's praise, then shifted the topic to hairpins. All the hairpins we had made outside of Freida's had the same design and differed only by color. But she was probably curious about the one I had made for myself, figuring I would go the extra mile on it.

"Uh huh, 'cause it's Myne's celebration. I worked really hard on it. I made three large roses, just like the ones on yours."

"May I assume, then, that our hairpins match each other?" Freida looked at me a little doubtfully, head tilted.

Tuuli didn't know what to say and pulled my sleeve nervously. "They both have large flowers, but Myne's are white, and um, it shakes? They don't really match, right Myne?"

"The thread is actually more of a cream color, but it does look white from a distance. I put tiny flowers around the roses too, but it doesn't look like yours, Freida. You'll see when the day comes. Right, Tuuli?"

"Uh huh. It wouldn't be fun if we told you everything!" said Tuuli, putting a hand over her mouth and smiling mischievously.

Freida broke into a smile as well. "My my, I will look forward to it then. I shall go all the way outside to see."

The carriage made good progress as we talked, and soon enough I saw Tuuli's workplace within the line of workshops. We stopped the carriage and Tuuli put her stuff back on. After getting her bag of tools in hand, she nervously glanced back at me.

"Fear not. I shall see Myne home safely myself."

"Good luck at work, Tuuli."

"Thanks for letting me ride your carriage, Freida. Sorry, Myne, for being pushy." She waved goodbye and ran to her workshop as the horses drawing our carriage resumed trotting.

"Welcome back, Myne. A pound cake I baked is ready for you. Lemme know what you think." When we arrived at Frieda's, Leise was waiting for us. She took us to the parlor and immediately placed tea and cake on the table.

I took one bite and was immediately in heaven. The dough was baked to be perfectly moist, and she must have mastered baking cakes with the oven, as it tasted significantly better than last time. "So goooood! This is way better than last time. You baked it perfectly."

"Glad to hear it. I was wondering if I could improve it somehow."

"Improve it? Mmm, I think it tastes plenty good already." I threw a piece of the cake into my mouth and fell into thought while enjoying the sweet flavor. There were some things she could do, like make it look fancier on the plate, add dry fruit, shave citrus peels to mix into the batter, etc, but Benno would probably get mad if I told her any of those things.

...Mmm, Benno would definitely get mad no matter what I do, and while I would be fine with the simple cake here, I really want to support Leise since she's invested in making better food.

"I don't know how much we can improve it, but... I'll trade you ideas for a bag of sugar." I suggested a trade, thinking back to the about one-kilogram heavy bag I had seen in the kitchen before. Leise looked at Freida, who had the ultimate authority here.

"A bag of sugar... Is that a trade I can make, my lady?"

"Yes, certainly."

"You heard her. Let's hear the ideas!"

I gasped a little at Leise's intensity, then started to explain. "If you add grated apfelsige peels to the dough, it should taste and smell different. Maybe better. The flavor can also be changed by putting different things in it, like dry fruit. Please experiment on your own to see what will taste the best. This is extra information, but if you're serving the pound cake to nobles, it will look fancier if you add whipped cream and sliced fruit on top."

"Okay. Let's give it a shot." Leise sucked in air and stood up to leave immediately. Freida and I were left behind. After blinking in surprise, we smiled at each other.

"Forgive me, Myne. To think she would behave like that in front of a guest. She's normally much more calm, but when new recipes get involved..."

"It's good that she has a drive to improve her cooking. The harder she works, the better our food gets." I could appreciate her enthusiasm. Tasty food spreading throughout this world would be nothing but good, so I wanted her to experiment all she wanted.

"Speaking of which, why are you working as an apprentice in the Merchant's Guild? Aren't you going to own a store in the Noble's Quarter when you grow up? You can be an apprentice even if you won't work there?" I didn't expect to see Freida working in the Merchant's Guild when her future plan was to own a store. I asked what was up while eating cake and Freida answered while drinking tea.

"I asked my grandfather to employ me. I need to learn and make connections if I am to hold a store in the Noble's Quarter. I will be all alone when the store opens. It will be necessary for me to be capable of running the store on my own, and the more connections I have the better."

"All alone? You won't have, like, Jutte there to help you? No servants?"

"Nobody but me will be permitted to reside in the Noble's Quarter. They will have servants of their own permitted for me, so I will not technically be alone, but I'm sure you understand."

It would be hard to expect any servants assigned to her to be wise in the ways of economics and business. Wouldn't it be a little cruel to make a young girl who had just reached adulthood run a store all by herself? Couldn't they at least let her bring a partner to work with and consult when necessary?

"In truth, I will not be entirely alone. My family is permitted to enter the Noble's Quarter on business. They will not be with me at all times, but still, they are strong allies to have."

"…That's true." They wouldn't necessarily be ideal allies, but I had to agree with Freida. She was charging forward and challenging her fate, how could I say anything else? Her sophisticated, mature ways of speaking and thinking were her sword and shield in the Noble's Quarter. She would have to gain skills now to survive an unfamiliar world.

"I am working in the Guild and in my family stores now so that once my store opens, I will be able to deal with whatever may happen."

"That's really impressive, Freida. I can tell you're thinking really far ahead," I said.

Freida's expression hardened. She looked at me quietly, eyes serious, and spoke. "There is something I would like to ask you as well. May I?"

Well, here comes the main point, I thought. I knew what Freida would be asking me. I smiled and nodded.

"What in the world are you thinking?" asked Freida. "A reasonable person would have cut off Benno and joined my side by now. I have been waiting for that, Myne. Waiting for you to come to me, seeking my help…"

The guildmaster and Freida would be stronger allies than Benno when it came to seeking help from nobles to survive. Otto pointed out the same thing. Anyone would think that way. A store with deep connections to nobles would be able to negotiate more in my favor, there was no doubting that.

"It is almost summer, but you have made no moves. Are you thinking about your future? If you do not negotiate with a noble soon, you will…" Passion crept into her voice as she tried to convince me, firm in her beliefs from her own history. I could tell there was a restless sense of urgency boiling within her. As a fellow sufferer of the Devouring, she was worried about me. It would take time for negotiations to end and the contract to be signed. If Freida was wanting me to hurry out of fear of delaying the tools that would save my life, I would feel a little embarrassed for worrying her.

I let out a dry laugh and looked into her eyes. "You know, Freida. I thought about it really hard, and decided that I want to die while living with my family."

Freida froze with eyes and mouth wide open. From her trembling lips came a slight whisper, "No way."

"I've mostly given up already. Tuuli cried and said we could search for a way to keep me alive, but there's no way to survive the Devouring outside of signing my life away to nobles, is there?"

If there had been another way, the guildmaster wouldn't have had to use all the power and resources at his disposal to save Freida. He must have researched ways to cure the Devouring while gathering magic tools and buying time. In the end he didn't find anything and had no choice but to give up, negotiate a deal with a noble, and sign Freida's life away. How could I do any better?

"...None that I know of."

"I actually do want at least one more magic tool so I can try to finish what I'm doing, but I'm not even considering signing myself to a noble. There's nothing but magic tools that can cure the Devouring, right?"

"If I knew of something, I would have used it myself," said Freida, glaring at me in frustration. I shrugged.

"What I wanted to ask you, Freida, was whether or not I could buy magic tools from someone other than a noble. Or could I make them myself...? Something like that."

Ideally I would make magic tools myself, but unfortunately, there weren't any books about how to build them back on Earth. I had played games and read fantasy books that brought up magic tools, but they obviously weren't useful here. And as far as I knew, there weren't any workshops that made magic tools in this city.

"Creating magic tools requires mana, so only nobles with mana can do so. Nobody who knows how to make magic tools lives on this side of the inner wall."

"Okay. I was thinking I could try making some myself if I knew how, but I guess that's not happening." If only nobles could create them with their mana, then the only magic tool workshops in the city would be in the Noble's Quarter. I had hoped that I could make things work with how much money I had now, but as expected, things didn't pan out that way.

"…I had not considered the idea of making them myself."

"That's because you're the daughter of a rich family. I'm poor and everything I've wanted I've had to make myself, so that was the first idea that came to mind." I laughed to myself. Rinsham, hairpins, paper, soot pencils, chopsticks. Every time I wanted or needed something, I had to make it myself, with help or not.

"Is your family that important to you? Are you not afraid of being consumed by the heat and dying?" murmured Freida.

"Hmm, I don't know. I want to live, but I'm not that afraid of dying." I had already died and I remembered it. My life here as Myne was basically just a bonus life given to me by a whimsical god or whatever. Living here was fun now, but dying wouldn't be a big deal to me. "…I don't have access to books, so there's nothing super important to me but my family. The people around me. I haven't chosen to die, I've just chosen to be with my family."

"Books?"

"Uh huh. I've saved up a lot of money by now, maybe I can buy one," I said with a joking grin. Freida gave a troubled smile in return.

"If you want books, why not go to the Noble's Quarter? There are plenty of books there."

"Aaah, maybe I would if the contract said I could read as many books as I want, but I don't think a noble keeping me as a slave would let me touch their expensive, rare books."

"That would be unlikely, considering your social status."

From the perspective of a merchant, I was a poor commoner in a city with a low literacy rate. Even if I did know how to read, they wouldn't want to let me touch their expensive and possibly irreplaceable books. It was likely they would have me killed if I touched them without permission.

And suffice it to say, I knew myself. I wouldn't be able to hold myself back in the presence of books. It wasn't hard to imagine myself lunging at the first book I saw and getting killed in moments.

"...My plan was to try and establish a mass production line for books before I died, but that's a bit beyond me now. I've basically given up. I just don't have enough time left. So inside, I want to earn as much money as I can and leave it behind for my family, since I've been such a burden to them," I said with a self-derisive laugh.

Freida's eyes flashed with a sharp light. "In that case, shall I buy the pound cake recipe from you?"

I looked at Freida, who had shifted entirely into merchant mode, and fell into thought. Pound cakes were a basic sweet and although I wouldn't mind her monopolizing them for a limited time, I didn't want her to own all the rights to it like Benno did with the rinsham. That would seriously interfere with the growth of confectionery culture here.

"...What would you say if I offered to sell you exclusive rights to sell it for one year at the price of five small golds?"

"I would take that deal, of course," she answered immediately, without a moment of hesitation.

"...What do you mean, 'of course'? Am I underselling it?"

"Well yes, I believe you are. Much like plant paper, there is no precedent to pound cake, no similar product. Exclusive rights to sell it would generally be in the measure of large golds. After all, it will certainly earn that much and more in profit."

"Large golds...?" It seemed that I had been giving Benno information for much, much cheaper than I should have been.

"So? Will your raise your price?"

"No, it's fine. We're only talking about a year here. Five small golds is enough for me." Despite being given the opportunity to raise the price, I shook my head.

"Then I shall prepare the contract."

"What? Do you mean a magic contract?!" Would I have to live in fear again, bleeding onto the paper and worrying about people I didn't know getting hurt? I started to subconsciously tremble and Freida let out an exasperated sigh.

"...Myne, contract magic is not used so frivolously. It exists as a means of security for when you are dealing with those overwhelmingly more powerful than you in mana and authority. A standard contract on parchment will suffice for us."

"Oh, I see." My first contract had been a magic one, so my sense of perspective was super off. But if Freida was right about that, why had Benno used a magic contract when dealing with me? Weird.

"Actually, Myne, where did you even learn about contract magic? It is very rarely ever used."

"...Benno would get mad at me if I told you, so it's a secret."

"Oh, I see you're learning." Freida giggled and reached for a bell on a nearby shelf. She rang it and Jutte entered the room nigh silently. "Please prepare a contract."

Jutte prepared a sheet of parchment and Freida ran a feather pen over it, recording the contents of the contract. The pen looked fancier than the wooden one I had bought, it was harder to use, from what I could tell.

Writing up contracts was a daily event for Freida given her work as an apprentice in the Merchant's Guild, and even I had gotten used to it by now. After checking to make sure everything was in order, we tapped our guild cards together.

"Might I ask why you went for just one year?"

"A year will be enough for everyone to learn it came from your store, right? But once sugar spreads out a bit more, I want newcomers to have a chance to make it too."

"Newcomers?"

"Once the recipe is made public, there will be people competing with your store and working out new recipes and sweets. I really like sweets, so my ideal is to have a lot of people making them and spreading them throughout the world."

"Haaah… You would not be a good merchant, Myne, as you do not prioritize your own profit above all else."

Freida and I signed the parchment that would soon be an officially recognized legal contract. With that, I had successfully sold to Freida the right to monopolize pound cake sales for one year.

"But well, I guess it'll only be publicized if I'm alive in a year. You can do whatever you want with it if I'm gone by then."

"I will prioritize my profits, so you would do well to survive and publicize it yourself in a year." Freida looked away, looking close to tears.

To the Baptism Ceremony

Everyone was busy the morning of the ceremony. Mainly Mom, though. We needed to hurry and eat breakfast, clean up, and get me changed into my outfit, so she got mad when I overslept and ate my breakfast slowly. So I basically shoved my food into my mouth and changed in the bedroom with Tuuli while Mom cleaned up my dishes.

Mom and Tuuli had been adding little touches to the outfit over time, so now it wasn't only the waves added by the bundled-up cloth that made it look fancy. They had decorated it with flowers we'd made during our winter handiwork, which made it look more decorative. If Benno hadn't given us more thread than we needed for the flowers, we wouldn't have had the money to spare for them.

After throwing on the dress like I would a t-shirt, I wrapped the blue sash around my waist and tied it into a bow. The end of the sash hung by my leg.

"Myne, weren't you going to double loop the sash?" asked Tuuli, pursing her lips.

I undid the sash and wrapped it around my stomach twice. But despite being able to manage it in the winter, it was now just a little too short for that. "Oh? Did I eat too much? Is my stomach sticking out?"

"Nuh uh. You just got bigger, Myne. We made it so the hem would go beneath your knees a little, but now it's exactly at your knees."

It seemed I had grown during the spring. That was normal for most children, but the Devouring slowed my growth so much that I wasn't used to it. I was struck by a sense of awe, moved at my own growth, but Tuuli was more focused on practical matters. She took a look at the sash and thought about how to fix it.

"...It's just not the right length. Letting it hang like that would look bad. Maybe we should cut it?"

"No way, that would be a waste. I'm only wearing it for the baptism, it won't be too long. I can just double it up."

"But you couldn't do that just now."

"Not the wrapping, the bow." I wrapped the sash around my stomach and gave it a double bow knot. Once it was all tied up, I shifted the sash so the ribbony knots were behind me. "So? Does it look good?"

"So cute! Wow! How did you do that?!" I started to explain how double bow knots worked to Tuuli when suddenly Mom came into the room.

"If you've finished changing your clothes, Myne, hurry and get your hair ready. I need to change too."

"Okaaay. I'll tell you later, Tuuli."

We moved to the kitchen. Everyone had used rinsham last night, so my whole family had silky smooth hair. Even Dad had seemed interested yesterday, so I washed his hair for him. I asked what had gotten into him, and it turns out Otto had bragged about washing his hair with Corinna. As always, Dad was competitive in the weirdest of places.

"Myne, I don't know how to bundle up hair with a hair stick, so at least let me brush your hair and stuff." Tuuli's eyes started shining after she saw me brushing my hair. I had braided Tuuli's hair for her baptism, and it seemed she wanted to return the favor however she could. I nodded and gave her the brush.

She started brushing my hair while humming, seemingly in a very good mood. "Myne, your hair is so straight and pretty. It smells nice, too."

"Your hair smells the same way, doesn't it?" I thanked Tuuli for brushing my hair and bundled it up like I usually did, making sure not to crush the swaying ornament. More complex hair styles wouldn't really work for me since any strings I tried to use would just come right undone.

"Okay, that's that." Despite the special hair stick, I was still putting my hair up the same way that I always did. It didn't take very long.

The hair stick was noticeably heavier, and I could feel the small flowers shaking whenever I moved my head. I shook my head, amused, and Tuuli clapped happily.

"Wooow! So cute! It looks so good on your hair, Myne! I love the way it shakes when you move."

"That looks wonderful on you, Myne," Mom added.

"How'd this little rich girl end up here?" Dad said jokingly. "You're gonna be the cutest girl in the whole ceremony, Myne."

Once I was dressed, my parents came out of the bedroom and flooded me with praise. I appreciated the compliments, but it felt kind of embarrassing too.

"Dad, you said the same thing to Tuuli."

"'Course I did. Both my daughters are the cutest," said Dad, lifting up Tuuli and I with one arm each. We flailed and giggled to try and get away, but he just tightened his grip while cackling.

"Gaaah! My hair's gonna get messed up!"

"Goodness! Enough playing, we need to go outside," said Mom. Dad let us go, but it was too late. Mom looked at my hair and sighed.

"Myne, your hair will fall apart if you don't set it up again."

Dad shrugged and said he was sorry. I laughed and took out the hair stick so I could redo the bun. My hair wasn't good for complex hairstyles, but it didn't tangle much, so a quick brush was all it took to fix it back into shape.

"Everyone's by the well already." Tuuli, who had run downstairs to check, threw the door open and motioned us outside. We went down the stairs to the plaza, and indeed a ton of neighbors were already there.

"There's Ralph and the others. Lutz is wearing hand-me-downs, as expected."

I looked to where Tuuli was pointing and saw Lutz surrounded by a huge crowd, wearing hand-me-downs from Ralph. I hadn't seen what Ralph was wearing for his baptism so I didn't know it was a hand-me-down, but Lutz was wearing a white shirt with white pants and a light-blue sash. Zasha, the oldest brother, had probably worn the same thing. The outfit and sash had been made for him.

"Hey, Lutz."

"M-Myne?! Gracious, what's with that outfit?! You look like a rich girl!" Karla caught me on my way to Lutz. Her loud voice drew attention to me and other neighbors approached. It seemed I wouldn't make it to Lutz without giving an explanation.

"This is a hand-me-down from Tuuli."

"That's a hand-me-down?!"

"Uh huh. It was too big for me, so we bunched it up and sewed it together so that the skirt would be just long enough for me. It was a really simple fix." I explained what we had done briefly as lady after lady gathered around me. I was much shorter than even kids my age, so it was a bit scary to have a crowd of adults squatting all around me to be on my eye level. I subconsciously grabbed behind me for my Mom's skirt.

"I wouldn't have guessed this is just a remade outfit. Your clothes look really fancy."

"Let's see here. Guess you could do this 'cause you're so much shorter than Tuuli. Couldn't do the same myself."

"Ahaha, I thought this was a super fancy sash, but you just had to double the bows up 'cause it's too long."

Everyone said whatever was on their minds. Some people threw in celebratory congratulations, but they didn't feel too sincere to me.

"That hair thing is a real piece of work, too. How expensive was it?" The topic shifted to the price of the ornament on my hair stick. Mom shook her head with a smile.

"We made it ourselves, it didn't cost anything. Since we just altered Tuuli's outfit instead of making a new one from scratch, we had extra thread left over."

"My daughter's asking me to buy one for her baptism. Could you tell us how to make them ourselves?"

"They take a really thin needle to sew the thread. If you have one of those, the rest is simple."

They must not have expected to hear that we made the ornament ourselves. All the questions shifted to Mom instead. I stealthily slid away while she was flooded with question after question.

...*Okay, escape successful.* The moment I let out a sigh of relief, I was surrounded by a group of girls interested in my clothes and hair stick. They were mostly older girls who had finished their baptism before I started going to the forest, so unlike Tuuli, I had basically never interacted with them before.

"Kyaaah, so cute!"

"Let me see, let me see! Tuuli made this hairpin, right? Woooow!" A girl who did indeed seem to know Tuuli touched my hair stick, which made it slide out of my hair and undo my bun.

"Ah, s-sorry. What should I do...?" The girl held my hair stick and paled, having completely undone my hairdo.

"It's okay. I can fix it really easily." I held out my hand and smiled. She gave me the stick and I redid my hair. I scooped it up, wrapped it around the stick, and twisted it all before digging the stick inside.

"Wha? Wha? How'd you do that?! Isn't it just a hairpin?"

"Eheheh. It's an ornament and a hair stick. That's just how great Myne is." Tuuli puffed out her chest with pride and smiled for some reason. The girls proceeded to observe and tug my clothes in awe while Tuuli proudly explained how it all worked. They were squealing and having fun, but they were basically doing and saying the same things that the older women were.

I slid out of that circle too and sighed. It wasn't normal for so many strangers to talk to me at once. Honestly, I was a bit exhausted already. In search of a place to rest, I headed in Lutz's direction.

"Luuuutz!"

"Oh, Myne. Finally got away from Mom, huh? Took you lo—" Lutz turned around to see me and gasped, freezing up in place.

"Hm? What's wrong?"

"Nah, it's nothing. Just..." Lutz faltered and Ralph walked up, pushing him aside.

"What's with that outfit? It's a lot different from what Tuuli wore."

"We remade what she wore so it would fit me, and… Hyaaah! Let me down, Zasha!" Before I could finish explaining my outfit to Ralph, Zasha stuck his hands beneath my arms and lifted me up.

"Congrats, Myne. You're still so tiny and cute. Not like Lutz's, he's all cheeky and mean now. Not cute at all."

"'Grats, Myne! That outfit looks great on you! But seriously, you are friggin' tiny. Don't look old enough for a baptism at all."

"You may not be able to tell, Sieg, but I've gotten a little bigger!" I went to Lutz for peace and quiet, but his older brothers were tossing me around. I pouted to show I was getting mad and Lutz started to panic a little.

"C'mon guys, stop! Look at Myne, she's getting sick!"

"C'mooon, Myne. Get a grip. You don't wanna pass out before your baptism!"

I let the strength drain from my body as Zasha kept me held up high. Zasha was reaching adulthood tomorrow and was basically as strong as an adult.

"Lutz, I want to go home."

"You haven't even left yet."

Suddenly, the temple bell rang three times, each ring echoing and sending vibrations through the city. That was the signal for the baptism ceremony to begin. Out of all our neighbors, only Lutz and I were going to this baptism ceremony. Celebrating adults surrounded us in an instant.

"Let's go, Myne! To the main road!"

Dad pulled me out of Zasha's arms and lifted me up high, leading the crowd to the main street. Lutz hurriedly chased after him, and over Dad's shoulders I could see the rest of my family and the adults following us. I looked around and, just like during Tuuli's ceremony, kids and their families and neighbors were pouring out of side alleys to flood the main street.

"You feeling okay, Myne? I'll carry you to the temple, get some rest."

"Okay. Thanks, Dad." And so it was decided that Dad would carry me to the temple. That seemed like the best idea to me. I still couldn't walk at the same speed as the procession and the ceremony would be ruined for me if I passed out on the way there.

I heard loud cheers approaching our direction. It seemed that the procession had reached us. The families were following the rows of kids from behind, so Dad's plan was to wait and try to get to the very front of the parent section. But if Lutz followed us there, he'd get buried and lose the ability to see anything past the crowd.

"You can go up front, Lutz."

"Nah, if I lose you two we'll have to search each other out at the temple. I'll stick around."

"Maybe you should stick to the side, then? So you can see Benno's store along the way."

"...Good point. I'll try that."

The procession passed by in front of us, and we joined in with Lutz beside us. I was so high up in the air that unlike before, I could see the city around me.

People on both sides of the main street waved enthusiastically, whistling in support as they cheered us on. The windows of the buildings facing the main street were thrown open and cheers rained down on us from above as people stuck their heads out. I could see the kids in front of me waving back with proud smiles so broad they barely fit on their faces.

"You wave back too, Myne. That's how you say thanks." Dad urged me to wave back, so I clung to him with one arm and used my other to wave while smiling. I tried to visualize how the Japanese emperor and his family waved to people, so I could copy what they did.

...Right! Peaceful smile! Calm attitude! Dignity! I wasn't able to wave with the same regal grace as an emperor, but just having an example I could copy gave me some ground to stand on. At the very least, nobody here would mock me for trying to copy the emperor. I smiled as peacefully as I could and tried waving my hand as gracefully.

...Oh no, people are pointing at me! Why are so many of them looking at me?! Maybe because Dad was lifting me up, it felt like I was drawing a lot of attention. Though it was likely I was just imagining things since everyone was looking in the direction of the procession.

"Myne, my arm's getting tired. I'm shifting you to the other side." He shifted me over while we waited in the main plaza for the other processions.

I had watched Tuuli's baptism up until this point. Once everyone was gathered in the plaza, we would walk to the temple by the inner wall.

The temple, visible from the plaza, was made of white stone and was as tall as the inner wall, which was even taller than the outer walls. It was a large and magnificent building, but judging by the tall, narrow windows lined up near the top and the way it was built into the wall, I could guess that it was originally built as a fortress or otherwise as part of the wall's defenses.

Mmm, but would they really use a military building for religious purposes? I would imagine in times of war the church participates as well, but they use this temple during peace times too. It was probably built with donations raised from believers, so...

Ultimately, though, my thoughts were founded in Japanese knowledge and no amount of thinking would give me a reliable answer in this world. All I could do was have fun looking at the temple, which I hadn't paid much attention to before now, and try to guess what it was used for based on how it had been constructed.

The processions from other streets fused with ours, so we headed to the temple. The kids coming from buildings around here looked noticeably different. Cloth that was visibly more expensive than others and embroidery decorating their otherwise solid white clothing.

A bit of walking later and the Gilberta Company came into view. Benno, Mark, Otto, and Corinna were standing in front of it along with a crowd of familiar faces. Otto wrapped his arm around Corinna with a grin and waved at us. Corinna did the same, wearing a gentle smile.

"Lutz, there's Benno and Mark. Everyone came out of the store to see us!"

"Really?" Lutz wasn't being held up in the air like me, so he couldn't see Benno's store yet. It was funny watching him jumping repeatedly to try and see.

Once Lutz finally found Benno's store and started waving, Mark raised a hand and all the employees started cheering. "Lutz! Myne! Congratulations!"

I had been caught off guard by how much they stood out among the crowd, but everyone cheering us on made me so happy that I waved back hard along with Lutz. I was so pumped that I wasn't even thinking about acting like the emperor anymore.

"I think we should drop by and thank'm on our way back from the temple," said Dad as he rustled Lutz's hair, seeming just as happy as I was. Naturally, both Lutz and I nodded.

"Hey, Myne. Is it just me or is Benno looking kinda annoyed?"

"You think so too?"

Amid all the broadly smiling workers waving at us, Benno alone was rubbing his temples and scrunching his face up while looking in our direction. It was the same expression he wore when he was exasperated at something I had done. *Mmm, I wonder why Benno is making that face? I haven't done anything, I promise!*

We were finally approaching the temple. From the distance it had looked pure white, but as we got closer I could work out more details. Reliefs were carved into the walls, and there were four statues on either side of the entrance. I couldn't tell if they were decorative statues or if they represented various gods.

We passed by Freida's house as the front of the procession began entering the temple. I could see the guildmaster and his family by the side of the main street. Leise and Jutte were there too.

The guildmaster lifted Freida up, as if competing with my dad. Freida blinked in surprise, then waved at me with a smile, yelling "You look splendid, Myne!" loud enough for me to hear through the crowd.

"Congratulations, Myne!"

It was so nice to have people I know congratulating me that I yelled back while waving. "Freida! Everyone! Thank you!"

Guards in firm poses stood in front of the gate blocking the temple steps. They wore basic armor over blue clothing. I could tell from the ornaments decorating their well-polished, shining armor and the beautiful thread composing their blue clothing that they were wearing ceremonial outfits as well.

The two wooden doors that served as the entrance to the temple steps were twice as tall as an average adult and had reliefs carved into them as well. We passed through the gate and saw a plaza of white stone spread out before us.

In front of us was a large building about five stories tall, with smaller buildings about three stories tall on either side of it, all connected by passageways. Each building was made of the same white stone as the inner wall, and only the inner building had reliefs and decoration.

"This is as far as I can go. Myne's in your hands now, Lutz."

"Yeah, leave her to me."

Dad let me down. I took Lutz's hands and walked at the end of the procession toward the wide-open temple doors. The once noisy, excited children fell silent as soon as they entered the temple, which meant it was getting rapidly quieter as we walked. Which was exactly why Lutz was louder than expected when he spoke.

"Hey, Myne."

I looked at Lutz and quietly whispered "What?", leaning my ear toward him as if we were discussing secrets. I kept looking forward and Lutz whispered back.

"Those clothes and the ornament look super good on you. You're so cute I couldn't believe it." When the others praised me I just smiled and said thanks, but him whispering that right before we entered the temple threw me off.

"Wha? Bwuh? Why now...?" I reflexively looked up at Lutz and he smiled at me with a truly relieved smile.

"I didn't get the chance before since my brothers got in the way, so I waited until now."

"O-Oh, really? Okay, thanks." I held my pounding heart down and kept walking up the steps while holding Lutz's hand.

To the Baptism Ceremony

Since we were at the end of the procession, everyone in the plaza could see us even if they couldn't hear us. It was only after I came home that I learned that Dad had been gritting his teeth while people had said "How cute, it looks like they're getting married" as they watched Lutz and I enter the temple holding hands.

A Quiet Commotion

"Woooah! Holy cow!"

I couldn't hear their voices from the outside, but the second I went into the temple the shrill cries of the children echoed and made my head hurt. I reflexively stopped in place, but Lutz pulled me forward.

"There's still steps, watch your feet."

I looked at the ground and took a few steps, whereupon the doors closed behind us with heavy creaks. I turned around in surprise at the sudden darkness and saw priests wearing gray robes closing the door. "Oh, right. We were the last ones in."

A blue-robed priest walked slowly to the front of the tightly shut doors. He then held up a wind chime-esque bell with a strangely colored stone on it and rang it. Immediately the children fell silent, with only the echoes of their voices still reverberating through the temple.

"What, happened?" Lutz couldn't speak either. Or more precisely, he couldn't speak above a bare whisper. Judging by his expression and body language, he was trying to speak in a much louder voice. He was surprised by his own quiet voice and held a hand over his throat.

"Maybe it's a magic tool? It happened the second the blue-robed priest rung the bell." Likewise, my voice only came out in a whisper. But I was calm, since I had seen the priest ring the bell and could guess what had happened. Lutz calmed down a bit once I explained. Realizing the same thing was happening to me seemed to have done the trick.

At the back of the procession, I let out a sigh of awe and looked up. The temple had a ceiling that loomed high in the air like an atrium, and rows of round pillars carved with complex designs were lined up next to each other. At about four floors worth of height there were tall windows from which light streamed in. The walls and pillars were white aside from the gold used to decorate them, which made the area look brighter. Only the inner wall was colorful.

Unlike the Christian churches I had seen in photos, there weren't any paintings on the walls or stained glass in the windows. Everything was made of pure white stone. It didn't even feel like a Japanese shrine or temple. As far as I knew, it didn't resemble the religious architecture of Southeast Asia either.

The wall furthest inside was covered in colored designs from the floor to the ceiling and gave off a divine aura thanks to the light shining on it. It somewhat resembled a mosque, but there was a staircase of about forty steps leading up to it, and the statues dotting it didn't feel Islamic at all.

…Maybe that staircase is supposed to symbolize a staircase to the heavens and gods? The statues kind of remind me of the emperor and empress dolls used in the Japanese Doll's Day Festival.

At the top of the stairs were two statues, one male and one female. They seemed liked a couple, and since they were at the top of the stairs, I could guess that they were the king and queen of the gods. They were both pure white statues, but the male god was wearing a black cape made with sparkling gold scattered like stars, and the goddess was wearing a golden crown with long pointed tips that resembled light shining from the sun in all directions.

...The Goddess of Light and the God of Darkness, I guess? Or maybe the Goddess of Light and the God of Night? Either way, their crown and cape make them really stand out from the other statues.

A number of steps down was a statue of a peaceful, plump woman with her arms wrapped around a gleaming yellow grail. Beneath her was a woman holding a staff, a man holding a spear, a woman holding a shield, and a man holding a sword all lined up next to each other. It was odd. All of the statues were pure white, except the one colored object they were holding. I could imagine there was some deeper meaning resting within which statues were holding which objects.

...Maybe those are like, the holy grail and the holy sword and so on?

Further steps below had statues surrounded by flowers, fruits, clothes, and other items that could have been offerings. The more I looked, the more I thought back to Doll's Day.

"Myne, don't daydream, we gotta keep walking."

"Bwuh? Oh, sorry." Lutz pulled me forward and I sped up my pace to keep up with the procession.

The center of the room was empty, allowing the procession to walk forward unhindered. On either side of us were thick red carpets with about a meter of space between them. There were several desks lined up by the inner wall and a number of priests wearing blue robes were standing beside them, performing some kind of ritual. Once the ritual was completed, the child would be guided by a gray-robed priest to either the left or right. I could see them removing their shoes and sitting on the carpet.

The procession moved slowly forward, and eventually Lutz could see what the ritual was. He let out a quiet "geh" after peering forward.

"What's wrong, Lutz? Did you see what they're doing?" I asked, but Lutz's eyes wavered and it was obvious he didn't want to say anything. Eventually, he sighed and looked at me.

"They're doing the blood seal stuff you hate. Must be a magic tool they're using. Everyone's pressing their blood on it."

I wanted to pretend that I hadn't heard anything, and I kind of wanted to about-face and flee, but Lutz held my hand tightly and wouldn't let me leave.

"Give it up. Looks like they're registering us or something. This might have something to do with that city citizenship stuff."

"Guuuh... You're right. I think that's probably what's happening." Otto and Benno had been saying that following our baptism, we would be recognized as citizens of the city and have our citizenship. That meant that whether I liked it or not, I needed to finish the ceremony if I wanted my citizenship. "...Why do magic tools like blood so much?"

"Who knows."

Whenever it came time to deal with magic stuff, I had to cut my finger and touch it with blood. But pain wasn't something I would get used to so easily.

I waited my turn while quivering in fear and eventually saw a curt-looking blue-robed priest take the thing that looked like a needle, poke it into a kid's finger, and press that finger firmly against a white, flat medal. The kid opened his mouth as if to scream, but nothing came out. He then was guided to sit down elsewhere while he trembled and held his finger down in pain.

"Okay, next. Come forward." The crowd thinned out and one of the priests overseeing a now-empty desk called out to me. Lutz pushed me from behind and I stumbled my way toward it.

The blue-robed priest narrowed his eyes somewhat suspiciously and, after glancing over me, held out his hand. "Raise your palm and hold out your hand. We'll be drawing blood, but it won't hurt much at all."

He said it wouldn't hurt, but nobody who ever said that was telling the truth. He poked me with the needle and a sharp pain similar to touching a burning pan shot through my finger before red blood started puckering out. I could feel the blood draining from my face as I stared at my hurt finger.

"Please press your finger against this." This priest didn't aggressively force my finger against the medal like the meaner one I had seen. He was more gentle and handed the small medal to me instead. I just had to get a little blood on it, and my finger didn't hurt as much as I had expected, which was a relief.

I'm glad he wasn't mean or rough, but my finger's still hurting a bit. It struck me that the quiet-inducing magic tool probably existed not to silence small talk, but to muffle the sounds of kids crying out in pain.

"You two are the last ones. Please follow me." A young gray-robed priest who had probably just reached adulthood called out to Lutz and I, then headed to the carpet. He explained that we needed to take our shoes off before getting on it, so we did.

A lot of kids were sitting with their legs thrown out, but I was sitting cross-legged. The temple was wide open like a school gym, and with so many other kids my age around me, I somehow felt that cross-legged was the right way to sit here.

Before long the blue priests left the desks, having finished registering all of us. They put the medals into a box that they carried out of the room. The gray priests proceeded to prepare the next step. They carried out the desks, and in their place set down an extravagant podium.

The blue priests returned and lined up on either side of the podium. The gray priests, having seemingly finished their preparations, lined up by the walls around us. It felt like they were teachers watching us to make sure we kept quiet during assembly.

"The High Bishop enters," intoned a blue priest as he waved a rod in the air. The sound of several bells ringing filled the air and a door to the side opened. From it came an older man wearing a large white robe decorated with a golden sash and blue embroidery. I could tell he was the High Bishop. He deliberately walked up to the podium and gently placed what he was holding onto it.

...*Wait, is that a book?!* I rubbed my eyes and squinted to make sure. Once I saw him start slowly flipping through pages, I was certain. It was definitely a book. Maybe it was this religion's bible, or some other holy scripture.

"Lutz, a book! They have a book!" I put my hand on Lutz's shoulder as he fidgeted, and pointed excitedly at the podium. He leaned forward a bit to get a clearer look.

"Where? What kind of book is it?"

"It's right there, the High Bishop is turning its pages. See?!" It was bound in leather, and the sensitive corners were bound in metal clasps for protection. I could also see a gemstone buried in the cover.

"That's a book? Looks super expensive. Nothing like the ones you make."

"My books are all about practicality, don't compare them to books that are basically art. It's like comparing the sword that statue has to your knife."

"Huh, alright. Guess you're surprised to see books here?"

"...Actually, I guess I'm not. Now that I think about it, it makes perfect sense for books to be here." I was your standard Japanese person without much interest in religions, so I hadn't really visited any temples in my day. But I knew that religious institutions tended to have bibles, holy scriptures, sutras, and basically just written records of the religion's teachings. They had books. I didn't have to force my weak body to its limits to make books in the middle of crushing poverty. Books already existed.

Just like the how Merchant's Guild was at the cutting edge of information, the Church was at the cutting edge of theology, math, music, sculpturing — all science and art that brought humanity closer to the divine. The Christian Church had likewise historically been the forefront of academic advancement, and in Japan, men of culture and wisdom had gathered at shrines and temples to push knowledge forward.

"Gaaaaah! I should have come to the temple sooner. Why didn't I think of this before? I'm so dumb! I could have read books without all that struggling!" It was probably a good thing that my yelling was kept quiet. I shouted on the inside and Lutz shrugged his shoulders, exasperated.

"I mean, looks like you forgot this, but kids aren't allowed in the temple before their baptism ceremony. Even if you figured this out sooner, the guards would have just turned you away." He had a good point. Only kids who had finished their baptism could enter the temple.

"But you know, I think it's fate that I'm meeting a book during my baptism ceremony, the first time I've been to the temple."

"All kids go to the temple once they hit seven years old, fate's got nothing to do with it."

"Geez, Lutz. Stop being a buzzkill."

"I get that you're pumped to see a book, so calm down. I don't want you passing out in here." Lutz tried to calm me down before I got too excited. But how could I calm down now?

"Nuh uh. There's a book this close to me, no way can I calm down. It's impossible."

"Impossible or not, calm down. Not like they're gonna let you read that book anyway."

"Oh… You're right." There was a book, but not one I could read myself. It had a gemstone on its leather cover even; they would never let me touch it. My excitement drained in an instant and my shoulders slumped.

"As of today," began the High Bishop, "you have all become seven years of age and officially recognized citizens of the city. Congratulations." He was an older man, a practical grandpa it looked like, but his voice was strong and echoed throughout the temple. He first congratulated us, then began reading aloud from the bible-like book.

As my heart and soul belonged to books, I leaned forward and eagerly listened to every word. He was telling us stories of the creator gods and the changing of the seasons, similar to what Benno had told me once before. He spoke with simple language so it would be easier for kids to understand.

"The God of Darkness lived a lonely life all by himself for so long it would numb our minds just thinking about it." Thus began the story.

The God of Darkness then met the Goddess of Light. A lot happened, and they ended up married with children. The Goddess of Water, the God of Fire, the Goddess of Wind, and the Goddess of Earth were all born, and in the process the world we lived in was created. The "a lot happened" part was probably touched up to be more appealing to children and was basically like a soap opera.

But well, that was how religious myths tended to go. Most mythology I was familiar with was chaotic and all over the place. You could spend all day poking fun at the stories.

This story was personally fun for me already since I hadn't heard it before, but I was making it even more fun by comparing it to the mythologies I knew already. On the other hand, Lutz was fidgeting with boredom and looking at me jealously, not getting what I found so fun about it.

"Why're you liking this so much, Myne? What's fun about it?"

"Everything about it is fun!" I answered with a full smile and Lutz sighed, shaking his head in exasperation.

"…Cool. Good for you."

"Uh huh! I love hearing new stories."

The creation myth was followed by a myth about the changing of the seasons. Benno had framed the seasons as thus: "In spring, snow melts into water that gives life to sprouting plants. In summer, the sun burns like fire and plants grow leaves. In autumn, the cool wind chills fruit as they grow. In winter, the life and earth of our land sleeps." However, the actual myth was quite different.

"The Goddess of Earth is the youngest daughter of the Goddess of Light and the God of Darkness. One day, the God of Life fell in love with the Goddess of Earth at first sight. He asked her father, the God of Darkness, for her hand in marriage. The God of Darkness happily accepted, hoping that they would give birth to many children." The myth explaining seasons seemed fun to me, but Lutz sighed with boredom as he listened, so it would probably be best to summarize it.

Put simply, the God of Life was far too possessive and froze the Goddess of Earth within ice and snow. He impregnated her, then felt jealous of even their unborn children. As her power was stolen, winter occurred.

The Goddess of Light began to worry for the Goddess of Earth, whom she had not seen since her marriage, and upon discovering her, freed her by melting the ice. The Goddess of Water flooded away the melted ice and the God of Life, who had been weakened by his own actions, was swept away too. Then the Goddess of Earth's siblings gave their strength to the children, the seeds. This was the spring where seeds bloomed.

The God of Fire lending his power along to help the planted lives grow was the summer, and soon the world became lush with plant life. This returned the God of Life's strength, and he came looking for the Goddess of Earth. The Goddess of Wind, seeking to keep him away from her little sister, combined their powers and brought about the autumn where crops are harvested.

Once all of the siblings were weakened, the God of Life gained the upper hand. He froze the Goddess of Earth in ice and snow once again. The other deities wished to just kill the God of Life, but that would prevent any new lives from being born. Winter was the brother and sisters waiting in frustration for their power to return.

This back and forth looped endlessly, resulting in the seasons. By the way, since Lutz and I were born in the summer, our patron deity was the God of Fire and we were characterized by being passionate and hot-blooded. It seemed that he also granted favor when it came to teaching and guiding others.

The High Bishop brought the tale to a close and shut the book. "Now then, I will teach you how to pray. Praying to the gods and expressing your thanks to them is the key to receiving stronger divine protection," he said with a fairly serious expression as he slowly walked to the front of the podium. Meanwhile, gray priests unrolled a carpet in front of the blue priests. The High Bishop stood in the middle of the ten or so blue priests.

"Now then, observe closely so you may do what I do… Praise be to the gods!" declared the High Bishop while spreading and raising his arms to the sky, holding his left knee up and looking upwards.

"Pfff!" I quickly put a hand over my mouth to hold back a laugh. It wouldn't be polite to burst into laughter during a religious ceremony. I knew that. But the more I knew it was wrong, the more I wanted to laugh. My stomach wiggled as I held the laughter in.

…I mean, come on, that's the G*ico Man pose! He's just doing the *lico Man pose! Why the Gli*o Man pose?! Why lift up your knee?! You're an old man, it's dangerous to stand on one foot like that. The fact he was keeping perfect balance without wavering a bit just made it more funny. Honestly, it was all over for me. I was confident I would laugh no matter what the High Bishop did next.

And indeed, I nearly died when he slowly lowered his leg like a tai chi fighter. Was he trying to assassinate my sides or something? They were already hurting so bad, and he just went and made it worse.

"Glory be to the gods!" The High Bishop fluidly shifted from doing the Gl*co Man pose to genuflecting on the ground. That was it. Some laughter burst out of my mouth.

"Pfhahah!"

"Myne, what's wrong? You feeling sick or something?"

"I-I'm fine. I'm still… still fine. I can do this. This is a trial the gods have given me." I held my mouth and ducked my head down while answering Lutz. Naturally, I couldn't actually tell him that the praying pose was so funny that I couldn't stop laughing. Only those who knew the Glic* Man pose at a glance would find this so funny. No doubt about that.

...This is religion. This is a real religion. Everyone's very serious about this, so laughing would be rude.

I managed to calm down the ripples of laughter hitting my sides by imagining opening a classroom door and seeing my classmates praying to Allah. The way different religions prayed always looked silly from an outsider's perspective. It was just pure coincidence that this religion happened to pray by doing the Gl*co Man pose. Laughing would be rude.

I took deep breaths and calmed myself. Once I managed to raise my head, I saw the High Bishop urging us to stand.

"Now then, children, please stand. We shall pray together."

...Together?! Please no, anything but that! Everyone around me stood up together. My mouth was flapping and my sides aching. I could tell I was on the verge of bursting into hard laughter. I couldn't let that happen. *I can't laugh,* I told myself repeatedly, which just made me want to laugh more.

"Praise be to the gods!" said the High Bishop as he made the Gl*co pose again.

That was fine. It was less impactful the second time. I successfully held back the waves of laughter and felt my success through my stomach muscles. But in the next instant, the blue priests all lifted their legs up in the same pose.

"Praise be to the gods!"

My sides instantly lost to the sight of ten priests in a row making beautiful Gl*co poses with serious expressions on their faces. The angle of their arms, the height of their knees, their blank expressions... Everything worked together to make my stomach muscles give in. I fell down on the spot.

"Pfffh! Nnnggh, pfffh!" *My stomach hurts…! Someone, else!* I held my mouth shut and tried to contain the laughter, but tears formed in my eyes and laughter slipped out. It would feel so relieving to just roll on the floor and burst into laughter while kicking the ground, but I couldn't, and that made me want to laugh harder.

"Myne, I knew you weren't okay!" Lutz worriedly hopped over to me on one foot as he continued making the Gl*co pose. That was it. He finished me off. I gave in and just pounded the floor with my fists in silent laughter.

"Sorry, ppfffh… I can't, breathe…"

"Myne! Why'd you wait until it got this bad?!"

"No, I'm… f-fine…" I waved my hands at Lutz to tell him I was fine, but a gray priest who must have noticed something was off came running over.

"What's wrong?"

"Um, Myne started feeling bad and then collapsed. She's really sickly, and the ceremony got her all excited, so…"

I had definitely gotten excited, but I wasn't feeling bad. I was just laughing too hard. I didn't need the priest's help.

"I-I'm fine. I'll get better soon! See?" I hurriedly tried to stand up, but the sudden movement was too much for my laughter-striken body, and my arms just gave in. I collapsed right in front of the priest.

"Whaddaya mean, see?! You're not better at all!"

"Ngh, I just slipped a little… I'm really okay." So I said, but given that I was literally collapsed on the ground, there was zero chance of them believing me. From an objective standpoint it was completely natural that the priest would believe Lutz over me.

"I will carry her to a medical room. It would likely be best for her to rest until the ceremony is over." I sensed that the gray priest wouldn't believe anything I said, so I just limply let him pick me up.

…I retired from the ceremony early after having my sides sent to orbit. *Thiiis will probably be a painful memory that I'll keep to myself for the rest of my life.*

Gated Paradise

The gray priest didn't take me to a medical room for poor commoners. It was a well-furnished room that, judging by what I knew from the gate's waiting rooms, was probably for merchants with connections to nobles and wealthy visitors.

The reason was probably my clothes. You could roughly tell how wealthy someone's family was by their clothes — how much cloth was used, was it embroidered, how it looked, and so on. My normal clothes were a different story, but my baptism outfit was extremely frilly, and while it lacked embroidery, it had small flowers sewn onto it and looked pretty fancy. My hair stick was clearly special and handmade too, so at a glance, I probably looked like a girl about as wealthy as Freida.

…But well, I didn't need to go out of my way and point out that I was a poor person. It was the priest who made the mistake, and to be honest, I had no idea how they would treat me if I corrected them. What was the harm in keeping quiet?

"Please excuse me." As I furrowed my brow in thought, the grey priest sat me onto a bench. I held my swaying body steady by gripping the armrest and immediately the priest took out my hair stick and delicately removed my shoes.

…*Um, what?!* He did it so smoothly that I didn't even know how to react. It was like when Jutte fussed over me at Freida's house. The gray priest was clearly used to taking care of other people.

I opened my eyes wide in surprise, forgetting to thank him, and before I knew it he had stood up, made the nearby bed, and princess-carried me onto it. "Awww. Um, I'm really okay."

"It is not good to lie before the gods. This is a temple."

But I'm not lying...

Once I was on the bed, he gently pulled the covers over me. He then placed my hair stick on a table next to the bed and my shoes in front of it. He seemed more like a trained servant than a priest. It honestly felt really weird.

"Please rest here. I will come check on you later."

The priest left the room and shut the door behind him. It was true that I still felt weak, so I just stayed in bed and waited for my energy to return. I could use the time to think of an excuse for why this had happened. My family would definitely probe me for answers, but I couldn't tell them I just laughed too hard. That would make Lutz mad too. But thinking about Lutz made me remember him doing the Gl*co Man pose, which made me laugh again.

I waited in bed, and my strength slowly recovered. I clenched my fists open and closed to test my grip strength. Unfortunately, I had to use the bathroom.

There was a chamber pot right by the bed, but I didn't see any water nearby so I didn't know how I would clean up afterward. I could imagine that the people who usually stayed here had servants and didn't clean up after themselves, but that wasn't the case for me. Plus, I didn't want a priest I had never met before to do it for me. Ideally I could ask someone where the water was and stealthily clean up myself.

I sat up and tried moving my legs, and they felt strong enough to not give in immediately. I did my hair and put my hair stick back in. Freida had a bell beside her bed to call servants, but this room had no such thing. This was an emergency — I had to go look for someone. I didn't know how long it would take to find someone, so I had to act fast before I couldn't hold it in any longer. I slid off the bed, put my shoes on, and escaped the room.

The pillars and walls had decorative reliefs, but in general the hallways were pure white and stretched on infinitely. My footsteps echoed loudly enough to be quite loud, but I couldn't hear anyone else walking. It seemed like the best thing to do would be to walk back to where the ceremony was being held.

...Wait, what? Did I turn the wrong corner? The temple was generally pure white, but I was starting to see bits of color here and there. It became clear that it wasn't just my imagination that the statues and reliefs were getting more fancy. I had seemingly wandered my way into an area for nobles.

The blood drained from my face. I could only imagine bad things happening if a noble found me here. *...Oh no. I have to hurry back!* I spun around and started nervously speed-walking back to where I came from, legs trembling. I wanted to get out of the noble zone as soon as possible. I made sure to look at distinctive parts of the hall to keep track of where I was. *...I saw that carving before, right? I think I remember this tapestry...*

As I turned corners looking for the medical room I had been in, I heard a steady set of footsteps walking in my direction. If I had left the noble zone I would have welcomed that with open arms, but I didn't want to be found right now. I wanted to hide. I would be fine if it was a priest, but what if it was a noble?

I looked around in a panic, but there was nowhere to hide in the hallway. I was found and caught in seconds.

"Who are you?! What are you doing here?!" A firm voice rung out, originating from a priestess with tightly bound hair. She had the sharp look of someone who knew how to do her job, but at the same time she felt kind of like a sexy secretary.

She wore a grey robe like the priest who had carried me here, but it had a different design. I couldn't tell if the designs distinguished men and women or if those participating in the ceremony wore different robes. Speaking of which, it struck me for the first time that there weren't any priestesses at the baptism.

I let out a sigh of relief that she wasn't a noble and immediately apologized for trespassing in the noble zone. "I'm sorry. My name is Myne and I was taken to a medical room after collapsing. I had no servants with me and there were no bells, so I left to look for someone. I got lost and before I knew it, I was here…"

The woman looked me over head to toe, then sighed. She put a hand on her cheek, and as she sighed wearily I found myself unable to look away from her. "I will take you to the chapel where the ceremony is taking place once I have finished my business. Can you follow me for a moment?"

"Yes, thank you."

The priest's eyes narrowed slightly and she continued walking, her footsteps echoing as she went. I jogged to keep up with her, but if I kept that up I would collapse in no time. It was a stroke of luck that she had business just a single room away.

"Please wait here for a moment. I will be finished soon."

"O-Okaaay…" I nodded, breathing heavily.

The priestess glanced at me with brows furrowed in worry, then pushed the door open. I put a hand on the wall to catch my breath and peered into the room she'd just entered since the door was still open.

Once I saw what was inside, I gasped hard and froze in place. "…Is this, a library?"

It wasn't a very big room, but the walls were covered in bookshelves. Most of the shelves were packed with wooden boards and loose pieces of paper. There were some closed shelves with locked doors that probably contained the more precious books.

There were two long desks in the middle of the room with slanted tops to make reading easier. The desks resembled those I had seen in college lecture halls and the benches were long enough for about five people to sit next to each other. And finally, on the tops of the desks were six thick books, lined up and connected by sturdy chains.

"...It's a (chained library)." It had been my dream back in my Urano days to go to a foreign library with a long history. This was a fantasy world and not a foreign country, but still, it would be fair to say that my wish had finally been granted. In the past I had wanted so, so badly to go to a foreign chained library and touch the history protected by linked metal.

I put a hand on my chest and trembled. My heart was pounding so fast I could feel the blood rushing through my whole body. Something I had wanted for my whole life was now miraculously right in front of me. Warm tears spilled out of my eyes one after another.

"I-I've never seen one of these before..." Not only was it my first time seeing a chained library, it was my first time as Myne seeing a collection of books large enough to be called a library. Again, it was only a single room and it wasn't that large, but for me it was basically a cavern of hidden treasure given how long I had lived without seeing any books. ...*This is the true paradise created by the gods. The gods I worship are here!*

"Praise be to the gods! Glory be to the gods!" When in Rome, do as Romans do. Overjoyed as I was to see a library, and a chained library at that, I made the Gl*co Man pose and then genuflected on the ground to express my gratitude. I was kind of shaky on one leg, but I wanted to believe that my overwhelming gratitude was being conveyed.

I rubbed my face and hands with my clothes to make sure I wasn't dirty. Once I had confirmed my hands were clean, I took a determined step forward to follow the woman into paradise.

"Excuse m— pbbhhh?!" My face slammed into something, as if I had charged right into an automatic door that didn't open. I hit it so hard that I was actually seeing stars in my eyes.

"Ooooww..." I crouched to the ground and held my face while using my other hand to search for an entrance. My hand couldn't move past a certain point in the doorway. There was some invisible wall blocking the way. I tapped it with my palm, but the invisible wall blocked me and stopped me from going inside.

"Bwuh? B-But why?" The woman from before went inside without issue. I couldn't understand why only I was being denied entry. I felt the world darkening around me and I hit the invisible wall as hard as I could. It didn't budge an inch.

There was paradise right in front of me, but I couldn't go inside. There were books in sight, but I couldn't read or touch a single one of them. Did the gods approve of torture this cruel and unreasonable? *...I've been denied books so long, and now this. Stupid gods! Give back my gratitude!*

"Come on, let me in! I want inside toooo!" Books were so rare and expensive that only nobles owned them. Said nobles also had magic tools they used just to keep kids quiet during the baptism ceremony. It wasn't strange that they'd use some magic to keep their precious books safe. I understood that, but it was just too cruel.

The despair of seeing a library I couldn't enter was so visceral that tears dripped from my face. I couldn't even work up the energy to wipe them away. "I want to reaaaad…"

The priestess from earlier returned, holding a bundle of what looked like work documents. She looked down at me clinging to the invisible wall, crying, and took a sharp step backwards. "…May I ask what you are doing?"

"Uwaaaaaaah! Why, why, why can't I go inside?!" I asked while pounding the invisible wall.

The priest looked back at the library and realized what had happened. "These books are precious, so only those given special permission within the temple may enter this room," she said, shining a light of hope down onto me.

If only those affiliated with the temple could enter the room, I just had to join the temple myself. The gods had not abandoned me yet. I would use the last months available to me to read these books cover to cover.

I wiped my tears and snot away, then shot my hand up. "Question, please. How can I join the temple?"

"…I suppose the simplest way would be to become an apprentice shrine maiden." It seemed that women were called shrine maidens, not priests. I had been mistaken in calling this woman a priestess.

"Okay then, I want to be an apprentice shrine maiden here! How can I become one?"

"You need merely get the permission of the High Priest or the High Bishop. Now, shall we go to the chapel?" The shrine maiden tried to cut the conversation short there, but I shook my head.

"Where is the High Bishop?"

"The baptism ceremony has ended by now, so he should be in his room. Would you like to go there now?" I could tell that the woman was getting completely weirded out, but she was a precious source of information and I didn't want to miss this opportunity.

"Yes! I can't go home like this!"

"…I will consult the High Bishop."

I didn't know if she had been impressed by my unshakable resolve or if she was dealing with me based on the wealthy appearance of my clothing, but the shrine maiden let out a defeated sigh and took me to the High Bishop's room.

I had apparently gotten lost pretty deep inside the temple, judging by how close his room was. I stood outside the extravagant doors, waiting for my entrance to be permitted. I looked around and saw expensive art and furnishings all around me, confirming that, indeed, the top dog of the temple was fairly wealthy.

"High Bishop, there is a girl who wishes to become an apprentice shrine maiden…"

"Willingly?"

I could hear some of their conversation through the slightly ajar door. I got a little nervous, like someone waiting for an interview, and I checked to make sure I looked okay. Part of my outfit was a bit stiff with dried snot and tears.

"Yes, she came here today for the baptism ceremony."

"Hmm. I may as well meet her."

"Please come in."

I wanted to stride in confidently, but the door was heavier than expected. Having no other choice, I pushed the door with all my body weight and slid inside once there was a big enough crack. "Please excuse me," I apologized for the intrusion.

The High Bishop's room resembled Freida's room. There was a table with chairs around it fairly close to the door for meeting purposes. The corner of the room farthest from the door had a bed with thick drapes, and on the other side was a workspace.

The workspace had a large desk and two bookshelves. There was also a decorative shelf where a thirty-centimeter-tall statue of a god rested, along with the bible I had seen during the ceremony. There was also a candle there, placed symmetrically such that the bible was exactly in between it and the statue.

The shrine maiden and High Bishop were in the workspace, so I walked in that direction with as much dignity as I could muster. I was so acutely aware that that the High Bishop was staring right at me that it hurt. I took deep breaths and steeled myself. I was about to have a job interview. This interview would decide whether or not I could enter the book room.

"What is your name?"

"Myne. Please, High Bishop. I want to be an apprentice shrine maiden. I beg for your permission to become one." I clasped my hands in front of my chest as I begged.

The High Bishop gave an amused smile and put his pen down. "In that case, Myne. Could you tell me why you wish to become an apprentice shrine maiden?"

"Because there's a room with books here," I answered, which must have been an unexpected answer given by how his eyes widened.

"...The book room? You can read?"

"Yes, though there's still a lot of words I don't know. My vocabulary will grow as I read more books. I would like to spend the rest of my life reading the books here."

The High Bishop sighed and rubbed his temples. He slumped his shoulders to an exaggerated extent and shook his head. "You seem to be mistaking something. This temple is a place of worship. Priests and shrine maidens serve the gods."

"That's right. I understand. That thick bible you read from today for us is filled with stories about the gods, right? Well, that bible is basically a god to me. I want to read about the gods until I die. I want to know all about the gods."

"You are a biblical fundamentalist?" The High Bishop's eyes flashed.

I wasn't sure if I should say yes or no to that. After a bit of thought, I decided that the average kid my age wouldn't know what that meant. At times like this, it was best to keep things simple and not say anything unnecessary.

"I haven't heard that phrase and am not entirely sure what it means, but I would like to read the bible and there's no doubt in my mind that I want to learn more about the gods. Believe in my passion as one who receives the God of Fire's divine protection. I want to become an apprentice shrine maiden and spend the rest of my life reading the books here to learn everything about the gods. Do my prayers and wishes reach your heart, High Bishop?"

The High Bishop, a little thrown off by my desperate and repeated pleas, looked me over and nodded to himself. "I feel your passion. If you so wish, you can indeed become an apprentice shrine maiden. However, a child from a family such as yours will need to match their passion with a donation of equal dedication. Do you know how much you will need to donate?"

He was probably trying to rip me off since I was wearing expensive clothing. *If you want to get in the temple, hand over some cash.* But I already knew that the church wouldn't be a pretty organization that ran off of dreams and rainbows. If I could get in by paying money, I just had to give some of what I had on hand.

Speaking of which, I had heard that a single book would cost several small golds. If granted access to the chained library, I would be able to read at least ten books as thick as that bible. My only source of context was Japanese rental libraries, but generally you could access all books in the library for the price of one book. Considering that I would be able to read all the stuff packed in that book room for half a year, and considering that I would still have plenty to leave with my family, I could donate a large gold without feeling too bad about it.

"I'm not sure what a normal donation would be, but... I can donate up to one large gold of my own money."

"A-A large gold?!" shouted the High Priest so loud spit came flying out of his mouth. The shrine maiden looked stunned as well and put a hand over her mouth, eyes wide. Judging by their reaction, I realized I had offered far more money than what was normal.

"Oh? Is that too much? Well, that's just my maximum offer. I can pay less too."

The High Bishop looked at the shrine maiden, coughed to collect himself, then looked at me with much more serious eyes. "Aaah, well, we of the temple consider your passionate desire to become an apprentice shrine maiden quite splendid. However, as today was the baptism ceremony, haven't you already decided on a job? Do you belong to any organizations?"

It was true that if I had already settled on a job, I wouldn't be able to suddenly drop it and become an apprentice shrine maiden out of nowhere. But I had planned to work at home, and thus had no obligations anywhere.

"I am registered with the Merchant's Guild, but I'm not working anywhere. I'm sickly and was planning on working at home."

"At home? Are you a merchant's daughter? You cannot belong to any organization if you are to become an apprentice shrine maiden. You can leave the Merchant's Guild and become an apprentice shrine maiden, but do you have your parents' permission to do that?"

"I just saw the book room today, so I haven't discussed this with my parents yet..." I faltered there. I couldn't answer about the Merchant's Guild either. I needed to be registered there to sell things. "I'm not sure if I can leave the Guild. What would happen to all the money I've saved and all the products I plan to make?"

The High Bishop overheard me murmuring to myself to collect my thoughts, and his eyes widened. "The money you've saved? Your products? Are you not helping your parents with their work?"

"No, not exactly." This was my chance to market myself to the temple. Thinking back to what I had read about interviews in the past, I summarized everything I had done and what I had earned from it. All in all it took about a minute.

"...Hmm. It might be wise for me to negotiate with the guildmaster to allow you to remain registered even after becoming an apprentice here." My efforts were successful, judging by the High Bishop's impressed smile. It would be a big help for me if someone with authority negotiated on my behalf. I said my thanks and left dealing with the guildmaster to the High Bishop.

"I'll ask my parents if I can become an apprentice shrine maiden."

"Certainly. If they refuse or you have any worries, don't hesitate to come to me at once. You can come here to read books as you desire. Entering the book room still is out of the question, but I will allow you to read my bible here."

"Really?! Yaaay! Praise be to the gods!" I made the Gl*co Man pose, and instantly I could feel body tilt. The blood drained from my face. It seemed that I had passed my limit without realizing it.

My energy slipped right out of my body. In its place, I could feel the heat starting to rampage inside of me. ...*Oh no. I got too excited.* Without Lutz around, there was nobody to stop me and hold me back when I got too excited.

"...I've really done it now."

Plop! I fell to the side and stopped moving. It sucked that I couldn't move, but at least I was still conscious. I shifted my focus to keeping the still-slight amount of Devouring heat within me bottled up.

"What?! Are you alright?!" The High Bishop watched me collapse with a shocked expression and shot out of his chair, knocking it back.

The shrine maiden calmly looked at me on the ground and murmured quietly to herself. "...Speaking of which, I believe she mentioned collapsing during the ceremony."

"She what?!" replied the High Bishop, eyebrows shooting up.

I apologized to them, still unable to move. "I'm sorry, I got too excited. Please wait a moment, I can't move right now."

Rejection and Persuasion

The High Bishop summoned a gray priest to carry me back to the medical room, and this time the shrine maiden stayed behind so that I wouldn't leave unsupervised.

As a result, I was forced to use the bathroom with her watching and cleaning up after me. It was so embarrassing I almost cried. I felt so bad about it that I couldn't even look her in the eyes. I would have buried myself in the blankets and rolled around if I had the strength, but I didn't.

I stretched out on top of the bed and stared at the ceiling, despairing over my incompetence, until eventually Lutz came to see me. The sight of me being watched over in such a fancy room caught him off guard and he rushed to the bed immediately.

"What did you do, Myne?!"

"Ummm, I went looking for water, and... collapsed." I lifted my head up and summarized what had happened.

Lutz narrowed his eyes and shook his head, arms crossed. "That can't be everything. Spit it all out."

"Ngh... Ummm, I found a book room, and got really excited..."

"What's a book room, exactly?"

"A paradise given to us by the gods. Or in other words... a room full of books."

"Aaah… Alright, that's enough. I can guess the rest." Lutz put a hand on his forehead and waved me away with his other hand. That was the end of that, so I grabbed my hair stick so that we could leave.

"You didn't tell him the most important part. This young lady collapsed after forcing her way into a meeting with the High Bishop," added the shrine maiden with a shrug, having listened in to our conversation.

Lutz paled and then pinched my cheeks, pulling them. "How could you be so dumb?!"

"Sorry. I know I got a little too excited."

It would have been better if I had proceeded more cautiously after thinking things through, but ultimately I had forged a path toward becoming a shrine maiden and been given the opportunity to read the bible inside the High Bishop's room. I knew I'd messed up, but I didn't regret what I had done.

"We're going home before you do anything else."

Lutz carried me on his back out of the temple with the shrine maiden escorting us. Dad was waiting for us in front of the temple garden, looking frustrated.

"It seems someone came to get you. I will take my leave, then."

"Thank you for your help."

I moved over to Dad's back and we started going home. As I listened to Lutz report to Dad what happened today, the steady up and down shaking of being carried encouraged me to sleep.

"I'm gonna sign my contract at the store before going home," said Lutz, snapping me back to reality.

We were in front of the Gilberta Company, but naturally, I wasn't in a state to drop by. Lutz and I split up so he could go inside to report what had happened and sign his apprentice contract. Before

Dad and I left, though, Mark came outside to greet us. I waved at him while still on Dad's back.

"Thanks for today, Mr. Mark. I'm a bit too weak to go inside right now, but I'll be back."

"Take care of yourself."

"Lutz, don't mess up the contract."

"Yeah. Get some rest."

I waved goodbye to Lutz and Mark, then went home with Dad. We finished lunch, which was somewhat fancier than usual for celebratory reasons. Then, as we all drank tea together, I looked at Dad. I had to talk to him about how I wanted to become an apprentice shrine maiden.

"Um, Dad."

"Yeah?" Dad took a sip of tea, looking like he was in a good mood.

"I think I want to be an apprentice shrine maiden, at the temple."

The second I said that, Dad's smile vanished. He then slammed his cup against the table so hard it shook. I flinched as the tea flew out of the cup and splashed onto the table.

"…What was that? Say it again." Dad's voice was so low and intense that I blinked in surprise. His anger and disgust were so apparent that my heart started beating faster.

"…An apprentice shrine maiden, at the temple."

"Don't joke around! I wouldn't send my daughter to the friggin' temple."

"D-Dad. Why are you so mad?" I could only blink in confusion at Dad's sudden change in attitude. I had expected him to oppose this, but I really couldn't imagine why he was so furious with disgust.

"Only orphans become priests and shrine maidens! Orphans don't have parents or guardians, so they have to. They have no choice. You're different!"

"Only orphans become shrine maidens?"

"Yeah, and priests. You have parents and family. You're not becoming a shrine maiden. Don't bring this up again!"

I could only sit in shock, stunned at Dad's extreme response. But at the same time, I could understand where he was coming from. I had noticed some things were off back at the temple. The High Bishop had been surprised that someone would "willingly" want to become a shrine maiden, and the apparent wealth of my family had thrown him off.

"Gunther, you don't have to be so harsh. Myne just didn't know."

"...Yeah, you're right." Dad took deep breaths to calm his frustration and ruffled my hair.

Mom started wiping up the tea while looking at me curiously. "Still, though. Why would you ever want to be a shrine maiden, Myne?"

It was clear that both Mom and Dad were heavily biased against priests and shrine maidens. I had thought both were honorable and respected professions, to be honest, so I was really surprised.

"Well, when I collapsed in the temple, I got lost looking for water."

"You were in some waiting room, right? There should've been water right outside of it." Dad, having heard the same thing from Lutz, rubbed his chin. It was true that waiting rooms for commoners tended to have water near them. But I had to shake my head.

"...My outfit was so fancy, they actually thought I was the daughter of a rich family and took me to the kind of room a merchant with a noble's letter of introduction would go. There wasn't any water nearby."

"Ah, yeah, can't help that with an outfit like yours." Dad nodded repeatedly. Mom and Tuuli both understood as well.

"While I was lost, I ended up in a part of the temple meant for nobles."

Both of my parents paled. We lived in a stratified society where those of different statuses were kept thoroughly separate. If I had gotten lost and annoyed a noble, that could have meant the end of our lives right then and there.

"A shrine maiden found me first, so I never met a noble, but I did find a book room. It was filled with books. I wanted to read them so, so bad, but I couldn't go inside…"

"Books, huh?" Dad's eyebrow twitched.

"I asked how I could get inside, and they told me I needed to become an apprentice shrine maiden…"

"And you decided to become one without thinking at all, huh? Sheesh. Give up on those books. Just keep trying to make them like you have been."

I couldn't believe that Dad was telling me to give up on the books I had been dedicating my whole life to obtain. I just stared at him. He was looking at me with a deadly serious expression, not a smile in sight.

"Which do you want more? Cutting off your family and living life in an orphanage to read books, or keeping on living with us like you have been?"

My head went blank. Books or my family, pick one. I wanted to live with my family as long as possible before my Devouring killed me. I wanted to use some of that time to make and read books if possible.

But I had found a room of books and got super excited at the opportunity to potentially read real books. I wanted to become a shrine maiden to enter the room, that was all. I didn't understand why I would have to cut off my family.

"...Cut you off? Why?" My voice was shaking and barely audible.

Dad gave a heavy nod. "Apprentice shrine maidens live in the temple. The work is hard and the orphans only get help from each other. You would never last there with your Devouring. What job could you do when you're so bad at managing your health that you collapse during a ceremony? Not to mention, books are expensive. They're so rare that they use magic tools or whatever to protect them from strangers in the temple. You think they would let you read them right away just 'cause you'd be an apprentice?"

Everything Dad said was right. I had no room for arguing. I knew in my head that it would be impossible for me to become an apprentice shrine maiden. But I didn't want to give up after seeing all of those books.

I bit my lip to hold back my tears and Tuuli held my hand. With tears brimming in my eyes, I squeezed her hand.

"Why do you want to be a shrine maiden that much? You promised to stay with us. Do you want to be one so much you'd break your promise to me?" said Tuuli, driving a stake through my heart.

I shook my head weakly, feeling the strength draining from my body. "...No. I just want to read the books I saw. I don't want to be a shrine maiden or anything, I just want in that room."

Becoming an apprentice shrine maiden was a means to an end, not the end itself. It wasn't important enough to me to hurt my family and cut myself off from them. My answer made Tuuli beam a smile, but I could tell she was still anxious.

"That's a relief. Myne... You'll stay with me, right? You promised, right?"

"Mhm. Once I get better, I'll... I'll tell the High Bishop I changed my mind."

Dad sighed in relief and gave me a tight hug. "I'm glad you understand. You're my precious daughter. I'm not handing you over to the temple."

On the one hand, I was glad that I wouldn't have to cut my family off, but the moment the door leading to a future in the book room firmly shut, I felt the Devouring heat start boiling within me.

"Myne, feels like you're getting a fever."

"She already collapsed several times today, remember? The stress of this conversation just caught up to her. Let her sleep."

My parents took me to bed and I gently closed my eyes while feeling the Devouring heat spread through me. ...*I never would have thought that I'd pick something else over books.* My entire life up until now had been focused around books. All choices led to books. Back in my Urano days, I would have chosen books in an instant and cut myself off from my family. No matter the cost, books came first.

And yet, I hadn't been able to pick books here. I had thought my family was only so important to me because I lacked books, but at some point they had become just as important to me.

...But still, I had finally found books. I wanted to read them. I couldn't pick them over my family, but I couldn't abandon them either. The pressure of being pinched between two desires made it hard for me to bottle up the heat like I usually did. The Devouring heat rapidly spread through my body, as if mocking my weak mental state. I felt frustrated at things not working out, and started thinking of a compromise between my family and books.

...Is there any way to read the books without becoming an apprentice shrine maiden? The High Bishop's attitude flipped around when I mentioned my donation, so maybe he'll give me permission to enter the book room if I save up some more money? I don't like the idea of using money to control people, but I have to do what I have to do. Or maybe I should just be satisfied with going to the High Bishop's room and just reading the bible there?

In the end, it took two full days for me to push the Devouring heat back down. I could finally get out of bed once my fever faded, but my body still felt heavy. I would probably get better after another day of rest since I had bottled up the Devouring heat.

Lutz came to check on me and scrunched up his face after seeing how I looked. "You still look sick. Benno wants to talk to you, but looks like that's not gonna happen today."

"Do you have any plans for tomorrow, Lutz? I want to go to the temple and then go to Benno's store afterwards," I asked, making Lutz tilt his head a bit.

"The temple? Sure, but why?"

"I want to read the bible there. While I'm there, I'll tell them I don't want to be an apprentice shrine maiden anymore."

"Huh? Apprentice shrine maiden? Where's that coming from?"

Right. The shrine maiden had told Lutz that I forced my way into a meeting with the High Bishop, but not about what I had been asking about.

"I told you I found a book room during the ceremony, right? Only people involved with the temple can enter it, so I wanted to join the temple. I was told that becoming an apprentice shrine maiden would be the fastest way to do that, so I jumped at the opportunity."

"That's dumber than me wanting to be a traveling merchant, y'know? Be a little more realistic. Aren't you the one who taught me not to charge ahead without thinking? To try and find a more realistic path forward instead?"

Lutz had transformed from a boy yearning for impossible dreams to a boy pursuing his goals with his feet planted firmly in reality. His words stabbed into my chest.

"...I was just thinking this would be the fastest way for me to get books."

"Yeah, you always stop thinking when books get involved. I'm thinking you should stop going to the temple at all. You're just gonna keep getting disappointed and that's not good for you. Won't that make your Devouring heat go wild?"

"I just managed to push back the Devouring heat by thinking about how I at least get to read the bible."

Lutz looked at me with a conflicted expression, then smiled and patted my head. "Worked out a compromise, huh? I didn't think you'd ever give in with books on the line. You did good. If going to the temple's all you need, that's fine with me. Not like you're healthy enough to work in the temple anyway."

"Mhm, I know that."

The next day, Lutz and I went to the temple. Since we would be going to Benno's store afterward, we wore our new apprentice clothes. The area around the temple was fairly fancy, too, so I figured they would be better than our normal clothes all around.

I told the guard my name and that I wanted to see the High Bishop. He must have been informed about me ahead of time, because soon a gray priest arrived to guide me through the temple.

"What about you, Lutz? You won't have anything to do if you come with me. Maybe you should go to Benno's to study? I'll go there once I'm done here."

"Okay, I'll come get you after fifth bell, so just wait here until then. Don't go wandering off on your own."

"Okay."

The gray priest took me to the High Bishop's room, but he was absent. In his stead, a blue-robed High Priest greeted me. He looked to be about as old as Benno and his face was like a carved statue, revealing no emotion whatsoever. He had light-gold eyes and pale-blue hair that extended to his shoulders. The High Bishop was a little overweight, but the High Priest was very tall and had a slender build. He looked exactly like the kind of skilled leader who could efficiently micromanage hundreds of priests if necessary.

"You are Myne? The High Bishop told me about you. Come inside."

"Thank you."

"The High Bishop requested that I read the bible to you until he returns."

Um… That's great, but why did he ask the High Priest to do that? Aren't there more important things for him to be doing? Why would he… Oh, right. The donation money. I was offering to donate so much money that they were probably treating me as a VIP now. My suggested donation really seemed to have left an impact on them. I could use this to my advantage — maybe a little negotiation really could open the way to the book room.

"Please, have a seat." The High Priest began reading for me at the table, but since he was sitting across from me, I couldn't see the pages. It seemed they wouldn't be letting me touch the book itself. I thought for a moment, then hesitantly decided to push my luck.

"Um, High Priest. I don't just want to hear the stories, I want to read the book too."

"Why is that? Are you not here to learn more of the gods?"

"I am, but I also want to learn to read new words."

The High Priest blinked in surprise, as if stunned by what I had said. Then, after some thought, he gave a deep nod. "...Very well. But know that this bible is very precious. Will you swear not to touch it?"

"I will. I promise not to touch it."

The High Priest sat me onto his lap and continued reading, positioned such that I could read the bible and he could stop me immediately if I tried to touch it. Beautifully written letters covered the pages of parchment, yellowed on the edges where people had touched them. I inhaled deeply the scent of old paper and let out a sigh of admiration.

Just as I had expected, the writing had been greatly simplified for the baptism festival. The words had a completely different feel to them. I learned new words while the High Priest read aloud from the bible. Nouns and verbs I had wanted to know how to read for so long rained down upon me in an endless torrent of entertainment.

Eventually, I started pointing at words I vaguely recognized (making sure not to touch them) and reading them aloud while the amused High Priest taught me what they meant.

"You seem to be a fast learner. I would love to teach one who absorbs knowledge as you do. Hm... Are you not a noble? Is it possible that either of your parents carries blood from a noble lineage?"

"Definitely not."

"I see, that is a shame."

I didn't know why the High Priest was disappointed with that. But I got the feeling that he taught the priests and shrine maidens here, just like Mark taught Benno's apprentices. He had a kind of teacher-like atmosphere and seemed to be used to teaching people, similar to Mark.

"Oh, you've arrived indeed. I appreciate you waiting."

The High Bishop returned, so I went back to my seat and the High Priest delicately closed the bible, locked the gemstone clasp, and placed it back on the bookshelf.

"I had a very fun time thanks to the High Priest reading the bible to me. I am very thankful."

The High Bishop sat comfortably where the High Priest had been sitting, and the other man moved to stand next to him instead.

"In any case, what did your parents say?"

"They got mad at me and said no, since only orphans become shrine maidens."

Hope drained from the High Bishop's eyes and he slumped his shoulders. He sighed and shook his head. The High Priest, standing beside him, replied in his place.

"It is not true that only orphans can join the temple. There are children of nobles here. Many orphans do become priests and shrine maidens, but that is merely because few other workplaces will accept them. With their options limited, they have no choice but to become apprentice priests and shrine maidens," said the High Priest, making me blink in surprise.

"Why can't they work anywhere else?"

"They have no one to introduce them, nor anyone to look after them."

I understood completely. This city was founded on parents and family members introducing children to workplaces, which wasn't good for orphans at all. It was difficult enough for normal kids to get jobs their parents didn't support, so it was hard to imagine how difficult it would be for orphans to find any job at all.

"You do not have to be an orphan to become a shrine maiden. That is all I want you to understand."

"But apprentices live in the temple, and I'm too weak to do regular apprentice work here."

"Are you saying that you weren't sick that day, you're just regularly weak?" The High Bishop furrowed his brows and stroked his beard. I nodded, while thinking in the back of my head that he would look perfect in a Santa suit.

"Yes. I'm sick with a disease called the Devouring."

The High Bishop, who had been listening to me calmly, suddenly shot out of his chair with his eyes wide open. The High Priest practically slammed his hands against the table and leaned toward me.

"The Devouring?!" they both said in unison.

"Y-Yes. What about it?" I reflexively leaned back, overwhelmed by their sudden intensity. As I blinked in fear of having said something I shouldn't have, the High Bishop pointed to the door with a trembling hand.

"High Priest, bring it here at once."

"I know."

The High Priest gave a small nod and strode quickly out of the room. His movements were graceful, but incredibly fast. He left the door open behind him, probably due to being in such a hurry.

I watched him go, stunned, and saw the High Bishop turn to face the shelf with the bible. "Praise be to the gods!" Out of nowhere, he started praying to the gods with the Gli*co Man pose, and I instinctively raised my arms to do half of the pose. "Glory be to the gods!"

I watched the High Bishop bend over to genuflect in a daze, baffled and scared by what was happening. This was definitely not a good development. I wanted to run away, but judging by how serious they looked, I probably wouldn't be allowed out of here.

I sat in the chair, frozen in place as I tried not to look at the High Bishop praying. I heard footsteps rapidly coming in this direction, and before I knew it, the High Priest had returned carrying something wrapped in cloth. He set it on the table and removed the cloth, revealing the holy grail a statue in the chapel had been holding.

"Please touch this chalice."

"Bwuh? It's okay for me to touch it?"

"Yes. Hurry."

I timidly reached out to the chalice on the table. Both of them were staring at me so hard it was scary. Ultimately, I just pushed my hand out. The second my fingers touched the chalice, it began shining with a brilliant light.

"Kyaaah! What's going on?!" I hurriedly pulled my hand back and the light faded. I looked between my hand and the chalice while the High Bishop and High Priest nodded at each other.

"Myne, I would like to talk to your parents."

Um... Mom, Dad, I'm sorry. I think things just got really bad really fast.

Benno's Lecture

The High Bishop and High Priest looked so intense that I ended up meek and timid in response. The High Priest must have noticed my fearful twitching and brought the bible over, offering to read it to me until someone came to get me. I appreciated the thought, but I felt some kind of weird pressure from him, like a determination to prevent me from escaping so intense I could feel it radiating off him. I really wanted to run away.

"A boy named Lutz has arrived at the gate, claiming he is here for Myne." A gray priest came to the room not long after fifth bell.

I sighed in relief, since that meant I could finally leave. "Well, now that Lutz is here, I have to get going. High Bishop, High Priest, thank you for spending so much time with me today."

"Before you go, Myne. Take this and give it to your parents."

The High Bishop gave me a letter of invitation. That was bad, since a letter of invitation from the High Bishop was the same thing as a letter of summons you couldn't refuse. The date was third bell, the day after tomorrow. I swallowed hard and took the board from him.

"Luuutz! Thank you so much for coming to get me!"

The moment I left the temple and saw Lutz, I felt an indescribable sense of relief flowing through me. I actually jumped into his arms and hugged him to show how glad I was. He stumbled a bit, but stayed upright without falling. I rubbed by head against his shoulder and he sighed.

"What'd you do this time?"

"…I don't really know, but I think this is the biggest self-destruction I've ever done."

Lutz patted my head and grinned. "Well, don't worry. Benno's waiting for you with a big smile and a bulging forehead vein."

"Um… Can I go home now? I'm feeling really tired."

"He told me to drag you there if I have to, and you look fine right now, so yeah. You're coming with me."

"Aaaaaah…" I was mentally exhausted from the temple, but Lutz was dragging me to be slammed by another one of Benno's lectures. I felt as if my one ally had betrayed me.

I followed him to the Gilberta Company like a fearful lamb to the slaughter. Benno was waiting for us and we were taken to his office immediately. He told me to sit in the usual spot. Benno was in front of me, Mark was standing behind Benno, and Lutz sat next to him instead of me.

"Been a while, Myne."

"…U-Uh huh."

"Alright. There's a mountain of things I wanna say, but…" I stiffened up, expecting his lecture to last a very long time. But Benno just sighed. "First, a message from Corinna. She wants to see the dress and hairpin you wore at the baptism. That was some weird fashion. You drew a lot of attention to yourself. Why'd you pick an outfit like that?"

"It was just a remade hand-me-down from Tuuli. There wasn't any deep meaning to it. I don't mind showing her my clothes, but she'll have to ask my mom about how we made it, since she did all the work."

"Alright. Go ahead and ask her to drop by sometime," said Benno casually before clasping his hands together above the table and leaning for a bit, glaring at me. "Alright. Just spit it all out. Depending on what happened in that temple, what I say here and your future are both gonna change a lot."

"Wha? Didn't you hear about it from Lutz?" Several days had passed since the baptism ceremony. I thought that Lutz would have talked to him by now.

"Hearsay always twists information. Why would I ask Lutz what happened when I could just ask you instead? Not to mention, who knows what information you hid from him." He glared at me like a carnivore who had found its prey, making me gasp a little. I could guess that he wouldn't be letting me off easy.

"...Where should I start?"

"After you collapsed in the ceremony. Say everything that happened after you left Lutz. Don't leave out a single detail."

I collapsed, left the room in search of water, and wandered into a zone for nobles. A shrine maiden found me and took me to a book room. When I reached that point in the story, Benno's eyes opened wide.

"A book room? Didn't think there was one of those in the temple..."

"You didn't know about it, Benno?"

"Normal people don't risk their lives by wandering into an area for nobles. Wake up and realize what an idiot you are. What do you think's gonna happen if you keep walking into danger like that?"

"Ngh..." It was true that most people weren't allowed to go there. Benno was right. Though I was glad I had wandered in there, since I wouldn't have found the book room otherwise. "The shrine maiden told me only people affiliated with the temple could go into the book room, so I decided to become a shrine maiden and went straight to the High Bishop to ask for his permission."

"You idiot! Think for just one second before you pull this garbage, come on!"

"Ow, owww!"

Benno leaned forward to pinch my cheeks and pull. Mark and Lutz watched calmly, making no move to help me. I rubbed my stinging cheeks and Benno urged me on, looking very frustrated. "So? What'd he say?"

"He said I could be an apprentice shrine maiden if my parents permitted it and I donated money."

"And? Did you donate?" Benno furrowed his brows with a strict look in his eyes. I could tell immediately he was worried that I had donated money and then failed to get my parent's permission. In order to calm Benno down, I puffed out my chest with pride and told him what happened.

"No, not yet. I just told them that I had enough money to donate about one large gold as payment for letting me use the book room, but I haven't given it to them yet. I'm not dumb enough to pay for something before they guarantee I can have it."

I intended to calm him down, but first Benno, then Mark and Lutz all held their heads in pain as if I had given them all headaches. "That price is so stupidly high, I don't even know what to say."

"I mean, they treated me really well thanks to it, so…"

"Obviously!" I had expected that my donation offer was a little high, but apparently it was so high that even a highly successful merchant got a headache thinking about it.

"Anyway, I went home to talk to my family about becoming a shrine maiden and they got really mad about it. They said only orphans become shrine maidens."

"They have a point, y'know."

"The High Priest said that there are noble children there too, though." I tilted my head, not understanding why Dad had gotten so mad.

Benno scratched his head and explained how the temple hierarchy worked. "You remember how some priests had blue robes and some had gray robes, right? The blue-robed priests and shrine maidens are nobles, while the gray-robed ones are orphans. Gray-robed priests and shrine maidens get worked to the bone for no pay, usually serving as the attendants or servants of the blue-robed priests and shrine maidens," he revealed, making me gasp. I had thought the color just signified the difference between apprentices and full-fledged workers. I never dreamed that there was such a big difference between them.

"You're not a noble, so if you join the temple you'll end up as a gray shrine maiden. What kind of parents would allow that?" he said, to which I nodded. Now I understood why Dad had gotten as mad as he did. I definitely wouldn't be able to last doing that kind of work, and any loving father would oppose their daughter being worked like a slave for no pay.

"So. Lutz said you were going there to turn them down. Did you actually manage to do it?"

"...Umm, after I mentioned that I had the Devouring, they brought in a golden chalice that a statue in the chapel had been holding. It shined when I touched it and they gave me a letter of invitation to give my parents," I explained.

Benno rubbed his temples hard and let out a heavy sigh. "...Yeah, you're stuck with them now. Just be glad you get to survive now. You're lucky."

I didn't understand why he called me lucky when I was stuck going to the temple. Benno didn't address my confusion and instead started thinking about something. Then, he shot his head up and looked at me firmly with a hard look in his eyes. "Myne, how about we sign another magic contract? One about how the products you make will be managed."

"...Why?" I ended up feeling defensive after he brought up magic contracts out of nowhere.

Benno rubbed his chin and kept looking at me. "It won't happen immediately, but you're going to end up dragged into the world of nobles sooner or later. Contract magic is the best tool we commoners have for dealing with nobles on equal terms."

"...Have you been expecting me to get wrapped up with the nobility ever since our first magic contract?"

"At first it was mainly just insurance for me. I didn't know what kind of kid you were at the time, and contract magic keeps things firmly in place. But... I did know that you might have the Devouring. If you did, you'd need to sign a contract with a noble to survive. I knew that a magic contract would be useful for dealing with that noble."

The reason Benno had signed a magic contract with Lutz and I despite us being kids was simply because he had expected nobles to get involved, potentially years in the future.

"But I have no intention of signing a contract with a noble."

"You've managed to live on your own terms up until now because you haven't met any nobles, but that'll be over once the temple drags you to them. You have to act on the assumption that you'll get involved with nobles sooner rather than later. There's not a noble in the world who won't try to get their hands on a Devouring girl with revolutionary product ideas like yours. Especially now."

"What do you mean, especially now?" I asked.

"This is information I only recently got my hands on," Benno said, lowering his voice. He explained, "This region ended up mostly unaffected since our Archduke kept a neutral position and didn't get involved, but a lot of larger regions got wrapped up into a fierce political war with the Sovereignty. Large scale political purges were held all over the country, and there are a lot fewer nobles alive now than there used to be."

That sure got violent really fast. I tried thinking back to what I remembered about world history, but I didn't know exactly what time period this world was in, and even with a frame of reference I couldn't guess what would be happening in the future. I lacked information, and without a bird's eye view of this mess, I was as good as blind.

"Naturally, the gap left by those dead nobles needs to be filled. The survivors are mobilizing. They're reaching out to branch families, adopting, marrying more, seeking out new connections and power. People, money, and products are moving faster than ever before. There's so few nobles that those forced into the temple as blue-robed priests and shrine maidens during internal struggles are flooding back to their homes en masse. What do you think that means for the temple?"

Benno glared at me and I tilted my head. I looked to Mark and Lutz for help, but Mark only smiled and Lutz was just as confused as I was.

"Ummm, is there a problem with there not being enough nobles in the temple? I can't think of anything since I don't know what goes on in the temple or how anything works there. Isn't it a good thing, since there will be fewer people to overwork the gray priests and shrine maidens?"

275

"First of all, they'll get fewer donations. Second of all, without nobles to give them work, they'll end up overwhelmed with unemployed orphans. It'll be harder for the orphans to survive there."

"That's awful!" I let out a shout and Benno sighed, shaking his head.

"That's not the worst part. Remember that chalice you said you touched? Those temple guys call it a divine tool, but it's actually a magic tool. Blue-robed priests and shrine maidens pour their mana into it so that it can be used during the spring blessing ceremony. But without nobles, there's no mana. That'll mean less crops to harvest."

"Whaaaat?!" I hadn't expected the chalice to be involved with such an enormous ritual. It shining surprised me, but I had thought it was just a fancy ornament meant to show off the power of the gods or whatever. In reality, it was an essential tool for survival directly connected to how many crops our farmers could harvest. If less food was grown in this region, poor people in the city like me would be the ones to suffer the most.

"Before this political shift, there were too many noble children to deal with. Those with the Devouring were just annoyances to nobles, who want to keep the power of mana all to themselves. But now that there's fewer nobles and using magic tools properly is a lot more difficult, kids with the Devouring are extremely useful and important to the temple."

"Um, what does the Devouring have to do with mana?" I asked, which shocked Benno so much that his jaw dropped and he held in his head in absolute disbelief.

"Don't tell me you haven't realized this yet. The Devouring refers to the state where someone loses control of the mana inside of them."

"Whaaat?!"

"You regain control of your mana by moving the excess into a magic tool."

"That's the first time I'm hearing of this." *Wow... I guess I'm like a witch or something. I guess I can beat my foes with bursts of mana and use all sorts of crazy magic! But um... who are my enemies?* My mind raced with the possibilities this new information had revealed and Benno thumped my head, telling me to pay attention.

"This is how nobles are separated, roughly. Laynobles tend to have low amounts of mana while Archnobles have a lot of mana. Poor nobles without much money can't afford magic tools for all of their children. It's common for them to entrust the future of their family to the kid with the most mana and send the rest of them to their region's temple."

In other words, the blue-robed priests in the temple were nobles abandoned by their families. They were necessary for the region to prosper, but at the same time, them being there was kind of sad.

"The temple has survived this long with weak nobles through sheer numbers, but now those numbers are going down. Each noble has to work a lot harder. It's possible they don't even have enough nobles right now. How many blue priests were there at the baptism ceremony?"

"About ten." I could still remember busting my gut at the sight of all of them making the Gl*co Man pose.

"They normally have over twenty, but now they have ten. And since the ones getting called back are those with mana, you can imagine how weak the remaining ones must be. There's no mistaking that they would kill for a Devouring kid overflowing with mana. But that's just now we're talking about. It won't be long before new nobles are born and this gap gets filled up. Don't think you have much time there."

"Hmm." I didn't mind working for the temple and offering up my mana for a short period of time. I wondered if they would let me enter the book room in return for my mana. I fell into thought about it and Benno, who had at some point gotten behind me, started grinding his fist against my head.

"Are you listening to me?"

"Ow! Ooowww!"

"You have mana, money, and knowledge worth even more money. Wake up already! Realize just how much nobles are going to want you for themselves!" His voice was so serious that I instinctively sat up straight. He sighed and took his fist off my head to wave his hand in exasperation. "And that's why it's in your best interest to sign a magic contract now before you get wrapped up with nobles."

"...What kind of contract?"

"A contract that the things you make will be sold by Lutz."

"Bwuh? But why?" I had no idea what that had to do with the Devouring and the church. Did he just want to exploit the situation to gain profit for himself? I tilted my head in confusion, and Benno sat back in his chair before beginning his explanation.

"For now, it'll just be insurance. It won't be long before a thoughtless idiot like you falls for a noble's plot and gets dragged to the other side of the wall. This will let us contact you after that happens. Think about what situation you'll be in after you're forced to sign a contract with a noble. Commoners need permission to go to the other side of the inner wall. You know that, right?"

I worked at the gate sometimes, so I knew one needed permission to go through the inner wall. I nodded and Benno grimaced a little.

"The guildmaster's granddaughter will still be able to meet her family after going to the other side of the wall. Makes sense, because her family consists of merchants approved by nobles. But what about your family?"

I could only answer in silence. I had specifically chosen not to sign a contract with a noble because it meant not seeing my family. If I got dragged to the other side of the wall, I might never see them again.

"I doubt your family will be able to go past the wall to see you. So at the very least, shouldn't you make a magic contract that lets you see Lutz now, before all this happens? We'll be able to use that contract as an excuse for Lutz and me to come see you. Not even nobles can defy contract magic."

I looked at Benno with wide eyes. I then looked at Lutz. We made eye contact and nodded at each other.

"With Lutz as an intermediary, you can send letters, messages, and so on to your family. You'll be able to stay up to date on how they are, too. And most importantly, your family will be able to relax more, knowing that they can make sure you're safe through Lutz. But I won't mind if you want to sign a contract with me instead."

"You won't be able to keep me updated on my family, Mr. Benno, so."

I didn't want to think that I would get wrapped up with nobles, but if that did happen, it would be a good idea for me to preemptively give myself the ability to see Lutz. Freida had said that seeing her family was enough to give her strength. But... did I really want to wrap Lutz into this too?

"What do you think, Lutz?"

"I wouldn't mind checking out the Noble's Quarter if I can, and passing messages is no big deal. I'd be more worried if I had to leave you alone over there. My head hurts just thinking about what you might do."

Lutz himself was already on board with signing, but we were talking about an anti-noble contract here. Considering how much of a dangerous burden it would place on Lutz, I couldn't be too enthusiastic about signing it.

"I don't think this contract is something we should take too lightly. Won't Lutz end up in bad, sometimes dangerous spots? And doesn't this put your profits in danger, Mr. Benno? If Lutz gets pulled out of the equation, that's it for you and me doing business, isn't it?" I pursed my lips, pouting, and Benno let out an exasperated sigh.

"You're not in a situation light enough to be worrying about others. Just be glad that Lutz benefits from this too."

"How does this benefit Lutz?"

"You don't have to worry about that. Just think about what will benefit you. I'm going to be honest — you already have a letter of invitation, and that means we barely have any time to prepare or do anything."

Benno had more information and a broader perspective than me, so he was more on edge about this than I was. He listed out all the things we needed to do before the temple got a hold of me.

"First of all, we need to officially create the Myne Workshop and register you as its forewoman so you can retain an avenue for making and selling products. If money can improve your situation, you'll want to negotiate with the temple to put you in circumstances where you can make money. That shouldn't be impossible, since they want money too."

It was true that wealth was a strong source of power. They treated me extremely well at the mere suggestion of a high donation amount. When it came to protecting myself, the more money I had, the better. But if the temple took control of all the products I made, they would keep all the profit for themselves. I needed a reliable avenue to sell products. Benno had tricked and tested me in a few ways, but right now he was the most reliable person I knew. I nodded, and Benno nodded back.

"Remember that the life of a commoner means nothing to nobles. Stay on guard. Prepare as many escape routes and avenues for survival as possible while you can. Get your hands on anything that can work as insurance and protection."

The temple had treated me well, letting me sit on the High Priest's lap and read the bible, but there was no harm in preparing insurance and escape routes just in case. Better safe than sorry. The fact that I knew so little about this world that I didn't know exactly how to prepare was really frustrating.

Benno looked at me carefully and continued, "You said there's still ten nobles in the temple, right? Find one of them that you can exploit for your own benefit as they exploit you, rather than just letting yourself be exploited one-way. If you're going to be kidnapped and enslaved either way, you're going to at least want to open up your options for a slightly better future. Look carefully. Pick carefully. Think carefully. Don't just sit in a daze and go with the flow. Flail as hard as you can to survive."

"Mr. Benno, why are you going this far for me...?" It wasn't a simple matter to gather all this information and give me such thorough warnings, not to mention helping me prepare a workshop. I didn't understand why he would do all that for me when I wasn't even going to be an apprentice at his store.

"The longer you survive, the more new products you can make. If I can keep my store connected to you, that'll mean profit for me. That'll be good for the both of us, right? That's all there is to it." Benno furrowed his brows and Mark laughed softly behind him.

"The master is merely worried about you. You are always putting yourself in danger and causing unexpected problems. It is truly poor for our health."

"Shut it, Mark," said Benno, turning around, but Mark continued on with his slight smile.

"Apprentices here tend to learn the fundamentals of trade at their own home, so the master had not met a child he needed to take of so dearly himself before now. I will refrain from saying you are like a daughter to him, but you are like the daughter of a brother, and he worries about you as if you were a family member. Of course, I do as well."

"Thank you very much, Mr. Mark!" I let out an emotional thank you and Benno spat out "Why Mark?" Mark and I looked at each other and laughed.

"Thank you too, Mr. Benno. I'm really grateful to you both. And... I'll do it. I'll sign the magic contract and register the workshop with the guild."

Contract Magic and Registering the Workshop

"Here you are, sir." Mark set a sheet of contract paper used for magic contracts and a weirdly designed jar full of special ink on the table. I recognized them both.

Benno put his pen into the ink jar and started writing out the contract. The ink was blue rather than black, just as I remembered. I watched carefully as he wrote the text of the contract.

Lutz holds the right to sell goods created by the Myne Workshop. In order to establish a representative, one must first gain the approval of Myne, Lutz, and Benno, then submit an application to the Merchant's Guild.

"What's this line for?" I pointed at the contract and Benno raised an eyebrow.

"Insurance. If a contract involves just kids, some people will try to get around it through violence or kidnapping. I'm getting myself and the Guild involved to prevent that kind of thing as much as possible. When making contracts like these, it's best to involve third parties that you can count on supporting you. Remember that."

"...Thank you." He didn't just suggest making a magic contract despite all the work involved for him, he even actively involved himself so he could help me if necessary. I took a pen from Mark and signed my name. Lutz followed with his, and after Benno signed his own name, we prepared to stamp our blood onto it.

"Lutz, please." I shut my eyes and held out my thumb so Lutz could cut it. Once he did, I pressed the welling blood against my signature.

The blue ink sucked up the blood and turned black just like last time. Once everyone stamped their name, the ink shone brightly, burnt away holes in the paper, and ultimately the paper itself disappeared. Again, just like last time. Benno let out a slow sigh as he watched the paper burn away brightly.

"At the very least, this ensures that you can keep selling products and see Lutz even if you get dragged to the Noble's Quarter. Learn how to protect yourself if you don't want that to happen, Myne."

I clenched my fist to show my determination and Benno, Lutz, and even Mark all grimaced with worry written on their faces.

"But remember. This contract will only work on people who know how valuable your products are."

"Wha?"

"If a noble only cares about your mana, they won't care at all about your products. Lucky thing is, I'm pretty sure there aren't any nobles here rich enough to ignore how much money you could make them. Also, like I mentioned before, magic contracts only work in the town they're signed in. Be careful."

Once that was done, we wrote up an identical contract on normal parchment. It wouldn't mean much to nobles, but it was important for reporting to the guild and proving that the contract existed in the event of something happening outside of the city.

"Let's get this ball rolling today while the iron is hot. We're heading to the Merchant's Guild right away. We'll register the Myne Workshop and establish you as its forewoman. That'll let you make and sell products without any problems. It'll also give you more power in negotiations by showing that you have options outside of the temple and are financially independent."

The Merchant's Guild was on the way home, so once we finished our business there, I would have time to relax. Benno hurried me up, and after watching Lutz go upstairs to his room to change, I looked up at him. "What can I do to make my negotiations with the temple go well?"

"First of all, start by thinking about the best possible result for you. Figure out what you need to get from the other side to make that happen, think about what you can offer them, and think about what they want."

As I listened to Benno talk, I thought about what I wanted from this. The first thing that came to mind was permission to enter the book room and read the books. Ideally, I would want to join the temple, but not as a gray-robed apprentice shrine maiden, in order to avoid the arduous labor required of them. I could offer them mana and money. If Benno was correct, the other side wanted mana and money. *Well... I guess these negotiations might work out, then?*

"That reminds me, the High Bishop told me that I couldn't belong to any other organization if I wanted to join the temple. He said he would try negotiating with the guildmaster, but do you think registering myself as a forewoman will get in the way of that?" I said, thinking about what the High Bishop had said, and in return Benno hit me with a sharp chop.

"Come on, Myne. Don't count on others to do anything for you. Get involved yourself and secure your own position. You don't know what kind of unreasonable terms they'll demand from you."

"You're right. To be honest, I never expected that the chalice would be able to extend my life like this. I just wanted to read books, and since I was dying in six months at best anyway, I didn't care about anything else. I'll accept that I was just counting on other people to do everything for me. But now that I'm probably going to survive and I've found a book room, I'm motivated to do whatever I can to get a better future for myself. I'll work hard."

"Use your head so that motivation doesn't get wasted on nothing."

"I'll do better."

Lutz came racing down the stairs. He must have really pushed himself, given how hard he was breathing. I looked up at the seven-floor staircase and felt awe in my heart for the heroic feat he had just accomplished. If I tried running up that staircase, I would definitely collapse before I even got to the top.

"Alright, let's go." Benno stuck his hands under my arms and lifted me up as if it were a matter of routine. Otto once told me that I walked far too slow for adults to bear, so lately I had just given in and accepted that it was my fate to be carried. Trying to resist would just tire me out more.

"If those joining the temple can't belong to guilds and the like, you'll end up as the only one in the temple capable of doing trade with the Merchant's Guild. If the fact that you're already registered isn't enough to push past them, flash some money and force them to allow you to keep running your workshop."

Benno continued his lecture even as we walked to the Merchant's Guild, not wanting to waste even a second of time he could be using to formulate plans and teach me how to negotiate. I wanted to write down everything he said, and it was really frustrating that I couldn't. I stared at Benno and worked every neuron in my brain to try and memorize as much of his advice as possible.

"Like I mentioned, it's very possible that the lack of blue priests is resulting in unemployed orphans and a decrease in donations. List off a bunch of rubbish like you want to give them a future in life, you want to give them work, or you want to improve their living situation, whatever it takes to get their permission to keep your workshop running and within your control. Those in the temple should at least be smart enough to know that everything runs on money."

"Right."

"While you're at it, mention that you need someone to watch your health and work for you directly. Take a fact with a kernel of truth and exaggerate it as much as you have to in order to get people who will do physical labor for you. Lutz works for my store now and will be busy for at least half of each week."

I nodded repeatedly and processed his practical advice. Exploit the moral high ground to secure rights for my workshop, exaggerate my weakness to get workers. It was true that I would need help to run the workshop at all, rights or not.

"Once they learn that even orphans will work hard in workshops, it's possible that other workshops might take orphans as well. Their attitude might change as they see orphans making the new products you think up. All this depends on your skill as a forewoman."

"Okay. I'll do my best."

Benno wasn't just thinking about me, he was even thinking about the orphans. That really impressed me, but he just shook his head and sighed. "Haaah... Do you ever think for yourself? Don't just nod and try to do everything at once. Figure out your priorities ahead of time."

"Bwuh? What do you mean?" I blinked in surprise at Benno's sudden backlash and he furrowed his brows. Apparently, he had been testing me on something again.

"Prioritize yourself over the orphans until you've established your position inside the temple. Really, consider the orphans as tools to exploit by appearing as a savior to them. I hate to put it like this, but more people will care about you getting hurt than anyone will about those orphans."

"...Okay," I said with a nod just as we arrived at the Merchant's Guild. Lutz pulled the door open to let us in and Benno grimaced a little.

"When you have stuff to sell, need some help, or are having problems, come talk to me. I'll charge you for what the help's worth, but I'll be generous."

"Thank you. This means a lot to me, Mr. Benno."

It was late in the evening, and there weren't many people in the Merchant's Guild. We passed by the first two floors in no time and headed to the third floor's counter. Then we returned our temporary guild cards and gave them the documents Benno had prepared since long before our baptism to register us officially. The documents identified the Gilberta Company as our affiliated shop with Lutz as the intermediary.

"Why hello, Myne. You're finally here?" Freida came walking down the stairs with her light-pink twintails bobbing and came running over after seeing me fishing through the bookshelf in the waiting area. "I thought you would arrive to be registered right after the ceremony, but I haven't seen you since. I had begun to worry that you had collapsed during your baptism."

"Ahaha, well, that's what happened. I actually did collapse. It took until now for me to get better," I explained, laughing a little at the fact that Freida had predicted exactly what happened. She glared at Lutz, who was looking at a spread-open map.

"To think that you would collapse with Lutz by your side."

"It's not Lutz's fault at all. Really, it's all on me." My sides exploding at the Gl*co Man pose and me going crazy over the book room were both entirely my fault. It was so much my fault that Lutz deserved a groveling apology from me, to be honest.

"Hey, Myne. Get over here."

Our new guild cards had been finished while I talked to Freida. She went back behind the counter to work and I stayed behind to get the details on my new card. I gasped in fear when they explained that the new card had carried over everything from the temporary card, but needed a new blood seal.

"Give it up, Myne."

I poked my finger with the given needle and pressed the welling blood against the card, making it shine. Thus completed the registration. It was simple, but painful. We paid the registration fee of five small silvers and the clerk began explaining the difference between a temporary guild card and a forewoman card. Freida overheard and peered over at me.

"My my, the Myne Workshop? Were you not becoming a merchant apprentice at the Gilberta Company?"

"I gave up on that since I'm too weak to hold a stable job."

"In that case, might I suggest that you sell your products to the Othmar Company as well?" Freida's eyes immediately shone with the sharp glint of a merchant seeking profit.

I looked away. "Aaah, sorry. We have it set up so Lutz sells what I make to Mr. Benno's store."

"...Lutz again, hm?" Freida pursed her lips unhappily, but what was done was done. I had given her exclusive rights to pound cakes, and that would have to be enough for her.

"I already gave you the pound cake, didn't I? How is it? Do you think it'll sell well?"

"Indeed, I am having Leise experiment with new flavors. I would like to hear your opinion before we put them on the market. Please come and taste-test them, if you would. How about tomorrow?"

I mean, I do want to eat the cake. I do think sweet things are just perfect when life is being particularly hard. But I won't have the time to taste-test sweets until I'm done negotiating with the temple.

"Thanks for the offer, but my plans are packed for tomorrow."

"What about the day after that, then? You could bring your sister if she would like to come. That will mean Lutz doesn't have to come, correct?" Freida was utilizing Tuuli to neutralize Lutz. He glared at her harshly, looking close to biting her. Which reminded me that she had blown Lutz off last time by having Tuuli ride the carriage.

"Freida, don't be mean. It'll taste better if everyone eats together. And if Leise is experimenting with flavors, there must be a lot of cake."

"That is true, but…" Freida looked unsatisfied, so I started thinking of how I could turn her emotional invitation into a business one.

"I think that the taste-tests will do better at predicting future sales if more people are there to give varied opinions. Kids and adults want different flavors, not to mention girls and boys, so."

"…More people? Varied opinions? A tea party will hardly last with a large group of people." Freida's eyes had the sharp look of a merchant. However, it seemed that now she was thinking about holding a tea party rather than feeling concerned with Lutz. I started piling on follow-ups to try and get her to agree to Lutz coming over.

"It doesn't have to be a big get together or anything. You can cut different pound cakes into bite-sized pieces and formally ask people which they liked the most. That way, Lutz can…"

"That's a perfect idea!" Before I could finish what I was saying, Freida clapped her hands together, eyes shining. Her expression made it clear that she was already completely on board with my suggestion. She looked really happy and excited, but at the same time, it felt like she wasn't even looking at me anymore.

"I'll contact you when the date of the taste-testing event is decided. Of course, your sister and Lutz can both come. Aaah, I will be ever so busy. Farewell, Myne, Lutz. Have a good evening."

Freida turned on a dime and raced back up the stairs, apparently wanting to immediately implement the plans she had just thought up. I could imagine that she was about to discuss the taste-testing event with the guildmaster. I wasn't sure why she was so excited about it, but since she ultimately invited Lutz with me, I had no complaints.

I watched Freida go, excited to eat all sorts of cake after all this business with the temple settled down, but my happy thoughts were interrupted by Lutz sighing.

"See? Freida and Myne are just alike, aren't they?" he said. I turned to see Benno cackling and nodding.

By the time we finished the paperwork and left the Merchant's Guild, even the long-lasting summer sun was on the verge of setting. The once-busy plaza now had just a few scattered people walking about. Lutz and I started heading home. As I watched our long shadows, I felt Lutz's hand squeeze mine.

"What's wrong?" I stopped and looked up at Lutz. He was looking back down at me, his expression twisted with a complex storm of emotions from angry to tearful. He let out a mumble that fell to the shadowy ground.

"…You're really joining the temple?"

"Mhm, probably. If Benno was right about all that, I don't think the temple will let me get away from them. You heard what he said, didn't you?"

Lutz squeezed his lips together tightly, then looked at me anxiously. "You think you'll be able to negotiate with them?"

The setting sun cast thick shadows on his face, making him look even more tearful and anxious. I could feel him squeezing my hand increasingly hard. I smiled, wanting to help calm him down as much as possible.

"I've never negotiated with nobles before, so I'm not sure. But if the grail really is a magic tool that can keep my Devouring in check, then joining the temple will be good for me, not to mention that I want to read the books in the book room. But I won't survive as a gray shrine maiden. It all depends on how negotiations go. I'll work as hard as I can to put myself in as best a situation as possible there."

"Yeah... Good luck." Lutz briefly scrunched up his face as if in pain, then lowered his eyes and resumed walking.

For a while we walked next to each other in silence. Lutz looked up, pretending to be curious about a passing carriage, but then swallowed down whatever he wanted to say. I was getting more and more curious as we kept walking in silence.

"Um, Lutz. If you want to say something, don't hold back. I'll listen."

Lutz stopped and opened his mouth, then closed it. After a moment of thought, he looked away from me. "...It's lame, I don't wanna say it."

As curious as I was, it would probably be wise to respect the male desire to act cool. I nodded and resumed walking.

Our silence continued. The sounds of people rushing home just like us clattered on the stone roads, and the bustle of home life could be heard from surrounding windows, but the air between Lutz and I remained heavy and silent. The sun finished setting and the shadows on the streets fused together, blanketing the city in thick darkness which made it harder to see.

"...You said we'd make paper and start selling real books together. Myne, you liar." Lutz's murmur was nearly lost among the clattering of a passing carriage, but I heard it. His complaint that he had wanted to say but never found the opportunity to until now pierced my heart.

"Sorry, Lutz."

"I know I'm too weak to do anything about this. Benno's right, and I want to help you as much as I can to keep you safe there." Lutz gritted his teeth. "But... I hate this. You said we'd start a bookstore together..."

"I did. But remember, I want to make books so I can read them. I won't stop making books because I'm joining the temple. Really, I'm going to work harder now that I'm going to survive longer. My dream won't come true unless I spread books across the world," I said, which made Lutz look up. He shrugged with a forced, tearful smile.

"Your dream of being surrounded by books so you can spend every day reading?"

"That's right. You want to be a merchant, right? You want to go all over the world as a merchant? I have my own dream too. Let's both work hard to make our dreams come true," I said.

This time, Lutz really did come close to breaking into tears. Despite the darkness, I could clearly see the tears welling in his eyes. "I want to help you. But... I've come this far because I was with you. I wanted to work hard in Benno's store with you. I want to keep doing things with you," said Lutz before hugging me and burying his face in my shoulder. I could hear him desperately holding back quiet sobs.

"It'll be okay. We can still do things together after I join the temple. I'll definitely keep making books."

"No. That's not what I mean. I don't want to sell books you made with someone else, I want to sell books we made together."

The dam had broken and Lutz was letting all of the frustration he'd been keeping inside come flowing out. He shook his head as if defying reality, and I felt a twinge of pain in my chest. Tears came dripping out of my own eyes. I hugged Lutz back, embracing him and his frustration as I patted his back gently.

"Nothing will be different from what we planned. You'll make the things I think up, right? When I have new ideas, I'll talk to you first. Before Benno, before anyone, I'll ask for your help."

"Even though I can't do anything?" Lutz looked up, shocked.

I wiped away the tears on his cheek and smiled. "If you can't do anything, what in the world can I do? Is there anything? And well, who else but you will stick around and help me make the weird things I come up with? I need you. I won't be able to do anything without you."

"...Nah. Everyone already knows the stuff you make is worth money. They'll help you." Lutz pursed his lips and hurriedly wiped away his tears, embarrassed that he had started crying. He then stood up straight, having calmed himself down by spitting out all his built-up frustration.

"Mmm, the only thing I can see happening is other people trying to help me, failing, and ultimately calling you over to get through to me. Will you still help me when that happens?"

I shrugged, and Lutz finally laughed. He squeezed my hand and walked forward, his bright smile contrasting with our increasingly dark surroundings.

"Don't sweat it. I'll make anything you think up, no matter what."

Strategy Meeting and the Temple

I returned home to find my entire family impatiently waiting for me with worry clear on their faces. The moment I opened the door, Tuuli and Mom sighed in relief, as did Dad moments before yelling at me in anger.

"You're late! How much will you have to make us worry before you're satisfied?!"

"Sorry for worrying you, Dad." Benno had told me enough about the temple that I knew Dad would be extremely worried for me. I apologized on the spot, then headed to put my stuff in the bedroom, eyeing the dinner already prepared on the table. My empty stomach had started making itself heard the moment I got home.

"I went to Benno's store and the Merchant's Guild after going to the temple, and it took a lot of time. I'm tired and super hungry."

I washed my hands and sat at the table to eat. Dad narrowed his eyes at me, brows furrowed.

"What in the world happened?" said Dad, speaking for everyone there. Mom and Tuuli were looking at me with their eyes full of worry.

"I'll tell you everything that happened, but can I eat first? I'm hungry and there's a lot to say."

"...Alright."

Everyone's expressions darkened as they realized that I probably didn't have many positive things to say. I could tell that they were all falling deep into thought. I tried searching my memory for something positive to say and remembered something with a start. I could definitely lighten the mood a bit by mentioning what Corinna said.

"Um, Mom. Benno told me this when I went to his store, but Corinna wants to see my baptism dress and hair stick. Can I show them to her?"

Mom dropped her spoon into her soup. Her eyes widened and she looked around in a panic, shaking her head with her cheeks blushing. "Wh-What?! Goodness, that outfit isn't worth showing to Corinna!"

"...Okay. I'll turn her down, then." I had thought Mom might be hesitant, but I didn't expect her to reject the offer so firmly. It would probably be best to just turn Corinna down if Mom was so upset about it.

But despite my kind intentions, Mom panicked even harder at that suggestion and waved her hands around with wide eyes. "Wh-What are you saying, Myne?! We can't turn her down. That would be rude to her. Wait just a moment. Aaah, goodness, I can't answer her right away."

Mom had fallen into a complete panic. She was happy to be recognized by Corinna, but she didn't know how to deal with someone who was practically a hero to her. I smiled at that, finding it funny. Mom never acted like this usually, and it was really cute.

I watched Mom murmuring to herself and barely eating, amused, when suddenly Tuuli poked me in the side. "Hey, Myne. Does that mean we'll be taking them to Corinna's house?"

"Probably?" Mom herself said we couldn't turn her down, so it was basically guaranteed that we would be bringing the outfit and whatnot to her. I wasn't sure if Mom would go or if I would be alone, but either way, someone was bringing the clothes over. There was basically no chance of us inviting her to our place, for obvious reasons.

Tuuli looked at me with eyes shining in anticipation and clasped her hands in front of her chest. She always made the cutest pose when asking for something. "Can I go with you this time, Myne?"

Last time, when I brought her the rinsham, Corinna had sent a letter of invitation exclusively to me, which meant that Tuuli had to stay home despite wanting to go. There wasn't a letter of invitation this time, so I could just mention that Tuuli was coming with me when I gave Benno our reply.

"Corinna is a nice lady, so I don't think she'll turn you down. But just in case, I'll mention that you made the big flowers on my hair stick and ask if you can come too."

"Yaaay! I love you, Myne! Thank you!" Tuuli's face lit up and she skipped with innocent joy.

Tuuli… You're so cute. Just what I'd expect from my angel. Tuuli was an apprentice seamstress, so Corinna with all her fame and charisma was probably an idol to her. I smiled at Tuuli and Mom held her hands out, shaking her head.

"Hold on, you two. Just hold on. I haven't decided on whether we'll be going or not yet."

"Huh? But you can't turn her down."

"That's true, but…"

"I think Corinna will want to talk to the person who actually sewed the outfit, but… if you don't want to go, you don't have to."

The words that came spluttering out of my Mom's mouth didn't contain any particular meaning. I started to say that Tuuli and I could go ourselves, but Mom shook her head hard. "I never said I didn't want to go."

"Okay. We can all go together, then," I said with a smile, leaving Mom speechless. Tuuli looked at her and giggled. I laughed too, and Mom ultimately gave a defeated smile and laughed as well. Dad watched us laugh with a complicated smile on his face.

"Okay, let's talk about what happened today," said Mom as she prepared the after-dinner tea. Immediately, a weight fell over us. Everyone looked at me, urging me to speak.

"Ummm, okay. I'll start with the temple. I told them I didn't want to be an apprentice shrine maiden anymore, but once they learned that I have the Devouring, they said they want to talk to my parents and gave me this letter of invitation. It's for the day after tomorrow at third bell."

I took the board out of my bag and the second Dad saw it, his expression twisted. As a guard, he knew how letters of invitation worked and he had seen many of them over his life. He knew exactly what meaning a letter of invitation from a noble such as the High Bishop meant. His mouth bent into a hard frown as he looked at what was ultimately a forceful letter of summons.

"Myne, what did you do?!"

"I didn't do anything. We just talked and they read the bible to me."

"You had a noble reading a book to you...?"

"...I mean, back then I didn't realize the High Priest was a noble. It wasn't my fault." I pursed my lips and continued on, telling them that the chalice in the temple shined when I touched it.

Both of them looked at me with shocked expressions and practically slumped against their chairs as if their souls had left their bodies. Apparently that was a bit too much for them to process. I waved my hands in front of their eyes and tilted my head as they stared at the ceiling in a daze. "Can I continue?"

Dad came back to his senses with a gasp and shook himself awake, then scratched his chin. "Yeah, keep going."

"I went to Benno's store after leaving the temple. He knows a lot more about the Devouring, nobles, and the temple than me, so he taught me a lot." Everyone was looking at me curiously, so I looked around and nodded before taking a deep breath. "Well, the thing is, the Devouring heat inside of me is actually mana. Benno said that there's probably no chance of me escaping the temple and nobles."

"No way…" Mom and Tuuli put a hand on their mouths and shook in fear. I wasn't sure if that was them being afraid of me for having mana, or afraid of how much control the temple had over us commoners.

I lowered my eyes and continued. "But the temple has magic tools, so if I go there, I won't die."

Dad, Mom, and Tuuli all looked at me with a mixture of hope and unease. The fact they were worried for me and not afraid of my mana was such a relief that I felt the tension drain from my body.

"Wait, Myne. If you went to the temple, does that mean we wouldn't be able to see you, even if you stay alive?"

"At this rate, probably…" I said, making Tuuli tear up and shake her head.

"…How is that different from a noble enslaving you? I'm not giving you to the temple," said Dad in a strained voice. It was true that normally, my only future was entering the temple as a gray shrine maiden, having my mana sucked up, my money stolen in the form of donations, and then spending the rest of my lifespan enslaved in the service of blue priests.

"Well, Dad. Do you know about the Sovereignty? Have you heard about a political shift that's had a big impact on the nobility?"

"There was a merchant talking about something like that a few days ago. I know a lot since I work as a guard at the gate, but that's got nothing to do with us."

It was possible that Benno had heard about this through Otto. I kept that possibility in mind and shook my head. "It's because of that shift that I'm being summoned to the temple. Benno said that right now there's a lot fewer nobles and the temple needs more mana. I'm not sure if he was right, though. What do you think?"

Dad gasped a little, probably due to having heard the same thing. He stroked his chin and closed his eyes as if trying to remember the details. "There's definitely fewer nobles now. A lot of nobles are leaving, but lately not many nobles have been arriving."

"So Benno was right? In that case, I might have a chance."

"What do you mean?" Everyone leaned forward, eager to hear the details.

"Benno said I was lucky. The temple's having problems due to the lack of nobles, so if I negotiate with them properly, I might be able to have them treat me like a noble or close to it."

"Details." Dad looked at me with the sharp, fierce eyes he wore when doing his job.

I told him what Benno had told me, as closely as I could remember. I mentioned the contract magic and workshop while I was at it.

"...So, I'm not sure how it'll work until I try, but if I exaggerate how weak I am and all that, it's possible that I can negotiate for better circumstances. Given their tight situation, they should be open to at least a little negotiation. Benno said I should flail as hard as I can to survive," I said, which made Dad's eyes shine.

"Flail to survive, huh? If you think about it, your situation's not too bad."

"Uh huh." *Focus on my mana and my weakness so they treat me like a noble. Exaggerate my magnanimity and weakness so they're more likely to agree to my terms. Use money as a sword to get them to accept the continued operation of my workshop.*

"There's some other things I want, like access to the book room and my own servants to do work for me, but if they just treat me like a noble and don't shut down my workshop, it'll be a win for me."

"Alright. Let's give it a shot. I became a soldier to protect my family and our city. What good am I for if I can't even protect my family? I'll make sure you win and have the best life you can." Dad grinned with a confident look on his face, the expression of a man ready for battle.

The next day, my parents went to work and asked for the next day off. I had walked around so much yesterday that I could barely move and needed to stay in bed.

Before I knew it another day had passed, and it was time to go to the temple. My parents wore their best clothes and I wore the Gilberta Company apprentice outfit. Once we were dressed, we headed to the temple.

"Dad, be sure to protect me." I clenched my fist and bent my knees a little in an attack posture, like I had seen soldiers doing at the gate. It was a pose that signified soldiers praying for each other's success in battle.

Dad widened his eyes, then laughed. He clenched his fist and bent his knees the same way before lightly hitting my fist with his. "You can count on me."

The temple was ready for us and as soon as we reached the gate, a gray priest guided us directly to the High Bishop's room. We passed by the chapel and the waiting rooms for commoners to go right through the area for nobles.

As the hall became more fancily decorated around us, I could see Dad clenching his fist tighter in determination with his brows furrowed. Mom paled as she nervously kept an eye on Dad. I squeezed her hand and felt how it was trembling.

"High Bishop, Myne and her parents have arrived," said the grey priest as he opened the door to the High Bishop's room. Inside I could see the High Bishop and High Priest sitting at the table, waiting for us. Behind them were four gray priests.

I hadn't known that the gray priests were orphans before, but now that I looked at them again, I got the feeling they were cleaner and looked better than I would expect for orphans. Maybe they weren't treated so poorly. Or maybe it was just that those serving nobles had to keep themselves clean no matter what.

"Good morning, High Bishop."

"Yes, hello Myne." The High Bishop greeted me with the expression of a friendly old grandfather, just like I was used to. But once he saw my parents, his eyes widened. He blinked in disbelief, and I could see his hands trembling a bit.

"...And these are indeed your parents?"

"Yes, they are."

"May I ask what their professions are?"

"My dad is a soldier and my mom works at a dye workshop," I answered.

He looked at my parents with narrowed eyes then snorted condescendingly. He didn't have to say anything for me to understand that he was looking down on them for being poor.

I blinked in surprise at his rapid change in attitude. He was looking down at my parents with condescending eyes, and there wasn't a trace of his friendly old grandpa expression from just a second ago. It was at that moment that I realized I had only been treated so well due to the power of money, and that in reality we were indeed living in a status-based society.

"Now, let us get this over with." There were no greetings, and we were not permitted to sit at the table. We had to stand as the High Bishop began talking. That was probably normal behavior, but I was so used to him being friendly that I couldn't help but furrow my brow.

The High Priest was just looking at us with a quiet, unmoved expression. He didn't have scorn in his eyes like the High Bishop did. But he seemingly had no intention of calling the High Bishop out, either. He was calm and unmoved.

The High Bishop coughed, then began speaking with an incredibly arrogant expression on his face. "It seems that you two have refused Myne's wish to become an apprentice shrine maiden."

"Yes, that's right. I don't want my precious daughter to be treated like an orphan." Dad looked at the High Bishop with sparks flying, but the High Bishop just stroked his beard while showing no interest whatsoever in my dad's hostile tone.

"Hm. That may be so, but Myne has the Devouring. She will not survive without magic tools. There are magic tools here at the temple. We will express our benevolence and take her in with us."

That was an order that left no room for negotiation. The High Bishop's smug tone and behavior were putting a lot of pressure on us. I wasn't used to dealing with this kind of status-based discrimination and I couldn't help but feel frustrated. I seemingly wasn't alone there, as I could feel Dad nearly bursting with anger.

"I refuse. Myne won't be able to survive here as a servant."

"That's right. Even without the Devouring, Myne is very weak and sickly. She's the kind of child that collapses twice during a baptism ceremony and ends up bedridden for days with a fever. She wouldn't last in the temple." Mom squeezed my hand protectively.

By rejecting the High Bishop despite his higher status, they were literally putting their lives on the line. The High Bishop had naturally not expected for a moment that they would refuse, and so when they both did, he exploded angrily, his cheeks and somewhat balding head bright red with fury.

"What rude parents you two are! Be quiet and hand over your daughter!" He was being so emotional and pathetic for a member of the church that I actually flinched at the sight of him. How was he a noble? Why did we have to bow before him just because we were commoners? I just couldn't understand.

Dad himself was shaking with anger, as was reasonable, but he repeated his rejection with a cold voice that gave no hint as to his feelings. "I refuse. There are many orphans in this temple. You can work them to the bone as your personal playthings instead. Under no circumstances will I throw my precious daughter into an orphanage," he said.

Mom nodded while squeezing my hand so hard it hurt. They were being so courageous that I couldn't help but smile with pride, but that just poured oil on the High Bishop's fire.

"Don't be ridiculous! Priests! Capture these impudent parents and lock Myne up!" The High Bishop stood up so fast his chair toppled and he turned to scream at the gray priests standing behind him. He went straight to using force to get his way, either due to having a short fuse or due to having no intention of discussing anything with commoners.

"Get back." Dad stepped forward to protect Mom and I just as the gray priests moved forward. They couldn't all come at once due to the table in the way, so there was a time gap between each one.

The High Bishop gave a smug grin as my Dad assumed a fighting posture. "If you lay a hand on a priest, I will have you executed in the name of the gods."

"I've been ready for that ever since I swore to protect Myne."

Dad drove a fist into the stomach of the first priest that reached him and knocked him out with a knee to the jaw. A priest came at him from behind, which he responded to with a backhanded punch and then kicked him away.

Dad didn't hesitate at all as he incapacitated the priests by hitting their vital points. In the first place, the orphans raised to be servants to the nobility had no chance of beating a trained soldier like my dad. The remaining two priests, probably not used to so much violence in their daily lives, looked at Dad fearfully and backed away.

"Hmph. You can handle a few at a time, but how about many at once?" The High Bishop opened the door as if to mock Dad's resolve. I didn't know how they had been summoned, but there were over a dozen priests outside and they all came rushing in at once.

I felt something snap inside of me as I saw the High Bishop smirk like he had just beaten us. *Enough of this already!*

My body heated up as if all the blood inside me was boiling, but despite that, my head felt oddly calm with a sharp chill. I could feel my entire body being painted over with fury.

"You're the one who's being ridiculous. Don't you dare touch my mom and dad."

I took a step forward, and for some reason, everyone looked at me with stunned, horrified expressions. The once smugly laughing High Bishop, the once calmly sitting High Priest, and even the priests that came flooding in were all staring at me in shock.

Confrontation

Despite my body feeling hot to the point of boiling, my head was so clear that I honestly felt better than I usually did. I could see the blood draining from the High Bishop's face, even though I was just calmly looking at him while he pressed his back against the door.

...If you're that much of a coward, don't be so cruel to other people. Idiot. The High Priest must have seen the High Bishop getting increasingly pale, as he broke his silence to stand up with a clatter and yell.

"Myne, your mana is leaking! Control your emotions!"

I shifted my gaze from the High Bishop to the High Priest. The moment I stopped looking at him, I heard the High Bishop collapse onto the ground like a heavy weight being dropped. The gray priests seemingly regained the ability to move when I looked away, and I could hear them rushing to the High Bishop while calling out to him. Their worried voices seemed to fade into the distance as I spoke to the High Priest.

"How do I do that?" I looked at him firmly with anger in my eyes.

The High Priest held down his chest and let out a grunt. "Ngh... Haven't you been doing it your entire life?"

"He summoned me here to talk, started ordering us around, got violent, and on top of all that, threatened to execute us when we fought back. How could I control my anger in a situation like this? You'll have to tell me, 'cause I don't have a clue."

I glanced back at the High Bishop. Now that he had collapsed on the ground, he was short enough that we could make eye contact. He flinched and shook with so much fear that it was actually comical, sliding backwards to get as far away from me as possible with terror covering his face.

...What a funny face. He doesn't look like a kind grandpa, and he doesn't look like a smug noble either. I'm just a weak little girl, but he's looking at me like I'm some kind of monster. I felt a little angry at how two-faced the High Bishop was, always changing his expression at the slightest thing, and took a step toward him.

"S-Stay away! Stay away! Stay away from me!" The High Bishop, gasping desperately for air, was so terrified that he was just repeating the same thing over and over. I heard the High Priest call out to me from over my shoulder, his voice panicked.

"Stop! If you give in to your emotions and continue hitting the High Bishop with mana, his heart won't last!"

I replied with an uninterested "Hm" and took step after step toward the High Bishop. "He can just die, then. You'll kill my mom and dad if I leave you alive, right? I'll just kill you first instead. I imagine that if you're willing to kill other people, you're prepared to be killed yourself. Just think of all the people who will be happy at your death. I bet there's a lot of people who want to be the High Bishop."

After I took four steps forward, the High Bishop's eyes rolled to the back of his head and he passed out while frothing at the mouth.

Within moments, the High Priest was on his knees in front of me, protectively blocking my line of sight to the High Bishop. His brows furrowed in pain and he looked at me with deadly serious eyes as sweat dripped down his forehead.

"Let us talk," the High Priest said.

"Talk? With fists? Or with mana?"

The High Priest's eyes widened, then he coughed, blood dripping from the corner of his mouth. My eyes were drawn to the red droplets trickling down his chin.

"You must not kill him. If you kill the High Bishop, your family will be stained with the crime of murdering a noble. That cannot be what you want," said the High Priest, snapping me back to my senses. I couldn't let my family end up as criminals due to me going on a rampage to save them. I blinked repeatedly and heard the High Priest sigh in relief.

"Back to your senses now, I presume?"

"…I think so."

The High Priest loosened up with relief and took a handkerchief out of his pocket to dab his mouth before moving his hair out of his eyes. That was all he had to do before returning to his cold, calm expression from before, as if nothing at all had just happened.

"Let us talk. Just as you wished for."

"Does that mean you'll listen to every condition we have?"

The High Priest frowned for a moment, then shook his head and placed a hand on my shoulder. "…You will need to control your rampaging mana for that. Can you manage?"

I took deep breaths and focused on the heat that had spread throughout my body, pushing it back inside of me. Doing so was harder than I expected and it felt that I had a lot more Devouring heat built up within me than I'd thought.

…Or wait, it's mana inside of me, not Devouring heat. As meaningless thoughts passed through my head, I managed to fit all the mana into a box within me and shut the lid tightly. Instantly, the strength drained from my body and I collapsed like a marionette with cut strings.

"Careful now." The High Priest embraced me to keep me from falling onto the floor.

"Myne!"

"Are you alright?!"

The High Priest offered me to my parents as they rushed in our direction. Mom bent her knees to take me and hug me close. Dad looked down at my limp body with worry in his eyes.

"I'm fine. My body just can't keep up with the rapid temperature changes that happen when my Devouring heat goes crazy. This happens all the time, I'm still conscious."

"It does?" said Dad anxiously. I let out a tiny laugh.

"It's not normal for me to get that emotional, but well, I lost control of the heat constantly about six months ago, back when I nearly died."

"I had no idea…"

The High Priest stood while I was talking with my parents and gave orders to the gathered priests. He left the High Bishop to them and instructed them to prepare a room for our discussion.

"Once you've put the High Bishop to bed, return to your own rooms and rest. You all must be quite exhausted after being directly hit with the Crushing of that much mana."

"But High Priest, you yourself are…" The priest's worry was justified. Out of all the priests there, it was likely the High Priest who was the most exhausted of all. Not only had he gotten in between me and the High Bishop, he had talked to me while looking me in the eyes.

"High Priest... are you okay?" I remembered the blood that had trickled out of his mouth and reflexively called out to him. He looked at me, surprised, and forced a smile.

"This is a punishment I brought upon myself. What else could I expect to happen after silently watching the High Bishop anger you, a child with the Devouring who somehow managed to survive until her baptism ceremony?"

After finishing giving out orders, the High Priest walked toward us. Up close I could tell from his thoroughly exhausted expression and heavy breathing that he was pushing himself.

"Why *did* you just silently watch us, High Priest?"

"Because the best possible result from my perspective would be you unconditionally joining the temple. I greedily sought the easy route with the most rewards. I did not expect your commoner parents to firmly deny the orders of a noble, and I certainly did not expect them to embrace an execution for the sake of protecting you." The High Priest shook his head and Dad grinned a little.

"Myne's my precious daughter. Didn't I make that clear?" said Dad, which made the High Priest look at me. He gave a complicated smile, one seemingly dripping with self-derision, and gently patted my head. It was like he had seen a dazzling sight too bright for him.

"...Myne, I am envious of how loved you are, of how deeply your parents care for you. This temple is filled with those abandoned by their parents, be they orphans or nobles, and we know no such warmth."

The High Priest's words, spoken within an ornately decorated room, filled me with sadness and stuck with me as my life became intertwined with the temple.

Since the High Bishop was put into his bed, we moved to the High Priest's room to have our discussion. It was fundamentally the same as the High Bishop's room. It had the same furniture, but there was no shelf with decorations and his desk was buried in a mountain of paper and boards. It seemed that the High Priest was doing the real work in the temple.

This time, he offered us seats as was proper, including a bench so I could slump in exhaustion. Then, the discussion began.

"You called what happened the Crushing, didn't you? What in the world was that? Myne's eyes shone like rainbows and a yellow mist was drifting off her body..."

...I had no idea that kinda bizarre thing was happening to me! Rainbow eyes?! A mist coming out of me?! What?! My dad's question stunned me. But I was the only one who hadn't seen myself, so nobody else was surprised and the discussion continued on normally.

"It is what happens when one with mana loses control of turbulent emotions. Mana races through their body, energizes, and crushes those they identify as an enemy by putting immense magic pressure on them. It should be a common event for children, as they are poor at keeping their emotions in check. Has it not happened before?"

My parents looked at each other and fell into thought.

"I've seen her eyes change color several times. Mainly when she's being unreasonable. But none of that Crushing has ever happened. She always calmed down after I told her why she was being unreasonable."

Those were good memories to my parents, but from a third party, I really stuck out as abnormal. Even I thought a kid whose eyes changed colors when throwing tantrums was borderline creepy. *...It would have made sense for me to be thrown out into the streets. I'm impressed they actually raised me well like they did.*

"The effects depend on the quantity of mana, so it is possible that the Crushing we saw was the result of Myne's mana growing bit by bit over the years. Please be careful to prevent her from losing control like that again."

"I won't get emotional like that unless it's something really horrible," I said, indirectly blaming the High Bishop for what happened.

The High Priest gave me a measured look and narrowed his eyes. "It is known that those with the Devouring have abnormal amounts of mana, but I still did not expect you to have enough mana to knock the High Bishop unconscious through the Crushing alone. Forgive my phrasing, but why are you alive...?"

That was a hard question to answer. I tilted my head in confusion and the High Priest elaborated. "The more mana one has, the stronger a mind it takes to control it. To be honest, the weak mind of a child unfamiliar with keeping their emotions in check can generally only withstand a small amount of mana. The more mana a child is born with, the faster they die. Mana increases as one grows, so Devouring children who survive until their baptism ceremony tend to have only slight amounts of mana. It is very unusual that someone with your quantity of mana is still alive."

"I should be dead already, you're right. But a kind person gave me a nearly broken magic tool that saved my life."

The original Myne died two years ago. I would have died six months ago if not for Freida. The High Priest was right; it wasn't easy for a kid with the Devouring to survive until their baptism ceremony.

"I see. But did you not seek a contract with a noble through that kind person? You will not survive without doing so. That is good for us, since it means you will be joining the temple as you are, but I cannot help but be confused." He did seem sincerely confused, but the same went for me.

"What would be the point in living as a noble's slave? I want to stay with my family. I want to read books. I want to make books. Living a life where you can't do what you want is the same thing as being dead. There's no point in it."

"…You want to live as you choose, hm? That is a hard philosophy for me to understand." The High Priest shook his head slowly, collected himself, and then spoke again after looking at all three of us in turn. "Myne, I would like you to join the temple. This is not an order, but a request."

"I heard from a merchant that there are fewer nobles and you're low on mana right now. Is it true that mana gathered in the temple impacts the crop harvest?"

"…That is one well-informed merchant. But I will put that aside for now." It seemed that the information Benno had gathered was accurate. In which case, their lack of mana would have a huge impact on the region.

"Can't you ask other nobles to help?"

"There are many magic tools that must be kept running. It is largely magic tools that protect our country and its cities."

I had thought the problem could be solved by making other nobles help, but it seemed that they were busy with other things.

"The High Bishop is a man of questionable character as you saw, but I handle the administration of the temple personally. It is rare for a Devouring child to have as much mana as you do. As promised, I will do my best to accommodate your needs."

"Dad, you can handle the rest."

We had already discussed what I needed. I would leave the rest of negotiations to Dad, the head of our household. Mom patted my head and said I could sleep if I was tired, but if I didn't pay close attention to the negotiations that would decide my future, Benno would karate chop my head right off. I decided to watch the discussion unfold, slumped against the back of the bench.

"These are our conditions. Since you need Myne's mana, we request that you treat her like a noble. Under no circumstances should she be given the hard labor of a gray shrine maiden."

The High Priest nodded to my dad's request without more than a second of thought. "I will prepare blue robes for her. Her primary job will be the upkeep of magic tools, just like our noble apprentices. That was what we initially intended to do had the High Bishop not lost his mind, after all. She will be assigned to the upkeep of magic tools and the book room which she so passionately desires to enter. How does that sound?"

My affection points for the High Priest shot up after he permitted me to enter the book room without any negotiation needed on our part. He looked like a cold person, but he was actually quite kind. *...He risked his life to stop my rampage, he's a skilled leader managing all the administration of the temple himself, he read the bible to me, he let me enter the book room, he let me enter the book room, and he let me enter the book room!*

"High Priest, you're such a good person!" I was so moved that I let out an explosion of joy, but it didn't get through to anyone. Dad and the High Priest just glanced at me once before returning to their discussion.

"Furthermore, we are worried about her living in the temple where we can't see her, so we request that you let her stay at home and commute to work each day. We have no intention of letting anyone take Myne out of our reach."

"...I see. Myne is not an orphan, so she can commute from home. That should not be an issue, as there are already many nobles who stay at their homes."

"Also, Myne is too weak and sickly to work every day. What are your thoughts on that?" Mom was holding my mouth closed with a hand, keeping me silent as they advanced the conversation on without me.

"She does not need to force herself to work when ill. But I recall her speaking of going to the forest when healthy, so on those days there should be no problem with her working, correct?" The High Priest looked at me and I shook my head, frustrated at myself for blabbing on about things I shouldn't have.

"Even when I'm healthy, I need Lutz to do anything."

"Lutz? The boy who came to get you the other day?"

"Yes. He manages my health for me. Without him, I'll pass out out of nowhere and catch fevers. I need someone to manage my health to do anything."

Before I could continue on and say I could only work when it was convenient for Lutz, the High Priest nodded with understanding. He started writing something onto a board near him as if it weren't a big deal at all.

"Ah, you need servants. That will be no problem, as it is customary for several servants to be assigned to each blue priest and blue shrine maiden."

Wait... Um, servants? Several of them? I-I don't want that.

"Are you still opposed to her joining? Do you have any other conditions?" The High Priest looked away from me and back to my parents as I floundered. There was no doubt that he was being exceptionally lenient with me. Benno was right when he said they would want me to join the temple no matter the costs.

"Um, High Priest. I'm registered at the Merchant's Guild right now. Can I continue running my workshop?"

"...Such things are unnecessary to those serving the gods. Or so the High Bishop would say, in any case."

For the first time, the High Priest showed hesitance toward a condition. He furrowed his brows and fell into thought. I tried negotiating along the lines Benno had taught me.

"But I've been making things for a long time. It's an important source of income for me. There's an orphanage here, right? I could give work to the orphans and pay them, or give a portion of my profits to the temple. Isn't there some kind of compromise we could make here?"

Unlike the High Bishop, who would probably say no without even thinking about it, the High Priest ran the temple and knew the state of their finances very well. Benno had said that with fewer nobles, the temple would be receiving less donations and be seeking alternative forms of revenue. I waited for the High Priest's answer. He frustratedly murmured "Just how much does she know?" to himself and rubbed his temples.

"...Very well. At a later date we will discuss your profit margins and how much of it you will dedicate to the temple. The final decision can be made then. As it stands, I have so little information on your work that nothing can be said."

"Okay. We can talk about money stuff another day, including my initial donation." I didn't really want to talk about how much money I had in front of my parents. The High Priest picked up on that and raised an eyebrow, but looked back to my parents without saying anything about it.

"Any other conditions?"

"No. If she will be treated as a blue shrine maiden and given work only on days when she is healthy while staying at home otherwise, as a parent I am satisfied."

"Very well. Come to the temple again in one month. We will need time to prepare her blue robes and such." The High Priest waved his hand, signaling us to leave the room.

Once we left the temple and the tall walls surrounding it, seeing the bright-blue noon sky made a sense of release flow through me.

Dad carried me home. For some time we all walked in silence, but after seeing the plaza and returning to our part of the city, Dad finally let out a murmur.

"It's over…"

"Uh huh."

"We won, yeah?" said Dad in disbelief.

I replied with a big nod and a full smile. "We won big. Mom, Dad, thanks for protecting me." I clenched my fist victoriously and bent my elbow, having finally regained the strength to move a little.

Dad grinned his usual grin and held me up with one arm while clenching his other hand into a fist. "You're the one who protected us, remember? With that Crushing of yours."

"Mmm, I just got so mad my mana went crazy. I don't really remember what happened exactly." I giggled and tapped my fist against Dad's. They had accepted all of our terms, and my money situation was up for negotiation. If I consulted Benno and formed a plan ahead of time, there was no way I could lose.

"I'm a little relieved, to be honest. I think you'll do just fine with the High Priest there," said Mom, making me tilt my head in confusion. The High Priest was definitely a capable leader, but I didn't know what about him would make Mom relieved. She went on, "He stopped you when you went on your rampage, didn't he?

You need someone to stop you when you run off on your own like that. I would be worried if something happened to make your mana go berserk and there wasn't someone who would stop and scold you."

That was just the kind of reason I would expect from Mom. She knew me well. I could already imagine that the High Priest would be lecturing me constantly in the temple with my Mom's silent endorsement.

"...He's probably going to get angry at me a lot."

My prediction made Mom and Dad laugh. It hit me that none of this would have been happening if I hadn't been able to stop the High Bishop from executing them. I sighed in relief. ...*I'm glad things worked out. I went on a rampage, but I wasn't wrong to do so.*

As relief that everyone was safe welled up in me, we walked down the main street and turned into the small alley that led to our home.

Tuuli was waiting by the well. She was walking around it in a circle, so obviously waiting for us to get back that I couldn't help but smile.

"Tuuli!"

"Myne! Yay! You came back!" Tuuli came running our way the moment she saw us, stepping on the somewhat overgrown weeds by the well. Dad set me down, standing such that I could lean my back against him. When Tuuli jumped into my arms, he was ready.

"Welcome back, Myne! I was waiting for you!" Tuuli smiled with tears dripping down her face and I smiled back at her.

"I'm home, Tuuli!"

Epilogue

There had been some trouble along the way, but now that the negotiations with the temple were finally over, Gunther thought that he would be able to relax and have a peaceful day at work for the first time in a while. Until he saw Otto's goofy grin, that is.

"Otto, shape up a little. You think that's the kinda smile a soldier should have?" he said, leading Otto to slap his cheeks a few times. But it had little effect beyond reddening them a bit.

Despite knowing that he was probably grinning due to something nice happening with his beloved wife, there was something about that smile that made Gunther want to give Otto a hard punch to the face.

Gunther let out a sigh and then heard a gravelly laugh from behind him. He turned to glare at whoever was laughing and saw the gate's commander, chuckling so much that his shoulders were shaking.

"Like subordinate like captain, huh? Right now, Otto looks just like you do when something good happens with your family. Give him a listen, would you? Usually it's the other way around. Should give you some good perspective," said the commander before patting Gunther's shoulder and walking away.

Gunther felt a little self-conscious that he had been obnoxious to Otto when, for example, Tuuli's baptism had overlapped with an important meeting.

…Oh well. He didn't want to, but Gunther decided to spend the day with Otto. It was annoying when he started talking for days about his wife, but what's done was done.

Luckily, Gunther didn't know that basically everyone thought of him the same way and were just glad that their two family-obsessed coworkers were bothering each other instead of them.

After his shift was over and someone came to take his place at the gate, Gunther went toward the east gate with Otto. The east gate connected to the main outside road, which meant that there was a constant flow of people through it and plenty of inns and restaurants nearby. The alleys leading off the main street had stores packed together tight and pretty much everyone who lived in the city had their favorite spots.

It was summer, so each restaurant had their doors thrown wide open and the loud voices of people drinking could be heard everywhere. Gunther and Otto walked through the throng of people on their way to a bar where most gate guards spent their time.

When Gunther stepped into the bar filled with the smell of alcohol and food, he saw a group of nearly twenty customers monopolizing two long tables pushed together in the middle of the store. There were several round tables for smaller groups, but most were filled.

"Oof, this place is packed." Gunther nodded as he passed through the noisy crowd to the back of the store and called out to the store owner, who was pouring beers behind the bar.

"Heya, Ebb. Two behelles and a decent platter of boiled sausages, please." Gunther placed the payment for the meal — a large copper — on the counter, and Ebb started pouring behelle beer into wooden mugs. They held their beers carefully so as to not spill any while moving to the only empty table they could see, a round one near the back of the store.

The last customer's utensils were still there, but a waitress deftly noticed the problem and had the wooden mugs and forks taken away before they could even sit down. The only thing left on the table was the hard bread they used as plates, which was a little softer due to sucking up meat juices. Gunther wiped the table with the bread and dropped it to the floor, whereupon the restaurant's dog came over with a wagging tail and gobbled it up.

They set their mugs on the table and sat down with a clatter. "Cheers to Vantole." They clinked their cups together, cheering the god of alcohol before chugging their behelles down.

Gunther drank most of his in just a few gulps. That was the best way to drink behelle; it gave it the most flavor. He loved the refreshing sensation of behelle going down his parched throat after a long day of work. The sharp, bitter taste of behelle spread through his mouth a second after he was done.

"Mmm, good stuff! So… what happened?" Gunther put his empty mug on the table and urged Otto on after wiping his mouth. Otto took the salted sausages from the waitress and asked for two more behelles. Picking up a sausage off the hard bread plate, Otto grinned and shrugged.

"Corinna told me not to tell anyone yet, so sorry Captain, I'm gonna have to keep it a secret."

"Hey, congrats on having your first kid."

"Wh-Wh, how'd you know?!"

"What else would your wife tell you to keep a secret? Not too hard to guess from that goofy grin of yours, too."

Otto scratched his head awkwardly. Gunther knew because he had done the same thing and everyone pointed it out to him, but there was no need to tell that to Otto.

...*Still. Otto, a father? Can a goofy guy like this really raise a kid well?* Those thoughts passed through Gunther's mind. But again, everyone had said the same thing about him.

...Being happy over a kid being born meant he would be a deeply loving father. He would be fine. Gunther mentally corrected himself after reflecting on his own life and nodded.

"Here's your seconds! Enjoy!" The waitress slapped the mugs on the table, causing their contents to stir. Some of the behelle sprayed out, but not a worker or customer in the store cared about something like that.

Gunther passed a middle copper to the waitress and he grabbed his mug with Otto. Unlike the first time, they took their time enjoying the multitude of sweet and bitter flavors rather than gulping it down all at once.

Gunther knew that Effa and Tuuli admired Otto's wife Corinna for her skill as a seamstress. Tuuli said she wanted to work at Corinna's workshop once her contract with her current workshop ended. On top of that, Corinna's older brother Benno was the head of the store that was helping Myne out so much. Gunther himself only knew Otto well, but their families were surprisingly linked overall.

"Otto. Take good care of your wife and kid. Your kid's gonna take over that big store, yeah? I remember Myne talking about that."

"...That's part of what I want to talk about, Captain." Otto's demeanor hardened in an instant. His goofy smile tightened and his eyes wavered as he searched for words. He looked just like Myne did when she was trying to finally talk about issues she had kept pent up inside her.

Epilogue

The alcohol flew out of Gunther's head, despite drinking so much his throat felt dry. He lifted his mug and took a slow sip. "…Go ahead. Talk."

"Aaah, well, this is kind of a long term thing. It'll take a few years, I think, but I'm going to quit being a soldier someday soon."

Otto had become a soldier in order to marry Corinna. A traveling merchant coincidentally falling in love with the heiress of a large store. Corinna had already been pursued by various merchants in the city because of her status, and she herself had been suspicious of Otto. But he proved his feelings by buying citizenship in the city and quitting his life as a merchant to be a soldier.

Suffice it to say, Gunther was sincerely shocked when that happened. It was about four years ago, back when he was guarding the western gate. A traveling merchant who said he was selling the last of his merchandise and going to the city where his parents lived to start a stable store came back just a few days later, saying he used all his money to buy citizenship and needed help finding a new job. Gunther couldn't believe his ears even after asking him to repeat himself multiple times with other guards nearby.

But Gunther had seen Otto passing through the gates with his parents ever since he was a child, and he knew from experience that one could fall in love at first sight with someone so hard that they would change their entire life plans to marry them.

Otto had learned to read and do math during his life as a merchant, and he wasn't bad at either of them. Gunther introduced him to his commander under the condition that he would mainly do paperwork. Most of the men who became soldiers tended to lack the skills necessary to do paperwork even if they had the enthusiasm to train. Otto joining the guards made it a lot easier to deal with passing merchants and people with letters of introduction from nobles.

...And now Otto was quitting his job as a soldier? Had his wife's family accepted him as a merchant? He knew that Otto was helping the store on the side already. He also knew that he was doing some trade with the traders and merchants that passed through the gate to keep his senses sharp. If Otto's efforts had finally been rewarded, that'd be something to celebrate, but Otto looked more troubled than anything.

"Your brother-in law finally approved of you after you made a kid?"

"...That more or less happened a while ago, so no. This is happening because of Myne."

Gunther's eyes widened at the sudden mention of his daughter and he set his mug down with a thump. In contrast, Otto's expression lightened a bit and he took a sip from his mug.

"Captain, the reason I chose to become a soldier over any other profession was to make connections with the people of the city. As I worked as a soldier people would remember who I am, and I would remember who they are. I also knew that a soldier would be in the best position to gather information on merchants and nobles going in and out of the city. In truth, I intended to keep working as a soldier for a long time after this, but the situation has changed. The insane products Myne keeps making like rinsham and hairpins are growing the Gilberta Company in directions we never expected."

"Oh? The products Myne's making?" Gunther was proud and happy as a father to hear his daughter praised, but he couldn't entirely agree. From his perspective, Tuuli was making the rinsham and Effa made better hairpins than Myne. It was more common for him to see Myne fail out of weakness or make things of questionable quality than anything else.

"But the Gilberta Company is ultimately a clothing store. The plant paper that Myne and Lutz brought us will be immensely profitable and impact probably the entire world, but that's not what our store sells. Benno wants to expand the store's scope. Corinna, though, is only interested in clothes and accessories. She doesn't want to expand the store's scope, so…"

"Is the stuff Myne's bringing you causing problems?" Gunther frowned and Otto hurriedly waved his hand side to side and shook his head.

"No no, this isn't a problem, it's just growing pains. The stuff Myne makes is more than any merchant could ask for. Anyone would go after them like Benno is. It's just that they're too much for Corinna to handle. So Benno wants to give the Gilberta Company over to Corinna and start his own shop while I help her out. He's in the process of making a new store so he can spread Myne's inventions even further."

The head of a large company making a new store and expanding his business demographic meant that there was an extraordinary amount of money being moved around. Tuuli had gotten excited early and desperately tried to explain to Gunther that Myne was super rich, but he just passed it off as her exaggerating. She had brought up some amount of money, but it was so unrealistic for a kid to have that he ignored it and had already forgotten what it was.

"…So it's true that Myne's making insane amounts of money?"

"It's true. But she's managing her money abnormally well for a kid, almost as if someone taught her finances already. I doubt you taught her with how loose you are with money, so really, I gotta ask. Who taught her?"

Gunther glared at Otto, who was raising a teasing eyebrow, and gave a derisive snort. There was only one possibility for who might have taken a liking to his cute daughter and made her abnormally smart with unnecessary mana on top of that.

"The gods must have taught her. Myne's a girl loved by the gods."

"I thought you'd give a dumb answer, but that's surprisingly convincing. Almost scarily so." Otto shrugged with a laugh and bit into a sausage. Gunther did the same.

"So, when are you quitting? There's nobody who can do your job for you right now."

"I can't just quit on the spot, so I think it'll be two or three years from now. I'm thinking about finding a good apprentice and teaching them to do math so they can take my place. Haaah... I didn't expect Myne to get snatched up by the temple like that. It happened so fast I had no idea what was going on."

Gunther remembered that Otto had taught Myne how complicated and difficult human relationships were in order to get her to give up on being a merchant apprentice. Just how nice would it have been if Myne had indeed just worked from home while occasionally going to the gate? Gunther had also never expected that the temple would steal Myne away.

"Same here. Myne was all about not wanting to deal with nobles, but then she suddenly started talking about being a shrine maiden out of nowhere. I know she wants to read books, but still... Sheesh."

Gunther remembered how Myne had talked about becoming an apprentice shrine maiden the moment she got back from her baptism ceremony. He tightened his grip on his cup. Myne was a fool for charging headfirst into a place she didn't understand just so she could read books.

"Benno gathered information and did what he could to put her in a good situation. You okay with her going now?"

"You think I am?" Gunther glared at Otto, who raised his hands in surrender and shook his head. No matter what good conditions they had secured, no parent would be happy about sending their daughter to the temple. "Like hell I'm okay with it. They said they'll treat her like a noble, but nobles have a sense of superiority and they'll never treat her well."

It was all talk. They might give her a blue robe for appearances, but there was no chance that they would actually treat her like a noble. Gunther had no idea how they would treat her.

"That said, they're not sending her to the orphanage. As long as she comes home, I can keep an eye on her. We're dealing with nobles here. I just gotta be happy that they didn't take her away completely."

"But still, Myne's in a dangerous position."

Things ended up fine because Myne went on a mana-fueled rampage and Crushed the High Bishop, but had that not happened he would have executed Gunther and Effa before sending Myne to the orphanage. The temple had really been generous by not killing them and letting Myne stay at home. They couldn't ask for better conditions than they were given. But regardless, there was no doubt that the High Bishop would resent being Crushed by a commoner. He would certainly hate Myne and make life hard for her. Gunther was scared just thinking about what would happen once Myne started going to the temple.

"Captain. This is something Benno told me, but it's likely that Myne will only have about five years of safety in the temple at best. Those with mana are precious right now due to the lack of nobles, but once the nobles come back she'll be in danger of being treated as a liability."

"Just five years, huh? Still, that's better than her not going to the temple and dying in half a year." Gunther's main goal in letting

Myne go to the temple was extending her life. That was the one thing he had absolutely no control over. Magic tools were necessary to keep her alive, but he didn't have the connections or money to get them himself. He considered himself a failure of a father.

"But right now, Myne's valuable. She has mana and she has the power to earn a lot of money. If she can prove her worth before her time's up, she might earn a better contract than one that just enslaves her."

"Myne said she wants to stay with us and not sign a contract with any noble, but… as a father, I want her to live as long as possible."

She had lived her whole life up until this point suffering with sickness. Now that she was finally following her dreams, Gunther wanted her to keep living and have the life she wanted. But would she sign a contract to stay alive? If she did, which noble would she sign with, and what terms would the contract have? It all depended on Myne.

Despite being her father, there was very little Gunther could ultimately do. Benno, by gathering information and lecturing her, and the guildmaster, by selling a magic tool he gathered for his granddaughter, were both helping Myne out far more than he was.

"…What can I even do? I've got no money, no options. No matter how much I love her, I'm just a soldier that can't even protect his own daughter. What a laugh." Gunther buried himself in the mug and let out grumbles he would never say at home. Despite confidently saying he would protect his family and the town, there wasn't much a single soldier could do.

Hearing that, Otto shook his head. "I don't think so. All things considered, it might be the will of the gods that Myne's father ended up being a soldier guarding the city gates."

"…What're you talking about?"

Otto narrowed his eyes, and after glancing around the bustling bar, lowered his voice a little. "Thanks to Benno's hard work, Myne is somewhat protected inside of this city by contract magic. The scariest possibility to Benno right now is Myne getting kidnapped by a noble from another city."

"Kidnapped?" Gunther swallowed hard. He had expected that a noble in the temple might try something like that, but he had never considered that nobles from other cities might go after her.

"A magic contract only has effect in the city it was signed in. If we're dealing with a noble of this town, the guildmaster or Benno could ask the Archduke to investigate Myne's whereabouts. But it's very possible that not even the Archduke will have any power over a noble from another city or region."

The reality that the owner of a large store, the guildmaster of the Merchant's Guild, and even the city's Archduke all had limited power was so shocking to Gunther that it felt like he had been struck in the head. *...If the Archduke can't do something, how could I? How in the world can I fight against nobles from other cities?* Gunther rubbed his temples and Otto gave a defiant grin.

"To stop that from happening, you'll need to investigate the priests in the temple who don't like Myne and the nobles they have connections to. Then you'll have to keep an eye on outsider nobles coming in and make sure there's no problem with them. Think about it. A guard looking over all the letters of invitation and letters of introduction passing through the gate is in the perfect position to protect Myne, isn't he?"

Gunther blinked and thought about his job. It was true that for a commoner wanting to keep track of nobles, there was no better job than guarding a gate. Nobles didn't enter foreign towns without letters of introduction or letters of invitation. They always rode on horses or in carriages, so they always went through the gate, then headed directly to the inner wall to enter the Noble's Quarter. High and mighty nobles did not deign to wander around the commoners' part of town. By keeping an eye on nobles who headed to the temple or stopped their carriage in the town, he could drastically reduce the chances of Myne being kidnapped.

Even if a noble hired some criminals to conduct the kidnapping for them, Gunther would recognize people who weren't from the city immediately. It was generally easy to tell at a glance whether someone lived off of criminal activity. He could ask the residents of the city if they had seen anyone suspicious, he could patrol looking for them himself, he could work together with other guards, and he could be ready to take action the moment anything bad happened. Of course, that was all part of a soldier's job already.

"You became a soldier to protect this town and your family, right? You just have to keep guarding the city like you have been."

"...Now that I think about it, I gotta say, it's pretty good luck that I'm being moved to the east gate next spring."

Every three years, each platoon of guards would move to a different gate. The goal was to strengthen the bonds between soldiers and prevent any negligence or collusion while standardizing the work everyone did, but that didn't matter to Gunther. Next summer, his platoon was moving from the south gate to the east gate. Since the east gate was connected to the main outside road, more people passed through it than any other and it was the easiest place to gather information. Given the traffic, it was the gate that needed the heaviest guarding.

"Keep your guard up and maintain a strong information net. You might want to use your connections with other soldiers to form a communication line where you can move as soon as you sense something dangerous. I'll help too. Benno's sticking his neck pretty far into this, so my family's just as involved in this as you are," said Otto, clenching his fist and bending his elbow. He was making the gesture soldiers made to wish each other good fortune in battle with a cocky grin on his face. "Captain. Let's protect our families."

Gunther returned the same confident grin, then gulped down the rest of his behelle before putting his mug on the table. He then clenched his fist, bent his elbow, and tapped his fist against Otto's.

"Yeah. I'm gonna protect this city — and my family."

Tuuli — Visiting Corinna

"I'm back, Tuuli! Corinna said she definitely doesn't mind everyone coming together. She'll be waiting tomorrow afternoon."

Myne came bursting through the front door, her heavy breathing a likely sign that she had rushed all the way home. After giving her announcement with a smile, she collapsed onto the floor in exhaustion.

"Ngh… I wanted to tell you as soon as I could, but maybe I walked a little too fast."

"We don't want you to get too sick to go tomorrow. Sit and rest for a bit."

Myne sat on a chair, leaning heavily against the table. Her silky blue hair fell onto it. I sighed in relief as I looked at her. …*Mhm, she'll be fine.*

Myne had thrown herself at all sorts of challenges and built up strength bit by bit over the last year or so, but she was still weak and small. She looked like a four- to five-year-old at best no matter how much time passed, and that worried me a lot. Lutz was the same age as her, but she looked like his little sister. The other day a kid two years younger than her had to help her with something, which made her depressed for the rest of the day.

Myne wasn't weak due to the Devouring it seemed, because she was still weak even with her Devouring cured. Lutz mentioned recently that she wasn't at all like Freida, who became entirely healthy after her Devouring was cured.

Myne was entering the temple as a blue apprentice shrine maiden. That meant she wouldn't die from her Devouring, and she wouldn't be thrown into an orphanage as a grey shrine maiden. For a long time I had been scared of Myne leaving me, but now I didn't have to worry anymore, and that made me really happy.

Today, Myne went to Benno's store to discuss how to deal with the High Priest and keep her workshop. While she was at it, she said she would talk to Corinna about when we could meet. I couldn't go last time since she only invited Myne, but this time Myne would ask if I could go with her.

…Aaah, I can't wait. I'm gonna brag to everyone at my workshop that I went to Corinna's place. Eheheh.

Corinna had owned her own workshop since reaching adulthood and she even made clothes specifically ordered by nobles. To an apprentice seamstress like me she was living the dream, a hero further out of my reach than the blue sky itself. I looked up to her and wanted to be like her one day if I could. Stories of her being passionately courted by a wonderful husband were told among apprentice seamstresses like minstrel tales. He abandoned his life as a merchant for her and threw away his life savings to prove his love for her. It was a girl's dream to be as loved and cared for as Corinna was.

…I wonder what kind of person Corinna is? Myne said she's really nice. I hope that's true.

"…Mmm, I think I'm better now?" Myne stood up while rubbing her forehead and unsteadily got to work. She delicately wrapped her folded baptism outfit and hair stick to keep them clean and put them in her favorite bag along with a thin needle. It hit me that she was preparing for tomorrow.

"Myne, what about me? Should I be doing anything?"

"Mmm, not really… I guess we should clean our hair before we go?"

Myne and I cleaned our hair using the rinsham I made. I never washed myself that much in the past, but lately I felt that I needed to keep myself as clean and neat as possible. Even at the workshop, it was always the clean people who got to guide visitors and talk to them.

"Um, Myne. Today I got to guide a visitor for the first time."

"Wow, really? That's great, Tuuli."

At some point I complained to Myne that only clean and tidy people got jobs that involved customers, and she replied that the first impression given to customers was very important to a business. Any merchant would be very careful about it. She said being dirty was fine for those working in the back, but if I wanted to deal with customers, I would have to keep myself clean and be careful about how I looked so I could give good first impressions. She also said I could put on nice work clothes that were presentable to customers, then put a long-sleeved apron over them to keep them clean. By taking it off before guiding customers, I could be clean at any time.

I listened to Myne's advice, and now the forewoman was giving me jobs that involved dealing with customers. I told Myne that it was thanks to her, but she just smiled and said it was thanks to me listening to her advice.

We were talking about how our days had been and cleaning our hair when Mom came home. Her eyes widened a bit after she saw what we were doing.

"Oh my, you're using rinsham? Does that mean…?"

"Mhm. We're going to Corinna's tomorrow," said Myne, which led to Mom pushing cooking duty onto us so she could vigorously clean her hair with a determined look in her eyes. Myne and I shrugged and went to cook, fully understanding why Mom wanted to be as clean as possible before meeting Corinna.

"I'm gonna go in my new summer clothes that Mom just finished making."

"That's a good idea. They look super comfy and cute."

The cloth we ended up not using on Myne's baptism outfit got used on my summer clothes instead. Unlike Myne, I was growing a lot each year and it didn't take long for old clothes to stop fitting me. There wasn't enough cloth to make an entire new outfit for me, so we just sewed different kinds of cloth to my skirt to make it longer. Myne said it just looked like patchwork, but to me it was cute. I liked it.

...I wonder if Corinna will think it's cute too?

We left early the next day so we could be on time walking at Myne's pace. We passed through the central plaza and headed to the north side of the city, where the people walking around had much fancier and more elaborate clothes. It was rare for me to go to the north part of the city, so I looked down at my clothes, worrying that I was standing out. Mom looked like she was getting self-conscious too. Only Myne was as full of energy as ever without a care in the world. That didn't stop her from walking slow, though.

"Corinna lives, like, right above Benno's store," said Myne, which made it all click into place.

Myne only ever told me about what she was doing, so it never felt real to me, but she was actually going to the north of town on a regular basis. No way would she get nervous after spending all that time here.

"Mm, what do you think I should say first?"

"Just say hello, right? And then thank her for inviting you, I guess. You should save anything you have to say about me for Benno and Mark, since I don't talk with Corinna much at all."

Myne gave a casual reply to Mom's anxious question. We weren't used to dealing with rich people, but Myne had met countless ones at the gate and at the store. She knew exactly how to talk to them.

"What about me, Myne? What should I say?"

"You can just give her a cute smile, Tuuli. There's not a person in the world who wouldn't get happy if you smiled at them and said you were looking forward to seeing them."

Mom and I practiced what we would say as we walked. Compared to us, Myne blended in with the rich part of town perfectly in her Gilberta Company outfit. It was like I was seeing a side of her that I knew nothing about. It made me feel kind of frustrated and panicky.

"Hello, Mrs. Corinna!"

Mom and I both had trembling legs from the tense walk up the stairs, but Myne knocked on the door without a care in the world.

...Please, wait a second! I need to prepare myself!

"Welcome, Myne. And hello to your mother and sister as well. I am Corinna. Please do come in."

The door opened before I was ready, and behind it was a lovely looking woman. She was much younger and prettier than I expected. She had light cream-colored hair that looked like gathered moonlight and her silver gray eyes were filled with kindness. Despite her hair and eyes giving her a faint, almost fairy-like atmosphere, her body was very womanly.

"It's nice to meet you, Mrs. Corinna. I am Myne's mother, Effa. Thank you for inviting me here today." Mom said the lines she had practiced while doing her best to curtsy. I copied her and said my own lines.

"Mrs. Corinna, I'm Tuuli. I've been really looking forward to meeting you. I'm so happy to be here."

"I have been looking forward to this as well. Myne's baptism outfit was so splendid that it caught my eye from afar and ever since I have been positively dying to see it. My apologies for making you come all this way."

She smiled at me with such a gentle smile that I ended up smiling myself. It was a smile as warm as spring sunlight.

"Please wait just a moment. I will prepare tea for us."

Corinna took us to a room that seemed to be for both visitors and work. There was a table for talking and another table further inside, probably for work. It was entirely different from our place, where we had to handle everything on our kitchen table. Also, the room was covered in delicately embroidered cloth and sample outfits Corinna had sewn.

...*Wooow! So cool!* Mom and I both had our eyes locked on the clothes and colorful tapestries hanging off the walls. I hadn't expected that she would show us such pretty things. I spun around, enraptured by everything I saw. Everything was so well made, so expressive and colorful. The hanging outfits had designs entirely unlike what I was wearing. I let out sighs of awe as I stared at everything.

"So pretty... How can you even make clothes like this? I can't get it at all. Do you just have to practice?"

"Skill is important, but it's also important to look at a lot of good things so they can inspire you with your own ideas," Myne said, sitting down unsteadily and turning her golden eyes toward me.

I spun around, confused by what she had said. "What do you mean, Myne?"

"You won't have ideas like these if you don't carefully observe what clothes rich people like and what's popular. Corinna was born rich, so she was naturally surrounded by good things. That gave her a natural instinct for what's good."

It felt like Myne was saying no amount of effort would be enough for me. I slumped my shoulders, asking if I was doomed then, and Myne shook her head.

"It may be important for you to go to the forest on your days off, but you should take some time to walk around the north part of the city too. There are a lot of rich people here going to stores for rich people, right? People wear all sorts of clothes here and you can learn a lot by watching them and seeing what's popular."

Sometimes I went to the forest on my day off, but I never went to the north part of town. I could count on one hand how many times I had gone north of the central plaza. I never realized that I could learn about what was popular among rich people by going to where rich people are.

"Also, the designs on some of these tapestries and the embroidered flowers are all things you can see in the forest, right? If you observe nature, you'll have an easier time thinking up designs."

Myne had been looking at the clothes and tapestries with an entirely different perspective than me. I had just been impressed by how pretty they were. I supposed that was the difference between a craftswoman and a merchant. I pushed down my excitement a little and started carefully observing Corinna's work, even if I didn't have the skills to copy what she was doing.

"Goodness, Tuuli. I will feel embarrassed if you stare at my work as you are," said Corinna as she entered the room with a servant.

"I've never seen clothes like this before. They're super new to me. I work as an apprentice seamstress, but they still haven't given me any big jobs like making clothes..." They had recently started letting me work on small parts of products that didn't stand out, but it would be a long time before I was making entire outfits by myself.

"Simple practice is the key. If you cannot sew pretty lines, sewing pretty clothes is out of the question."

"I'll do my best. Um, Mrs. Corinna. How did you sew these two parts together?"

As the servant placed snacks and tea on the table, Corinna explained her clothes to us. At some point Mom had walked up and was listening next to us. Only Myne remained sitting at the table, seemingly uninterested.

"Please, drink."

At Corinna's encouragement, I had a sip of the tea. It had a really nice smell, unlike our tea. I could feel the flavor spreading through my mouth.

"So good! This tastes really, really good."

"I am pleased you like it." Corinna smiled at me. I looked at my mom and Myne hoping they would agree with me, but Mom looked more worried about the price than the flavor and Myne was just savoring it with closed eyes and a smile.

"Feel free to eat as well." She pushed a plate of lightly baked bread mixed with fruit and covered with honey toward me. I took a piece and put it in my mouth.

...Mmm, this tastes good too, but the sweets Myne makes taste better. Myne had taught Freida a sweets recipe, and got a bag of sugar in return. We were using it to make all sorts of sweets I didn't know about like "crepes," "compotes," and "faux-cookies." She said something about making "pudding" if it were colder. Apparently it wasn't good to make in the summer since it needed to be chilled. She was also packing fruit and sugar into jars and soaking them with wine. She said in the winter it'd end up super sweet with a summer flavor. I couldn't wait.

"They're sweet and super good. Aaah, I wish I could use lots of honey like this," said Myne as she ate the sweets, making Corinna smile.

"You could buy as much honey as you want, could you not? Benno was looking quite bitter about how much he was paying you."

"I keep my personal money and my work money separate."

After finishing the snacks, we spread out Myne's baptism outfit. Mom and Myne pointed to parts of it and explained how they had made it from the hand-me-down. Corinna held it up, took a good look, and observed it carefully while turning it around and flipping the hem.

"This is quite a unique way of repurposing old clothes."

"It's a lot simpler than resewing it all from the start."

Corinna was writing something on a wooden board as Myne continued her explanation. She looked just like Myne did when she was writing on paper or her slate. For some reason, it hit me that I should learn to read and write too. That would probably make me more cool, somehow.

"This is the hairpin, I see. I cannot say I have ever seen something like this before," murmured Corinna as she picked up

Myne's hair stick. The small white flowers hanging from it shook in the air.

"I made the large white ones on it."

"I see. They are very pretty, Tuuli." Corinna's compliment made me break out into a goofy smile. Her white fingers traced the flowers.

"I would like to take orders for these ornaments and make them in my own workshop. Would that be acceptable, I wonder?" asked Corinna with a warm smile. I hadn't expected that she would like it enough to start making them in her own workshop. I was so moved it felt like I had been hit by a wave of emotions. I beamed a smile and started to say "Of course you can!", but Myne shook her head before I could.

"That depends on your payment."

"W-Wait, Myne?!" I couldn't believe that Myne would charge Corinna for making the hairpins, but she just held up her hands to calm me down.

"We make these hairpins for our winter handiwork and they're an important source of income for us. We can't just let other people make them willy nilly. If you really want to make them, Corinna, you'll need to buy the rights to them and pay us the money we would lose from your competition."

Myne's explanation cooled me down. She was right, hairpins were a very important source of income for us. With thoughts of how much money I'd earned over the winter, I lost the motivation to stop Myne.

"In that case, I will summon Benno." Corinna rang a bell to call for the servant, who she sent to get Benno. It wasn't long before we heard footsteps coming up the stairs.

"What's up, Corinna? Did something... Ah, Myne's family. It's nice to meet you. I'm Benno, Corinna's older brother."

...So this is Benno, the merchant Myne's been working with. He had light hair the color of milky tea, a gentle-looking appearance, and dark-red eyes. His smile really resembled Corinna's. I got the impression he was a bright, nice person.

"I am Myne's mother, Effa. Thank you for taking good care of my daughter."

"I'm Tuuli. Nice to meet you." I hurriedly introduced myself after Mom did so herself. Benno nodded at us with a smile, then looked down at Myne with a raised eyebrow.

"What is it this time, Myne?"

"Mrs. Corinna wants to buy the rights to make and sell this kind of hairpin. How much will you buy it for, Mr. Benno?"

"A business discussion, now?" Benno said, and Myne nodded.

"Yes, a business discussion."

Immediately Benno's gentle expression turned into the hard expression of a merchant. His eyes narrowed and he got kind of scary. He roughly pulled back a chair and sat down, glaring at Myne and holding up a few fingers. "How about this?"

"That wouldn't be worth it at all. I would get more money selling it to Freida."

Benno was so scary I got shivers looking at him from the side, but Myne just laughed him off. Despite him being in full merchant mode, Myne wasn't scared at all. She was negotiating with him on equal terms and having fun doing it.

"C'mon, wasn't Lutz gonna sell the stuff you make anyway?"

"That's for products I make in the Myne Workshop. It doesn't include recipes and other forms of intellectual property."

"You little!" Benno gave a furious yell so intense that Mom and I jerked, but Myne just tilted her head with a smile.

"Speaking of which, Mr. Benno. Freida said that if I had any other unique products not found anywhere else, she would start negotiations with several large golds. It looks like you've been really ripping me off up until now. Eheheh."

I had heard about Myne doing this kind of thing, but this was the first time I was seeing her actually working as a merchant. Seeing was believing, and I honestly felt immense respect for how Myne could negotiate with adults this scary.

At home she always just laid around and got fevers after doing anything, making her a dead weight when it came to chores. This was the first time I was seeing her being so successful at something. It was honestly shocking to me.

...She said she gave up on being an apprentice merchant because she was too weak for it, but maybe she actually really wanted to become one? It feels like she would be a great merchant.

"Tuuli, Effa, it seems that this discussion might take some time. Follow me, if you would."

Corinna stood up and headed to the table further into the room. Mom and I looked at each other, then stood up to follow her. I was worried about Myne, but their discussion was so intense that I didn't see either of us finding an opportunity to get involved.

"Benno always stretches out business discussions when he's having fun. Still, I have to say that Myne is quite impressive. Not many can handle business discussions with my brother like that," murmured Corinna as she looked at the two of them, dazzled.

For the first time, I realized how amazing Myne really was. *...I'm Myne's older sister, but I didn't know about this side of her at all.*

"We can leave the business talk to them while we return to our sewing. We were just discussing the shape of the skirt, yes?"

On one table business talks reigned, while on our table we discussed sewing while drinking tea. Corinna told me about clothes and accessories popular among the nobility. There were many different forms of sewing, and hearing their names wasn't enough for me to imagine what kind of skirt they would make. When talking with Corinna I heard word after word that never came up when I talked with the other apprentices in my workshop.

When I asked what she was talking about, Corinna would smile and kindly teach me. That made me happy, but it also made me feel kind of pathetic. One year had passed since I began my apprentice work, and there was still so much I didn't know. Just talking with Corinna made me painfully aware of how much I had left to learn about sewing. If I didn't study and practice more, I would probably never be trusted to make clothes for customers.

"This is a style of dress that just recently became popular," said Corinna as she showed us a commissioned dress she was in the middle of making. It was apparently a kind of dress nobles wore during tea parties. I couldn't help but sigh in awe at the quality of the fabric, the thin thread, and the detailed embroidery.

"It looks amazing. But I really can't believe they have different dresses for different things. That just seems like a waste to me."

"It seems so, doesn't it? But we have different clothes for when we sleep, when we go out, and when we work, yes? The more money one has, the more narrow categories they can develop for their clothing."

Suddenly, our discussion was interrupted by the sound of chairs screeching backwards from the other table. We looked over in shock and saw Benno and Myne standing up and looking at each other, a short distance away from the table.

"You're not as innocent as you used to be."

"This is all thanks to you teaching me, Benno."

"Sheesh, you sure got too smart for your own good."

"Isn't it standard practice for merchants to gather information from various sources to improve the accuracy of what they know?"

The two of them shook hands with meaningful smiles. I could practically see a dark aura radiating from both of them.

...*Mmm, I definitely wouldn't be a good merchant,* I thought, taken aback by the intensity of their back and forth. Myne saw me watching them with wide eyes and came walking over.

"Mom, you can teach Corinna how to make the hairpins. Haaah... Now my throat's all dry." Corinna prepared a cup of tea for Myne and she thanked her as she took it.

"Impressive work. How much did you settle for, in the end? That will impact how much we charge for them."

Myne glanced at Mom and me, then held up some fingers. "The agreement ended up being that your workshop has the exclusive rights to make and sell them—not only during the winter, but the other seasons as well."

"Consider me quite impressed that you squeezed this much money out of Benno." Corinna looked at Myne's fingers with awe and a quiet gasp. She must have been giving some kind of sign that merchants used to state prices. It was kind of frustrating for me since I didn't know what they meant.

"Hey, Myne. How much does that mean?" I asked, curious as to how much the rights to the hairpins were worth. Myne looked at me really awkwardly, then at Mom, and then finally at Corinna while letting out a tiny groan. It was obvious she didn't want to say it.

"Is it something you can't say?"

"It's the fair market price, so it's not a secret, but I don't really want to say it…"

I begged Myne over and over to tell me, and eventually, with a clearly reluctant expression, she let out a quiet murmur. "…One large gold and six small golds."

"Whaaat?! Hold on. Did you just say golds?" I thought it would be worth a large silver at best, so the immensely larger price she'd stated made me feel like I had been hit in the head by something. Mom was looking at Myne, just as shocked as I was.

"It sounds like a lot of money, but it really is the fair market price for exclusive product rights. I'm not Benno. I don't rip people off. Also, this is money for my workshop, it's not my own personal money." Myne waved her hands and desperately tried to make excuses, but I really didn't understand how she could so confidently negotiate with amounts of money that large.

…I mean, that's a large gold. She said it's not her personal money, but just how much does Myne have saved up?! Maybe Myne really should have become a merchant, not a shrine maiden.

The visit to Corinna's home ended with me feeling overwhelmed by many things: my own ignorance, the depth of the art of sewing, and how incredible my little sister was.

Leise — Confectionary Recipe

"Leise, I will be returning with Myne, so please prepare the pound cakes for us."

"I'll get all the recipes ready." I gave Miss Freida a short answer and went right for my cooking tools.

My choice to become a chef was the natural result of my parents running a restaurant. When I was young they did their best with a little food stand, but it wasn't long before they opened up a small restaurant by the east gate. I grew up watching them cook. Thanks to them I could cook before becoming an apprentice and I had enough math skills to handle sales, which was rare for kids who hadn't been baptized.

After my baptism I started work at a restaurant owned by a family friend and absorbed recipe after recipe. I loved to learn and I loved to think about how to improve the recipes I had been taught and the recipes I had learned by watching others cook.

I explored various stores to hone my skills, and eventually I was asked to cook in a noble's mansion. My parents told me not to do it since I wouldn't be able to return to the commoner's part of the city, but I went anyway. I didn't want to miss the opportunity to learn the recipes served to the nobility.

I started off being worked to the bone as a dish washer, and slowly over time I stole the techniques held by the head chef. The ingredients and spices used for nobles' meals were a league above anything I had ever used myself. Even their dishes were fancier than anything you'd see in a normal restaurant. I learned more every day.

But that only lasted for a few years. No matter how much I trained, I never moved up in the kitchen. In noble mansions, you needed not just skill but connections and a dignified bloodline to move upwards.

I was stuck in the mud when the guildmaster called out to me. The head chef had recommended me, as he knew I was skilled enough to be a head chef myself, but didn't have the connections to make it there. He asked me to make food fit for a noble for his grandaughter, so that she would be better prepared to live in the Noble's Quarter when she reached adulthood.

...I said yes on the spot. Finally, I had a chance to show off my skills as a head chef. Not to mention that I would be working for the Merchant's Guild guildmaster, who had more money than some laynobles. His kitchen was built just like a noble's and he had all the same ingredients and spices. There was no better place for a chef to work.

To show my thanks for being given such an opportunity, I worked my hardest. Every day was enormously fun and rewarding, and I built up total confidence in my skills. I was confident that nobody would be able to beat the recipes I had built up.

Until Myne appeared, that is.

I couldn't believe it. Sugar was a newly developed sweetener that the guildmaster had just recently managed to purchase from the Sovereignty. Nobody in the world that I knew of had managed to accomplish much with it. I tried experimenting with it in various ways without much success. And yet, Myne made something great with sugar like it was the most natural thing in the world. I had to do all the making myself since she lacked the strength to do so, but her instructions made it clear that she knew the recipe by heart.

The pound cake she'd had me bake was fluffy, moist, had a refined sweetness, and broke apart in your mouth. It was unlike anything I had seen or made before. Not even the noble's kitchen had made anything like it.

But when I asked Miss Freida where Myne was from, she told me that she was a commoner girl with a soldier father and a dyer mother. Her family would be too poor to partake in extravagant sweets. At most, she would be able to eat the fruit and honey she gathered in the forest. Where had she learned a confectionery recipe?

Ever since then, I had been experimenting with the pound cake recipe she taught me by altering the batter and changing the oven's heat. After baking countless cakes, I finally made one that I could consider my masterpiece. Even Miss Freida was saying that this was food fit for nobles.

Miss Freida said that she would have Myne taste-test my pound cakes and negotiate for the rights to sell them. There was no doubt that Myne would be seeking connections with nobles. Miss Freida would introduce her to a noble that would treat her well in return for exclusive rights to the pound cake.

But contrary to her expectations, despite the approaching summer, Myne never visited a single time. When Miss Freida panicked and forcibly dragged Myne here, she didn't look worried at all about the time limit on her life.

When Myne ate the pound cake I had worked tirelessly to improve, she just shared ideas to improve it further in return for sugar. She said the flavor would change by putting stuff into the batter before baking, and that creams and fruits would make the cake look more fancy.

As I made a pound cake with ground apfelsige peels in it, I clenched the bowl. Myne had known how to improve the pound cake off the top of her head. She definitely knew more recipes.

...I wanted them. I wanted her new recipes. I wanted to know every recipe Myne had.

"Leise, Leise! I've brought Myne!"

Just as I was lining up plates with small slices of my cakes on the table in the corner of the kitchen, Miss Freida came bursting through the door with a broad smile on her face.

Miss Freida was born weak, and when I was first hired, she rarely ever left her room. She had changed so much after meeting Myne that it was hard to imagine she was the same girl who considered counting gold coins in her room to be her greatest joy. She had become a merchant with as much enthusiasm as Benno, a young man growing in power and influence every day. Her mission was to make Myne join her store.

Miss Freida had been pushing herself to surprising limits after deciding to hold her first taste-testing event. She had her entire family wrapped around her thumb, ordering them every which way. Myne seemed to have gotten wrapped up in this too, and Miss Freida had brought her to participate in the taste-testing.

"So, Myne, you believe I should consider children as an important demographic?" asked Miss Freida.

"It'll definitely be too expensive for commoner kids to buy, but merchant children might understand the value and have the money to buy some," Myne replied while looking around the kitchen. "Those of apprentice age will be able to read, so... The thing to remember here is that food you eat in your childhood will stay with you until adulthood."

"Is that so?" murmured Miss Freida while scribbling something on a board, the sight of which made me feel curious. Myne's growth had been slowed by her Devouring, and she looked like a five-year-old at best. But she was talking entirely as if she had already experienced reaching adulthood.

"Also, when you sell it, you don't have to sell the entire cake at once. You can lower the price and get more buyers by selling individual slices. That would be good for couples who only want two slices, or when someone wants to celebrate their baptism ceremony. Stuff like that."

"I intend to sell primarily to nobles at first. An expensive confectionery will do well with them, I expect."

Miss Freida wanted to keep the price as high as possible since she had exclusive rights to selling it. Myne, on the other hand, wanted to lower the price so more people could eat the cake. Despite being two young girls of the same age, they both had very different philosophies.

"Exploiting your exclusivity isn't a bad idea, but I think lowering the price and spreading it around is the best thing to do if you want your brand to be well known."

"My exclusivity only lasts for one year. Within a year it will spread regardless of what I do, no? I want to spend this year profiting as much as I can with nobles as my core demographic."

"Mmm. In that case, you could use seasonal fruits to make new cake flavors limited to each season. That'll distinguish you from competitors and make your core consumer base happy."

New cake flavors, limited to each season...? I didn't let Myne's offhand suggestion slip by me. I immediately started thinking about seasonal fruits.

"What about winter, when fruit don't grow? What can you do then?"

"I mean, you can't talk about sweet things in winter without mentioning parues, right? There's also (rumtopf) y…" Myne froze mid-sentence and covered her mouth.

I raised an eyebrow at her. With a finger over her mouth, she said anything else would cost money. It seemed she had realized that she had gotten so caught up in the conversation she was slipping out valuable information for free.

Miss Freida giggled at Myne's awkward expression. "I wonder what you were about to say? I have a sizable sum prepared to pay for your information, Myne."

When offered a price that she considered fair market value, Myne tended to throw in extra information for free as a "bonus." Miss Freida said that was much better for forming friendly, long-term relationships than trying to greedily maximize profit or attempting to cheat others. Considering she used to say that cheating people was the bread and butter of merchants, it was clear how dramatically she had changed.

"Mmm, I was going to talk about (rumtopf). Put simply, it's fruit you put in jars with alcohol. It takes a lot of time for the soaking to make them taste just right, but I think they would be perfect for winter pound cakes."

"How does five large silvers sound?"

With the core knowledge of soaking fruit in alcohol obtained, everything else could be handled through experimentation. Even if negotiations broke down, I would be fine. Or so I thought, right as Myne glanced at the sugar.

"…I guess since sugar hasn't spread very far, nobody knows how to make or use (rumtopfs) either."

Despite just mentioning fruit and alcohol, it seemed what she was talking about also used sugar. Asking for details would probably be smart, then. Recipes involving sugar demanded a lot of trial and error. There weren't many recipes out there using it. I looked at Miss Freida and she nodded.

"How about eight small golds, then?"

"Okay. I'll teach you how to make and use them. You'll be able to keep it to yourself until sugar spreads around, so no need for a contract this time."

They tapped guild cards to exchange money, then Myne pointed at a jar in the kitchen. "We'll need a jar like that. Do you have any others?"

"We can just use that one, it doesn't have anything in it. What else do you need?"

I moved around the kitchen at Myne's instruction and got what we needed. I washed some rutbers, a fruit that only grew in this season, and chopped them into pieces before putting them all in a bowl. We filled about half of the bowl with sugar and left it sitting. Myne said it was important to let it sit until the water drained out from the rutbers and sugar started melting into them.

"Do you know how much sugar costs? You sure we should use this much at once?"

"It's for preservation. The fruit will go bad if you don't put enough sugar in. Also, the fruit will rot if you don't put super strong alcohol in it, like distilled alcohol."

I got the feeling that Myne's sense of money had been damaged by how much she was making from selling recipes and product rights. Sugar was worth its weight in silver, yet she was using this much on a single batch of sweets.

"Once the water is drawn out of the rutbers, put them in the jar and add the alcohol. Mmm... You have to make sure all of the fruit's under the liquid, or the parts sticking out will grow mold. Also, you should add a different kind of fruit after about ten days. Pfirsloches and prunbeers are about to be in season, right? You really want to pack summer flavors in here and eat them once winter comes. Oh, right. Fruit like apfelsiges aren't too good for this I think."

Miss Freida wrote down all the warnings she was giving us. I carved them into my memory while stirring the bowl. I could tell liquid was getting slowly drawn out.

"You're making these too?"

"Mhm. Using the sugar you gave me earlier. It's my first time making them too. You can put these in pound cakes or use them as jam. They're also good for making (parfaits) or putting on (ice cream)."

Myne smiled to herself, murmuring something about looking forward to winter, when suddenly Miss Freida shot up and looked at the table.

"Oh no. We have gotten off track. I forgot all about the taste-testing."

"That reminds me. Mr. Benno said he wants to try taste-testing the cakes too. Can he come?" Miss Freida gave Myne a look, eyes narrowed. Myne scratched her cheeks and looked up a bit, as if trying to remember what Benno had said. "Ummm, taste-testing is still pretty rare, right? He's interested in what kind of sweets you're going to sell, but he's even more interested in how taste-testing events go."

Miss Freida fell into thought, then looked up with a smile. She must have thought of something. She spun around and headed to the kitchen door. "I have something I need to ask Grandfather.

You will have to excuse me for a moment. Leise, please keep Myne entertained."

Miss Freida had an odd rivalry with Benno, and him coming over had apparently lit up her defiant, flaming heart. She speedily left Myne in the kitchen, maintaining her graceful aura the entire time.

"...Well, there she goes," Myne said.

"She doesn't usually act like that, you know."

"Freida said the same thing about you when I told you how to improve the pound cakes."

Myne giggled and I let out a sigh. People had been pointing out for years that I could never stay still after learning a new recipe, but I showed no signs of growing out of it.

"That's your recipe's fault."

"...Aww. I'm sorry."

"You don't need to apologize. I'm the one who wants to learn new recipes. So, mind telling me how these cakes ended up?"

I placed a piece of cake in front of her that best represented the advice she had given me: one with added apfelsiges for smell and flavor, one with some of the sugar changed to honey, and one with walnuts. On top of that, I had prepared tea that matched each pound cake.

"They all look so good! Thank you." Myne's eyes sparkled as she smiled and took slow bite after slow bite, enjoying the flavors to their fullest. The graceful way she held her fork made me think of a noble daughter who had been taught strict manners. At the very least, she didn't look at all like a poor commoner, considering how they tended to stuff their faces with sweets when given the opportunity to eat them at all.

Myne sipped her tea as she ate and let out a satisfied sigh. "Out of all of these, I think I like the apfelsige one the most? I like how the smell blossoms in my mouth," she said with a warm smile after finishing her tea. "...Oh, the tea leaves that made this tea would probably go well with pound cake too."

"Tea leaves? Aren't those too hard to eat?"

Myne held a hand over her mouth. Apparently, that was some valuable information. I let out a "hmph" and placed a bag of sugar on the table.

"I'll give you this bag of sugar if you talk. I want to know all I can to make the best cake possible. I'm guessing you're running low on sugar thanks to making that rumtopf?"

To be honest, I had never even dreamed of putting tea leaves in sweets. Sweets were, well, sweet. My understanding was that chefs in the Sovereignty were operating under the principle that if you were going to be using expensive sugar, the sweeter the better. It was hard to think that tea leaves would make anything sweeter. I didn't have enough time to experiment with the leaves and figure out how to use them properly.

"...Well, a bag of sugar is probably worth it, maybe. This can be my way of saying thanks for all the cake."

After thinking for a bit, Myne explained what she meant. "You can grind up the tea leaves so they don't hurt the food's mouthfeel when you mix them with the batter. You'll end up with some nice-smelling cake."

"You mean tea leaves like these?" I held up a bottle stuffed with the tea leaves I had used for Myne's drink and she gave a big nod. After looking at the bottle for a bit, I lit a fire in the oven. I started grinding the tea leaves up while Myne ate pound cake beside me. I wanted to try it out right away. That meant leaving a guest alone for a bit, but she would be the first one taste-testing it, so it all worked out.

"Hey, Myne. Mind if I ask something?"

"Not at all, what is it?"

"Do you maybe have some secret tips for making good soup, too? It seems like you do, judging by how you ate while you were staying over here. You always left the soup, but nothing else. I thought maybe you didn't like vegetables, but you eat them no problem in other things. What's the secret to making good soup?"

Myne looked up at me with wide eyes, fork still in her mouth. "...You're sharp, Miss Leise."

I raised an eyebrow while beating eggs. "So, will you tell me about the soup?"

Myne took the fork out of her mouth and placed it on the plate. "...That's a little harder for me. Things are different from before, and I'll be stuck dealing with nobles soon whether I want to or not. I want to keep as many trump cards as I can up my sleeve, for self-defense."

Her defeated expression made it impossible for me to push further, so I just shrugged my shoulders. I knew what she was going up against thanks to my time working in a noble's mansion. There was danger in a status-based society, and the hardship it produced was no laughing matter. It made sense that she would want to keep trump cards, and I agreed that she should.

"I'm fine sharing sweets recipes if Freida buys timed exclusivity for them, though."

"Really?!" I leaned forward with the bowl still in hand and Myne nodded repeatedly, leaning back in fear.

"Only after the pound cakes get popular, I mean. Maybe a good time would be when the pound cake exclusivity runs out."

"Won't Benno get in the way of that?" I said, knowing that Miss Freida was always talking about Lutz and Benno attempting to monopolize Myne's knowledge, but she just tilted her head.

"Mmm, I don't know about that. He probably won't be too happy about it, but I don't think he'll be able to get in the way. To be honest, I don't think the recipes will mean anything to him even after being made public."

"Why's that?"

"Benno doesn't have strong connections with nobles yet, so he won't be able to get the ingredients or the talent necessary. It looks like there aren't really established trade routes for sugar yet, and to get a chef of your level, he'd need to snatch someone away from nobles, right? Freida said that's how the guildmaster hired you."

Myne's analysis of Benno, who could basically be considered her guardian, left me at a loss for words. It seemed that Myne was actually properly thinking about who she gave information to. In which case, maybe there was a chance she would teach me more recipes.

I glanced at Myne while sprinkling the bowl with flour. "You don't mind giving me your recipes?"

"A chef needs to be as skilled as you to replicate a recipe from word of mouth. Also, you're so passionate about your work, so it makes me want to help you out," said Myne, making me so happy I wanted to shout. She was basically saying that she recognized my skill as a chef. She would teach me recipes that she wouldn't teach Benno, who she owed so much to.

"...But it'll end up unfair to various people if I teach them for free, so that's kind of a problem." Myne wasn't too obsessed with profit herself, but the same couldn't be said for those around her. Not only that, but her recipes made big waves around her in more ways than one. Her recipes probably weren't the only thing she made with no historical precedent.

I mixed in melted butter to the bowl and tried asking Myne something that had been on my mind for a long time. "Hey... Myne. Who in the world are you? Where did you learn all these recipes?"

"...Mmm... I learned them from dreams."

"Say what now?" I glared at her hard, thinking she was joking around, but she just gave a troubled smile.

"...I'm not kidding. Up until now, these are all things I've only been able to eat in dreams." Myne gave a nostalgic smile that looked so mature, my suspicions only got bigger.

"I would really like to just explain all my recipes at once and have talented chefs like you make them all, but oh well."

Myne closed her eyes, then looked up and gave a bright childish smile. But it was the kind of awkward smile that was clearly forced. Guessing that that was a topic she didn't want to talk about, I changed the subject a bit while pouring the batter into the mold.

"You can't make these yourself?"

"I don't have the strength, stamina, tools, or skills to replicate them myself. So I need a skilled chef helping out so I can teach countless recipes to them. Or well, I can't right now, but you know what I mean."

Myne swung her legs while frowning with a sad look on her face. I looked down at her slender, weak looking arms, remembering that she lacked the strength to even mix a bowl of flour. It was hard to imagine her cooking anything with those.

"Just ask if you ever want to eat something. I'll make anything for you if you tell me the recipe." My heart danced at the opportunity to recreate recipes that only existed within Myne's dreams.

...Aaah, I'm so excited. What kind of recipes are sleeping inside this girl? I looked at Myne eating more pound cake while sticking the new tea leaf cake batter into the oven.

Benno — Pound Cake Sampling

At the conclusion of the meeting held with only those running stores large enough to pay taxes above a certain set amount, the Merchant's Guild guildmaster looked at all the participants one by one. The dang geezer.

"Is that all we have to discuss today? In that case, a reminder that the Othmar Company is holding a taste-testing event in the larger meeting room for a confectionery I plan to sell soon. Drop by if you have the time. My granddaughter said that there would be enough for everyone here and their servants. Benno, Freida put her all into this knowing that you would be coming. You wouldn't betray her expectations, would you?"

Having no other choice, I stood up and headed to the larger meeting room. The meeting had consisted exclusively of rich store owners, which meant they all had the money to buy expensive sweets, and good eyes for valuable products. It was doubtful that many of them would go all the way to the guildmaster's house just to taste-test food, but holding it in the guild right after a meeting all but guaranteed a good number of them dropping by. He was so clever with this kind of thing it was frustrating. No doubt the event would draw a lot of attention.

The taste-testing event could be traced back to Myne leaking the recipe to something called a 'pound cake' to the geezer's granddaughter, then giving her the idea to have a bunch of people taste-test variations on the original recipe. *Seriously, will that idiot ever stop messing up?! Doesn't she realize her products are big enough to shake the market?! I'm breaking my back so nobody realizes she exists but nooo, she's just gotta spill secrets without thinking!*

When she sold products to me, I didn't announce them ahead of time since I wanted to monopolize them for myself. Announcing a product before selling it brought extra attention to the identity of who created the product. Doubly so if nobody else can replicate said product.

And frustratingly enough, sugar wasn't a healthy market yet. The only company who dealt with sugar from the Sovereignty was the Othmar Company. This pound cake would probably be a huge hit with nobles who were riding the trends of the Sovereignty and searching for sweet stuff to eat. By holding this taste-testing event, the guildmaster wasn't just revealing his intent to fill that niche, he was marketing his granddaughter's skill at the same time. That girl inherited her nose for money from him.

"Welcome to today's taste-testing event. Please select your favorite pound cakes and put these cards into their boxes."

Boys and girls wearing identical handkerchiefs on their heads were standing by the door to the large meeting room and giving three wooden cards to everyone who entered. "You may put all three into the box of your choosing, or you could select three different ones."

I gripped the cards they gave me and looked around the room. You could tell who was a staff member for the event by the handkerchiefs on their heads. As of yet there weren't many visitors in the room, and the few who were there were cautiously keeping an eye on each other without trying the pound cake.

There were five tables lined up, and each had a different kind of pound cake on it. The cakes were sliced into bite-sized pieces, but still, there were many more kinds of cake than I expected.

"Oh, it's Mr. Benno!" Myne, the one at fault for all this, saw me and came walking over (waving hard) with my apprentice Lutz. He was wearing our apprentice uniform, but Myne was dressed as one of the event staff members. I raised a hand casually, which I then used to grab Myne's head once she was close enough.

"What do you think you're doing here, Myne?"

"Ow, ow! I'm helping them. Can't you tell from my outfit?" she said with a tilted head. I ripped the handkerchief off her head.

"Get changed right now. Don't leave an impression on the merchants coming into this room. Why do you think I hid you and didn't publicize who made the paper and hairpins? You wanna come back to my store and make a big fuss about who you are? Should I throw a big ad campaign for you?"

"Aww... I'll go change. Stay here, Lutz." I gave back her handkerchief and Myne speed-walked out of the meeting room. I sighed as I watched her go.

Myne was an abnormally smart girl who picked up on things a lot faster than you would expect from a kid who just finished her baptism. She knew so many things she had no business knowing. And yet, she so often acted seemingly without thinking at all. That was normal for a kid, but she was so abnormal in other ways that acting without thinking put her in a lot of danger.

She stuck out, and the less she stuck out the better. Nothing good would come from a kid with no protection sticking out. Even when my father died and I took over the business immediately after reaching adulthood, I got mocked as a greenhorn and went through hell to keep the store running. A kid who just finished her baptism would get eaten alive out there.

"Master Benno… You sure are hard on Myne."

"Lutz, if you want to protect Myne, remember this. Right now Myne doesn't have a merchant backing her up and she doesn't have a noble in the temple supporting her. She's dangling in the air, completely exposed to danger."

Considering the magic tools there and the connections she would form over time with blue-robed nobles, entering the temple now was a good idea for Myne. But it was hard to think her good situation would last for more than a few years.

"Huh? But Mr. Benno, aren't you backing her up…?"

"To some degree I'm considered her guardian given my relationship to her workshop, but that's a thin connection. I would have more options if she were an apprentice like you, but now that she's entered the temple there's not much I can do. She'll be harder for you to keep an eye on too, now. It's better if she learns not to stand out like she has been. Don't forget that nobody knows what she's thinking, and she runs off to do who knows what the second you take your eyes off her. The harsher she's managed, the better."

"Aaah, that's definitely true." Lutz nodded with a solemn expression. He looked so much like Mark I couldn't help but laugh.

Once Lutz finished his baptism and started apprentice work, his language shaped up and he began acting a lot more like Mark. Apparently he was using Mark as an ideal to model himself after. Unlike the children of merchants, Lutz was lacking in a lot of places necessary for a merchant due to the difference in his upbringing. He was desperate to catch up to the others. I noticed him carefully watching Mark and me to copy as many of our mannerisms as possible. I was fairly fond of his strong ambition.

"What do you think of pound cakes, Lutz? As a product."

"...I think there's no doubt it will sell really well. I imagine nobles will love it."

"Your proof? How do you know what nobles like or what they normally eat?" I said antagonistically, but Lutz replied in an instant without showing any signs of hesitation.

"Myne told me that the guildmaster is working to make Freida's living conditions as close to a noble's as possible to help her when she needs to move to the Noble's Quarter. It seems that even their chef used to work in a noble's mansion. If both Freida and that chef are confident that the pound cake will sell, I trust their assessment."

I knew that the guildmaster was spending a lot of money on his home, but I didn't know that he was fashioning it after a noble's home. My eyes widened reflexively. One couldn't look down on the information network provided by children chatting with each other.

"I'm back, Lutz." Myne came back, dressed like one of my apprentices. Now people would assume that I had brought her with me and not think twice about her, just like Lutz.

"Master Benno, this is a pound cake with nothing in it. It's the first kind I tried myself," said Lutz, pointing at the rightmost pound cake. He was practically drooling as he stared at the sliced-up cake with excitement in his eyes, probably remembering how it had tasted when he first ate it.

"Leise is really passionate about improving her recipes, so it tastes a lot better than it did back then. The cake on this table was made with apfelsige. This table is mixed with honey, and that one has nuts. The last table has the newest kind, made with tea leaves. Try them out! They all taste really good," explained Myne with her chest puffed out in pride, as if she had made them herself.

I snorted in amusement and looked down at the pound cake. "Judging by how many different kinds there are, I'm guessing you just let a bunch of info slip for free?"

"Ngh... I-I traded the information for sugar, so I didn't let it slip for nothing."

It seemed that she was using her information to trade for sugar. I wasn't sure if I should praise her for acting like a merchant or chop her for giving the guildmaster more valuable information.

"Also, I only told her about the apfelsige and tea leaves. I didn't even tell her the measurements; she found them on her own through experimentation. This isn't all my fault," said Myne, pouting and looking away from me. She then reached out to some of the cake on the table. Lutz went after some cake of his own after seeing her plop it in her mouth. Judging by the surprised cries around me, there was no mistaking that the cake was pretty good. I grabbed a piece for myself.

...The heck is this?! I figured it would be good the second I grabbed a piece, but the cake was fluffy and so soft it melted in my mouth. It looked like bread on the outside, but no bread was this soft. Normally you ate bread with soup to soften it.

On top of that, it was so sweet I couldn't believe it. It had a solid sweet flavor, but it wasn't dense sweetness like something soaked in honey, or sharp sweetness like that of a fruit. A gentle sweetness spread throughout my entire mouth. It smelled of butter mixed with a sweetener and stirred my appetite, making me want more.

"Does it taste good?" Myne looked up at me, golden eyes sparkling with anticipation of my praise. It felt kind of wrong to just give her what she wanted, so I ignored Myne and reached for the apfelsige cake.

It was fluffy, and the smell of apfelsige spread through my mouth. It had a refreshing sweetness that made it easy to eat. Just a little flavoring changed it so much. I lifted my head up and looked at the pound cakes on the other tables.

"Isn't Leise amazing?" I avoided Myne, who was praising another store's chef, and moved to another table to try the honey pound cake. Unlike the prior two cakes, it was a bit heavy and the sweetness was thicker. I was used to sweet things, and this was the sweetest of anything I had eaten so far, so it would probably be a favorite for children and those who cared more about sweetness than anything.

"It's sweet, but not too thick, right?"

Next was the nut cake. It resembled bread with nuts in it and thus looked more familiar than any of the other cakes. But it wasn't anything like the cake I normally ate. It was much more soft and that made the hard nuts stick out more. The cake melted in my mouth immediately, leaving only the nuts. Over time the mixture of crunch and softness might end up pleasant, but I didn't like it very much.

"Come on, Mr. Benno. Tell me what you think."

"Shut it. Be quiet." I headed to the next table while Myne circled me, being loud and annoying.

At first I hesitated to try food with tea leaves in it, but once it was inside my mouth, the smell and flavor was surprisingly good. Unlike the nuts, the tea leaves were completely ground up and didn't have bad mouthfeel. The cake did taste of tea, but it was still a sweet, which made for a weird combination. It wasn't that sweet, but it tasted good. Out of everything, I imagined that the tea cake would be the favorite of men. Or at the very least, it was my favorite.

"Which box are you going to put your cards in?" Each of the pound cakes tasted good enough to be surprising. There was no doubt that pound cake would be spreading throughout the noble class in no time. Anyone would want more after trying it once. The cake was so much better than any other sugar-based confectionery I'd had that it wasn't even funny.

"Myne. Why did you give this recipe to the guildmaster?" The pound cake recipe was a sizable weapon for those wanting to push into noble society. I would have wanted it for myself.

I glared at Myne and she tilted her head, blinking in confusion. "But I gave it to Leise, not the guildmaster."

"That's the same thing as giving it to the geezer and his store." The pound cake would doubtlessly give the geezer yet more influence within the nobility.

Myne, noticing my frustration, frowned with worry. "You really don't like the guildmaster, do you? Why is that?"

It hit me that I had never told Myne about my long and not so pleasant history with the guildmaster. "He has been picking fights with my family's store ever since it started growing. The second my father died, that geezer tried to marry my mother so he could take over the store."

My father had been killed on his way to do trade with my grand-uncle's store by bandits looking for money. Since he died close to his city, his body was returned to us, but it was so brutalized that my mother ended up bedridden. The only person happy about my mother's hurt heart was the guildmaster, who saw it as an opportunity to exploit.

"Wait. L-Like, he would marry her himself?"

"Yeah. She turned him down, and ever since then he's been bothering us in every way he can. You remember how he held up my applications in the guild and blocked me himself?"

Myne and Lutz both grimaced in understanding as they thought back to all the times they had gotten wrapped up in that. He wasn't just bothering me, he was bothering everyone associated with me.

"Do you think you could be nice to a guy who greeted you with a full smile after your fiancée died, offering one of his daughters for you to marry? You think I can forgive him for trying to marry my little sister to one of his sons before she reached adulthood? A son older than me?"

He had messed with my business in countless awful ways, but there wasn't any point in complaining about that to Myne. I just wanted her to know that the guildmaster was a flat-out messed up person.

"...Ummm, if you look at it one way, doesn't that mean he has a very high opinion of the Gilberta Company? He's definitely more forceful and persistent than he should be, though." Myne was avoiding the truth in a pretty painfully obvious way, but at least she recognized what a pain in the ass he was.

"So. Why did you give this recipe to a guy as annoying as the guildmaster?"

"Well, like I said before, I made the pound cake with Freida at her house because I promised to make sweets with her."

"But you signed a contract with her, didn't you?"

"Only to give her exclusivity for one year. It's not that big of a deal." The fact she added a time limit to the contract was fairly clever on Myne's part, but who knew if that would be upheld. Knowing that geezer, it wouldn't be a surprise if his granddaughter did everything she could to keep her monopoly going.

"...Are you really gonna publicize it in a year?"

"Uh huh. Sweets shouldn't be monopolized, and I want a lot of different people making them." Regardless of her recipe, given how difficult it was to get sugar right now, the guildmaster's store would keep their monopoly for some time. I didn't want their store getting ahead of mine too much, but it felt like another big gap had just opened up between us.

"Hey, Myne. You said you know a lot of other recipes, yeah? Would you sell any of those to my store?"

Myne looked up at me with a surprised expression, then shook her head. "There wouldn't be any point to selling you the recipes right now. You don't have the sugar or the chefs for it."

"What're you talking about?"

"The sweets recipes I know about almost all use sugar. And what's most important is having a good chef. If you don't have a chef skilled enough to have worked in a noble's mansion, you won't be able to recreate the recipes even if I tell them to you."

"A noble's mansion…?"

"It's absolutely required that you have an oven you can work freely with. As far as I know, ovens aren't that widespread out here. Only bakeries really have them, right?" Almost no homes had personal ovens. They weren't necessary unless you were fairly rich and quite the gourmand. Both of which, in fact, the guildmaster happened to be.

"My my. It seems I will need to buy all of Myne's recipes before Benno can organize what he needs. My chef has quite the love for new recipes."

I turned around after hearing a little girl giggling and saw the guildmaster's granddaughter, her flowery pink hair bundled into tails above both her ears.

"Good afternoon, Benno. Nice to see you, Lutz." She looked up at me with defiant eyes just like the geezer's.

I thought my chances of winning would be boosted with the geezer out of the picture, but I couldn't let my guard down around his granddaughter. She was using every trick in the book to get closer to Myne, and her nose for money was just as sharp as her grandfather's. I had my guard up around her, but Myne just waved with a friendly laugh. They looked to be on such close terms that I felt a sizable burst of anxiety. Myne was going to be eaten alive.

"Hi Freida. How's the event going?"

"Splendidly, thanks to you. Everyone is positively loving the pound cakes. More than a few of them are eagerly awaiting the recipe's publication in a year."

...How many times do I have to tell this idiot she needs to be more on guard?! Will she ever listen?! I had tricked her myself several times already, but that always just ended with her pouting. I was the one testing her, and she was so defenseless that it honestly made me worried. She was definitely lacking something inside her that made most people wary toward others.

But regardless, the two of them looked like two young girls talking as friends. It would reflect poorly on me as an adult to get in their way. Lutz and I had to settle for listening in on the conversation and glaring at Myne before she got wrapped up into one trap or another.

"Hey, Lutz. How come Myne can keep smiling like that when her life's on the line and everyone's tricking her?"

"...I have no idea. I don't like Freida that much either." It was written on Lutz's face that he didn't want Freida anywhere near Myne. I couldn't tell whether the possessive fire in his eyes was him being protective over a friend or a sign that he had already started falling in love.

Either way, seeing Lutz be so protective of Myne reminded me of all the warm feelings within me that had died with my fiancée years ago. It put me in a hard to describe, sentimental mood.

"Looks like you've got a hard road ahead of you, Lutz. It won't be easy to keep Myne to yourself." I ruffled Lutz's hair. My words must have inspired him somehow, as he nodded with a fire burning in his green eyes.

"How's the cake taste, Myne?" said a sizable lady in a friendly tone as she approached Myne and Freida. She was radiating a sweet smell and was wearing a staff handkerchief. Lutz and I both stiffened up, on guard since we didn't recognize her, but Myne nonetheless beamed a smile and ran up to her.

"They taste great, of course! I just had some, but the tea pound cake was super super good. You never cease to impress me, Leise!"

The woman grinned at Myne's praise. It sounded like she was the chef working for the guildmaster and making these pound cakes. I took a close look at her, my merchant instincts compelling me to size up the chef who was about to earn the guildmaster a preposterous amount of money, and she looked at me in turn.

"You're Benno, then?"

"Yeah, what of it?" I didn't know why a chef would know my name and address me in particular. Myne must have done something. I narrowed my eyes and Leise looked me over.

"...Hmph." Her judging eyes reminded me of the guildmaster's, putting me in a bad mood. I had been holding back since it wouldn't be mature to go all out on a little girl, but an adult like Leise was another story.

"So you're the one who locks up Myne's knowledge and keeps it all to yourself, huh?"

"Clearly not. She gave the pound cake recipe to you, remember?"

I would have wanted to keep Myne's knowledge to myself, but she wasn't making it easy for me. Not to mention that I was only "locking it up" because a spare word from her was enough to flip the marketplace upside down. Introducing her products to the world bit by bit was safest for everyone.

"Really, you guys are pushing all the hard stuff about managing Myne to me and reaping the benefits of my hard work yourselves."

I was working hard in the shadows to protect Myne: signing magic contracts to carve her relationship with me into stone, gathering information to help her protect herself, making the Plant Paper Guild to hide Myne's existence, and so on and so on. Her thoughtless nature was forcing a lot of hard work onto me, not the guildmaster.

"Well, you're the one who was ripping me off, Mr. Benno," said Myne with pursed lips. I flicked her on the head.

"I threw away all the money I ripped off from you for your rinsham on those two magic contracts, y'know?"

"Bwuh?"

"...Two magic contracts, you say?"

Myne and Freida's mouths opened wide as they looked up at me with the same expression. I looked down on them and shrugged. "Seriously, you don't know how hard I'm working for you."

"I don't care how hard you're working," interjected Leise. "Myne said she'll only give recipes to people she thinks can recreate them well. You can have the other things, but her recipes are mine."

Even the guildmaster's chef was declaring war against me. It seemed that everyone involved with him felt compelled to treat me like an enemy.

"Not a chance. They're mine." I wasn't going to let the guildmaster keep this pound cake all to himself forever. I would get my hands on sugar and search for a skilled chef while the one year contract was in effect. It would be difficult, but getting sugar through my somewhat distant family members shouldn't be impossible. I glared at Leise while doing calculations in my head.

Myne nervously pulled on my sleeve. "Mr. Benno, Mr. Benno. It'll be really hard to find a good enough chef. You'll need a noble's help, I think."

"I don't need any help. I just need one with ambition and the ability to work an oven, yah?" They just needed enough skill to work at a noble's mansion and an opportunity to practice with an oven. They didn't absolutely have to have worked in a noble's mansion before.

"You're the one who said you would just make books if you couldn't buy them, right? What would you do if you wanted a good chef as much as good books?"

"...Train one myself?"

"Exactly."

I would prepare a kitchen, search the city for a skilled chef, and train them specifically for making sweets.

"...Let's do this thing."

Mark — The Master and I

My name is Mark, and I serve the master at the Gilberta Company. If my memory does not fail me, I just recently turned thirty-seven. As the years go on, one's exact age becomes increasingly difficult to remember.

Considering that I joined the Gilberta Company as an apprentice for the store's previous head, thirty years of my life have been spent in service to the store. Master Benno was born the year I joined the store as a lehange apprentice. Truly, time flies.

Apprentices of merchants and craftsmen were split into two broad categories: lehanges and leherls. Put simply, lehanges signed a contract of employment with the owner, whereas leherls signed a contract of clear apprenticeship that promised future work within the store. The contracts differed greatly in content and payment, but a detailed explanation would surely be a waste of your time.

The Gilberta Company generally hired children from other stores as lehanges. It was tradition for merchant children to gain experience by working in other stores. The length of the contract was determined by the store and the children's parents. They generally lasted three to four years. The contracts had many goals: to expand their world view, to help them understand what would be expected from them, to remove them from a coddling environment, to build relationships with other children who would go on to take management of the stores, and so on. The contracts formed bridges connecting stores.

I was originally one such lehange apprentice with plans to return to my family's store after my contract was over. But my father died, and my older brother who inherited the store handled business so differently from him that after repeatedly renewing my contract as a lehange, I signed a leherl contract after turning fifteen and reaching adulthood.

Leherl contracts lasted eight years. Under normal circumstances, one would return home from a lehange apprenticeship and sign a leherl contact before turning twelve. At age twenty, they would be given management of the store in place of the current head.

I was so late in signing my contract that I had eight years of training ahead of me after reaching adulthood. That said, I had already worked as a lehange for eight years and knew how to do my job at the Gilberta Company. The head of the store graciously treated me differently than a standard leherl, and modified our contract such that I would be paid about the same as a full-time worker. Thanks to that, I did not feel particularly troubled during my eight years of extended training. I merely rejoiced at my better pay and spent each day dedicating myself to my work.

However, unfortunately enough, the head of the store died before I finished my apprenticeship. Master Benno had just reached adulthood and was hardly in a position to run an entire store. The majority of lehanges signed to Master Benno's father declined to renew their contract with him.

I was still in my training period, so I requested that my family assist the Gilberta Company so that I might continue working there. My older brother, however, not only refused to send help, but mocked the death of Master Benno's father and announced that he was cutting ties with the Gilberta Company.

It would be hard to describe the wrath I felt that day. I still clearly remember the moment I swore to protect Master Benno and the Gilberta Company to spite my family.

When my leherl apprenticeship ended, the master asked if I would return home, but having cut my family off I had nowhere else to go, and the Gilberta Company needed me more than anywhere else.

I said that I would stay at the Gilberta Company, and Master Benno and I proceeded to work in a nonstop flurry of sleepless nights to restore the store to its former glory. With great speed, we accomplished that and even grew the store larger than it was before.

Surely enough years have passed since then that it is safe to say that I pulled the strings behind the scenes in order to collapse my family's store and use it as a stepping stone for the Gilberta Company's growth.

The previous head's youngest daughter Corinna married, but his eldest son Master Benno had lost interest in marriage itself after his fiancée, Liz, passed away. Before I knew it, I myself had passed the age for marriage as well. Life never goes quite the way you expect it to.

The store had plenty of work and the master agreed that Corinna's child would take over once they were old enough, so it could be said that the Gilberta Company was no longer in great danger of collapsing.

Which brings us to the present day, where Master Benno was absent due to a meeting with other large store owners. In such cases, important decisions were given to me in his place.

"Mr. Mark, we have received word that the next rinsham delivery will be late."

"That is reasonable, considering the last leeve shipment was late. Tell the foreman to deliver what they have completed and finish the rest as soon as possible."

"Er, Mr. Mark. An order for Mrs. Corinna has arrived from Baron Blon."

"That's unusual, given that it is summer. There is no time to waste. Contact Corinna at once."

As I passed the somewhat busier time than usual, the master returned carrying Myne.

"Mark, we have to talk. Follow me!"

He marched right to his office. His eyes were shining and filled with enthusiasm, whereas Myne was limp with exhaustion and Lutz was breathing heavily as he chased after him. That was all I needed to see to know that yet another difficult challenge had been put in front of us.

Gathering the materials to operate a rinsham-making workshop, securing craftsmen, blasting the market wide open, running around the city to get the tools and materials Myne and Lutz needed to make plant paper, working to calm the conflict with the Parchment Guild, creating yet another workshop for plant paper... Thinking back, my past year had been spent doing quite a lot of unreasonable work. What would it be this time?

"Mark, we're training a sweets maker! Get ready!"

Training a sweets maker? It seemed this had nothing to do with our earlier work. I was suddenly struck with a very bad feeling. Given how sudden this was, Myne was doubtlessly involved.

I observed the master cautiously as he took out various wood boards with gleaming eyes, checking various things. It was good to see him motivated, but his motivation here would probably give those around him a lot more work.

"You say a sweets maker, but what exactly do you intend to have them make?"

"Ask Myne."

Aaah… Of course, Myne. It seems she has done it again.

The Gilberta Company was initially a clothing and accessory workshop founded by the master's great-grandmother, Mrs. Gilberta. Historically, the wives of the family made clothes while the husbands sold them. Although the store was registered under their husbands' names, the women ran the store in reality.

The Gilberta Company initially sold clothes to wealthier commoners, but ever since laynobles began to notice clothes designed by the master's mother, it has become increasingly focused on selling to the nobility. It was about ten years ago that this shift first happened — very recently, all things considered. Corinna's talents were equally favored among the nobility, which secured the Gilberta Company's safety. To sum things up, the Gilberta Company was a clothing and accessory store that also dabbled in beauty products.

Myne's rinsham was a high-quality beauty product, and her hair ornaments (now being made in Corinna's workshop) were already fairly popular throughout the city. With higher-quality thread and more refined designs, they would even be possible to sell to noble wives and daughters, which made Corinna quite happy.

However, the plant paper Myne brought wasn't quite the kind of merchandise the Gilberta Company dealt with, nor was sweets.

"Once again! You need sugar to make my sweets! How many times have I said this by now?!"

"You don't need sugar to bake bread. They've gotta practice using an oven first, yeah?"

"But there are already bakeries throughout town and even a Baker's Guild! You're going to clash with the vested interests again! Just for practice! I'm betting you're going to try and steal a baker from the Baker's Guild, aren't you?!"

"You'll never start a new business if you're scared of the vested interests!"

Myne and Master Benno's heated argument, with Myne standing on her chair to be at eye level with him, reminded me of the master's arguments with Liz. They say that the more two people fight, the closer they are. Perhaps this argument showed how much they had grown to trust one another.

At times, it seemed like the master looked the most alive when he was furiously arguing with Myne about business. I couldn't help but wonder if arguing on equal terms with Myne, clever at speaking as she was, felt as good to him as arguing with Liz had. Though with Liz, he had never been able to win a single argument.

"Lutz, could you explain the situation to me while those two are busy? What has compelled the master to train a sweets maker?" I asked, snapping Lutz back to reality. He straightened his back and began to explain.

Lutz was so used to being dragged every which way by Myne that he was quick to shift gears when necessary. He was a fast and compliant learner when it came to just about everything, which when combined with his serious, determined nature made him quite a valuable apprentice. He had a good head on his shoulders, and at times like this he could concisely explain what had happened in order.

According to his explanation, there was a taste-testing event after the meeting at the Merchant's Guild, and there he'd had a confrontation with the guildmaster's chef. The master had ended up angrily declaring that he would just train a chef to make sweets for him. It would be impossible to ask him to give up on it, given how much he hated to lose.

"Judging from what Myne has said, to make her sweets we will need an oven at our disposal and a skilled, passionate chef that will work hard to improve recipes through experimentation. Master Benno is already thinking about hiring a baker used to using ovens, but that won't go well unless the baker is interested in making things other than bread and has the passion necessary to experiment," explained Lutz, which led me to finally understand the core of Myne and Master Benno's argument.

"And the master said that nobles would buy those sweets?"

"Yes. But..."

"No buts, Lutz. Now that the master is invested, we have no choice but to follow through with it."

Though my assessment was somewhat influenced by favoritism, I considered the master to have an inhuman sense for business. Every time he determined a product would sell and threw himself at making it happen, he was right and earned immense profits. I clapped my hands to get Myne and Master Benno's attention.

"Master Benno, you say that you will train a sweets maker, but how long do you intend to train him? Will this be profitable?"

"...Yeah, it'll be profitable. I intend to nab a baker and have him teach the chef, so it won't take too long for him to learn." Master Benno nodded. His eyes were brimming with confidence and his expression made it clear he wasn't even considering that he might fail.

"I hear that the sweets will need sugar. Do you have a plan for acquiring sugar?"

"I'll manage to get some if I talk to my relatives, though I've been distant with them lately. Pretty sure Uncle Emile has some connections in the Sovereignty, yeah? I'm also talking to one of Otto's childhood friends that's still a traveling merchant. I'll have the chef bake bread for now to get used to the oven."

"I see. So sugar isn't entirely out of our grasp, then." He hadn't thrown himself into this without any hope for success. Ever since Myne had first mentioned sweets, he had been researching avenues for getting sugar.

Purchasing an oven from a workshop and getting it installed would be complicated and frustrating, but not overall a large challenge. The biggest problem before us was the inevitable negotiations and conflict with the vested interests. There was no doubt that the guildmaster would come complain again.

I thought back to the conflict that broke out with the Parchment Guild and felt like sitting down. Continued conflicts over paper and sweets unrelated to our main business simply wouldn't be good for us.

"Myne, do you have any suggestions to reduce friction with the Baker's guild like you did with the Parchment Guild?"

"Bwuh?! You want me to think of an idea?!" Master Benno was so focused on staying on the offensive and not budging an inch that Myne would be a better choice for the job, given that she tended to dislike conflict and always sought ways to avoid it. Most importantly, sweets were outside of my area of expertise and I had no idea where to even begin with such negotiations.

"You are more familiar with sweets than anyone here, Myne. You would be better than Master Benno at finding compromises, so please, if you have a suggestion that will bring both parties profit, please don't hesitate to say it."

I knew that I was giving an unreasonable request to a little girl who had just finished her baptism, but just like Master Benno, I did not consider Myne to be a normal child.

"Bwuuuh?! Ummm, a compromise? That's kind of hard actually, um…"

"Perhaps suggesting that our bread will be different bread? Or that we will be using the oven for something other than bread?"

As Myne fell into thought, I tried turning Myne's paper compromises into their bread equivalents. Nothing really came to mind for me, but perhaps they would help Myne think of something, considering how she came up with strange idea after strange idea all the time. My guess must have been right, as Myne turned with her dark-blue hair swaying and her golden eyes sparkling before raising her left hand high in the air.

"I've got it! I want to eat (Italian) food!"

She said a word that I didn't understand. Lutz and Master Benno didn't seem to recognize it either, but Myne continued on talking nonetheless.

"You want to practice using the oven for food that doesn't take sugar, right? (Pizza), (gratin), and (lasagna) all fit that bill. Oh, right, right. We can probably make (quiches) and (pies) too, not to mention just cooking meat in the oven. Wow, now I'm excited!"

Myne was excitedly listing name after name, which was nice, but given that she mentioned cooking meat in the oven, she probably wasn't listing sweets. Lutz, seeing Myne's shining eyes and blissful almost-drooling expression, groaned next to me and held his head in his hands.

"It's too late. Myne's started going crazy. She has a goal in mind and now she's gonna rush right towards it… Master Benno's done for." The complete lack of hope in Lutz's voice made it clear just how much suffering Myne's rampages put him through. It seemed that Myne and Master Benno were even more alike than I thought. They both ran straight forward after setting their sights on something. Neither of them were concerned with the work they put those around them through.

"Mr. Benno, you should give up on sweets and just make a restaurant. Like, a fancy restaurant for selling fancy food."

"Hey, hold up! You're not the one deciding things here!"

"It'll be fine. You can use your sugar to make sweets for dessert. Let's just calm down and make an (Italian) restaurant."

"What's fine about that?!"

Just as Lutz feared, Master Benno was losing control of the situation. I thought to myself that Lutz being dragged around by Myne resembled me being dragged around by Master Benno, and internally wiped a single tear off my heart.

"Lutz, please grow strong. Don't just let her drag you around. Pretend that she is going on a rampage and prepare accordingly so that you maintain some control of the situation. Doing so will lessen the burden on your heart."

"Mr. Mark?"

"There is a knack to being properly dragged around."

Lutz looked at me with his green eyes shining with respect. His sincerity made me swear something: *I will raise Lutz such that he will survive, no matter how hard these two drag him around.*

Myne continued to talk as Lutz and I shared in our mutual suffering. She was listing off the various reasons why a restaurant would be superior to a sweets shop one after another.

"I mean, won't you cover more demographics if you sell food *and* sweets? Not to mention that this will make the oven practice more fruitful and the chef more motivated. You can also have customers eat food experimentally and hear their thoughts before introducing new recipes to nobles."

As I stood there, impressed at her skillful use of persuasive language, Lutz looked up at me with his brow furrowed. "You know... When Myne gets passionate about things and starts ranting, I somehow always start to think that she's right."

"An important skill for merchants to learn is making their customers want to buy their products," I said, nodding.

Lutz shrugged with a laugh. "...Too bad Myne only uses her talent to get stuff she wants."

"Observe carefully and learn how you can make the one you're talking to agree with you. Examples to follow in life are all around you if you look."

Many desired to have the skill to persuade others to agree with them, but as we had a store to run, we couldn't allow ourselves to be swept up in Myne's desires.

"More importantly, Lutz. How does Myne look right now? I think she might be getting too excited."

"Gaaah! Myne! Calm down a little!" By the time Lutz called out to Myne, she was in the process of faceplanting onto the table. As expected, she had gotten too excited. But she was still trying to talk with her face pressed against the table, her words ending up muffled as she tried to persevere.

"There's a world of difference between the food rich people eat and the food nobles eat. A lot of people will definitely come eat if you have food as good as what the nobility eat, even if it's a little expensive."

"A world of difference? Really? When have you ever eaten noble f... Right, the guildmaster."

"Seeee, Mr. Benno, you're interested too. The food really is incomparable. But don't worry, you still have hope. I haven't told Leise anything about cooking this kind of stuff. Eheheh." Myne giggled victoriously, and I knew that a major blow had been dealt to Master Benno.

But I couldn't let him agree to her suggestion through inertia alone. We needed to calm down and listen to Myne's suggestion after she could give more concrete details. It was a universal law that something with advantages carried with it some kind of flaw.

"As Myne has been saying, I believe we should think carefully over whether or not it would be worthwhile to train a sweets maker. Thank you for your wonderful suggestion, Myne. What would we do without you? On that note, I think it would be best for you to return home and collect yourself. You seem to be quite exhausted."

"Awww, Mr. Mark, you're so nice. Thank you." I directed Lutz to take Myne home, and thus got them both out of the store.

After seeing the kids leave, I returned to the office and discovered Master Benno face-planting against his desk as Myne had been. He looked up at me, but didn't lift his head.

"Sheesh. Myne never stops surprising me."

"I did not expect her plan to avoid conflict with the Baker's Guild to shift in that direction."

Master Benno slowly sat back up in his chair while scratching his head. He looked at me, his dark-red eyes gleaming sharply. "... What do you think, Mark?"

"I believe that a restaurant will be much simpler than your sweets plan. A restaurant will not cause friction with the Baker's Guild, for instance. In their stead, we will need to think about how to approach the Eatery Guild, but establishing a restaurant should not be difficult if we follow the proper procedures."

Myne had suggested that we build a high-class restaurant. We weren't going to use our status as a large store to disturb cheaper restaurants, so it was unlikely that the Eatery Guild would reject our application.

"A restaurant's not a bad idea. It's usually rich people that hire chefs, but most chefs are commoners. Having more money at their disposal just means they'll make more food, not different food. Nobles hire the best of the best and teach them recipes only shared among the nobility, so their food's more varied and tastes different. If we pay special attention to our ingredients and flavors, there's no doubt we'll get customers even if food's priced a bit high."

I had never eaten food cooked for a noble before, so I wasn't entirely sure myself, but Master Benno had been invited to dinner at noble estates a handful of times. If he said there was a big difference between the food of rich people and the food of the nobility, he was almost certainly correct.

"But why does Myne know all that? She only spent a few days in the guildmaster's house. Why does she know so many different kinds of recipes? How does she know so many recipes that need an oven?"

"Because she is Myne." I responded to Master Benno's question with a sigh. He didn't look satisfied, but that was the only answer.

"Mark, y'know…"

"Thinking about it will only be a waste of time. It does not matter who Myne truly is if we can use her knowledge for profit. You said so yourself when she brought us the rinsham. Rethinking that strategy won't change the situation we are in. It would be much more constructive to plan out ways to stop Myne from leaking valuable information elsewhere," I said with a shrug.

Master Benno looked away awkwardly, then clapped his hands to change the subject. "Yeah, that reminds me. I'm thinking about adopting Lutz. What do you think?"

"The fact that you have recently begun saying what comes to mind without thinking makes me believe Myne is influencing you in a negative way."

"Huh?! As if! Don't lump me in with that thoughtless buffoon!" Master Benno was quite furious, but what could adopting Lutz be considered if not a thoughtless suggestion? If he were to adopt a child in his position, third parties would consider that child to be his successor. He would be starting a war of inheritance with Corinna's child before said child was even born.

"In that case, may I ask what thoroughly considered line of thought led you to concluding it would be wise to create unnecessary conflict with Corinna?"

Master Benno sighed and complained about my sour tone, but nonetheless began explaining his reasoning. "First of all, we need to secure Lutz on our side so we don't lose our connection to Myne. You know what I mean, right?"

I understood that it was important to keep Lutz on our side since there was a magic contract that compelled products created in the Myne Workshop to be sold through Lutz. I also knew that as Lutz was a lehange apprentice, Master Benno wished to prevent him from leaving the store after his contract ended.

"I thought about making him a leherl, but if I'm gonna be entrusting a store to him, I might as well adopt him and put myself in a position where my opinion holds a lot of weight to him."

"Will a leherl not suffice for that? In fact, if Corinna's child is a girl, could we not just have them marry?" There would be less opposition from our surroundings if we trained him as a leherl and he then married into the store, compared to just raising him as an adopted son. But Master Benno just shrugged while waving a hand.

"That won't work with Lutz. He's only got eyes for Myne. Plus, his real dream's to be a traveling merchant. He's waiting for an opportunity to leave the city. I'm thinking it'll be real hard to keep him tied down to just this store."

"...A traveling merchant? Goodness." That was a fairly surprising dream for one born and raised in a city to have.

Master Benno shrugged and grinned. "I'm thinking it all comes from his insufferable home life, but either way, once Myne's not chaining him down here anymore, Lutz won't have any reason to stay with us. It won't be long before Myne gets taken by a noble. Might be a noble from this city, might be a noble from another city, might even be a noble sent from the Sovereignty. There's no way to say which it'll be, but it's beyond likely that Myne will be leaving this city."

At the moment, Lutz was an apprentice under Master Benno's protection. He had no skills or business knowledge. But once he reached adulthood and had the wisdom of a merchant, he would realize his own value. If at that time Myne had left the city and rendered their magic contract moot, it was very likely that he would leave to travel to stores in other cities.

"When Myne leaves this city, I want Lutz to be there ready to go with her."

"Why would you go so far for them?" I narrowed my eyes slightly and Master Benno gave a conflicted laugh.

"Corinna's the real successor of the Gilberta Company, I'm just standing in her place for now. Myne keeps talking about how she wants to make a book, but our store's not about making books. It'll take some time to set up, but I want to leave this store to Corinna and Otto so I can start up my own store."

The Gilberta Company was run by the female side of the family, so in a future where Corinna and Otto ran it themselves, Master Benno starting his own store made sense. But still, I couldn't connect that to his attitude toward Lutz. I looked at him in confusion, and after a sigh, he murmured that he couldn't hide anything from me with a nostalgic smile on his face.

"Myne and Lutz remind me of how my life used to be. Back when Dad was still alive, and I was free to live however I liked... Back when I was with Liz."

Myne and Lutz running around did indeed remind me of Master Benno and Liz having fun themselves, so I could empathize with his feelings. I closed my eyes and thought back to how I had seen them stealthily hiding behind the store, acting like adults and coming up with little plots.

"They've reminded me of so much. Even the dream I forgot after I had to dedicate everything I had to protect the store and my family after Dad died."

"You wanted to be the kind of merchant that held influence over the entire world, was it?" I said, causing Master Benno to open his eyes wide and get so flustered it was amusing.

"Wh-Why do you remember that?!"

"I remember everything about you." I would not like to be underestimated. I had known Master Benno since his very birth.

I lifted my head with pride and Master Benno groaned, holding his head. It was hard to deal with people who knew details of your youth. Understandable.

Master Benno finally escaped his embarrassment after groaning for some time. He coughed once, then spoke. "If I keep making the products in Myne's head a reality, don't you think my dream will come true? I'm pretty sure it will."

"The scale here is quite large, but if you do indeed make all of what Myne says into reality, you will no doubt hold immense influence over the world."

"I'm thinking about starting by going to the city my siblings live in and making a plant paper workshop there too, so I can start the spread of plant paper. So, Mark. What are you going to do?"

Master Benno looked up at me, his fingers intertwined and his back leaning against the chair. The sight of him waiting so seriously for an answer nearly made me laugh out loud. He had adopted the same posture and looked at me with the same expression when he asked me if I would leave the store after my training period as an apprentice was over, following the death of his father.

"I believe Theo will work better with Otto than I would. I will stay with you, Master Benno. You need someone to train Lutz, yes?"

Master Benno sighed in relief, which made me smile nostalgically. He had abandoned his dream to protect his family and his store, but now Myne was pushing him to grow the Plant Paper Guild and venture out into the world with a new business. She was certainly his Goddess of Water, just as Otto had said.

Thanks to this, I had also remembered my own dream. If Myne is Master Benno's Goddess of Water, then I would like to be his God of Fire, assisting his growth from the side.

The Life of an Apprentice Merchant

A bell rang loudly in the middle of the dark city, announcing that it was time for working citizens to wake up early in the morning.

"Ngggh, morning already...?" In the past, I slept right through first bell and stayed in bed until Mom shook me awake. But now that I was an apprentice merchant, I had to wake up.

I forced my tired body up despite its complaints and started moving. As a lehange, contracted until the age of ten, I had to work every other day. Today was one such other day, meaning I had to go to the Gilberta Company.

"Guuuh, I'm so tireeed..."

"This is what you wanted, Lutz. Quit your complaining."

I headed to the kitchen and grabbed breakfast while Mom complained at me. I dunked hard bread in yesterday's leftover soup and ate away. To finish the meal off, I gulped down some milk we got by trading eggs from our chickens and wiped my mouth with a sleeve. It was then that I realized my mistake.

"Oh, crap..." I reflexively looked at the milk stain on my sleeve, remembering how Mark had told me to eat gracefully and use a cloth when wiping my mouth.

To the wealthy customers of the Gilberta Company, I acted and talked too crudely to work on the floor yet. Despite trying to follow the advice given to me and get rid of bad habits, I always ended up acting like normal whenever I wasn't paying attention. Myne told me to follow Mark's example and I was trying my best to do just that, but I had so many bad habits that I didn't even realize were bad.

...It's hard to notice these kinds of things unless someone points them out to you. As someone raised by a family of builders, I knew nothing about what kind of world merchants lived in. It was only after making paper and opening up a path to being an apprentice in the Gilberta Company that I started getting little bits of advice from Mark. Nobody in my entire life had warned me to clean my mouth after eating, to keep my clothes and hair clean, to speak politely, to have proper posture, or even to treat things carefully.

Thanks to that, I finally understood how Myne felt when she said she had memories of living in another world and had trouble understanding how to live here. If you asked me, I was a lot closer to Myne than I used to be. You really couldn't notice these things unless someone told you.

"Thanks, Mom. See you!" I quickly finished my breakfast and dashed out of the apartment.

The gates would open once second bell rang. Farmers who woke up at first bell to come sell their crops, along with merchants who had to spend the night in the villages after the gates closed, would start pouring into the city. The Gilberta Company opened exactly at second bell to do business with these customers, which meant we had to be there even earlier to get the store ready.

My dad and my eldest brother Zasha both worked in construction, so their work depended heavily on the weather. They left once the sun rose. Sieg and Ralph were apprentices in carpentry workshops, and Mom wove fabric in a textile workshop. The opening of the gates was irrelevant to workshops, so those who worked in one tended to leave after second bell, right around the time kids going to the forest started gathering outside.

Basically, now that I was a lehange apprentice in the Gilberta Company, I was waking up and working super early.

I passed through small, dimly lit alleyways and ran down the still-dark street. Each day was hotter than the last since my baptism was in the early summer, but the air was still cool thanks to the early hour and it hit my cheeks pleasantly as I ran.

The Gilberta Company's employees were generally the kids of wealthy merchants, which meant they all lived to the north. I was the farthest, down by the south gate. It was common for me to end up late despite getting up and moving the moment I heard first bell. At least it was still summer. Things would get even harder once winter came and each day would begin with me having to leave my warm bed.

When I reached the Gilberta Company, it was early enough that nobody was inside preparing yet. The door for employees — lehanges — was still closed. I let out a sigh of relief and started climbing the stairs next to the store, at which point I heard the heavy sound of the door opening.

...Oh crap. It's open now. Hurry! I raced to my rented attic room and washed my face with the small jug inside, then wiped it with a towel. I pinched some salt and rubbed it against my teeth, then wiped them off with the towel too before gargling. Once that was done, I grabbed a pair of my apprentice clothes from a hanging thread and hurriedly changed before using a comb Mark bought for me to fix my hair up as much as possible.

"Nmm, yeah, I should wash my hair today." I touched my hair while brushing it and sighed. It was a little greasy. Mark would probably give me a warning if I didn't wash it soon. I had some rinsham that I made myself, but since my brothers made fun of me whenever they saw me using it at home, I always did it here. Tonight I would wash both my clothes and my hair.

After getting myself dressed, I grabbed my bag which had my ink, pen, calculator, and so on before rushing back down the stairs and entering the store.

"Good morning."

"Good morning, Lutz. Mr. Mark's already in the back," warned a leherl who was cleaning the front section of the store, where customers went. I hurriedly rushed to the back section. Pretty much every store kept most of their products in the back of their stores to prevent theft. They only put a few samples out front. Customers would point out what they wanted, then more of it would be brought out from the back of the store or the basement storage area. Basically, the back of the store was much larger than the front of the store, and was filled with products.

"Lutz, you are somewhat late."

"Sorry, I w— Forgive my lateness, Mr. Mark." I apologized to Mark, who was directing nearby lehanges as they organized the storage area, then got to work alongside them. Managing the storage area in the back was the job of newly hired lehanges. You couldn't do anything if you didn't know what was in the back, where it was, and how to handle it. The first thing lehanges needed to do was learn how to handle the numerous different products, ranging from accessories to types of cloth. Who knew how long it would take to have everything memorized like Mark.

"Lutz, take the hairpins to the front."

"Yes sir!" The hairpins that Myne and I had made over the winter were selling very well. Myne had mentioned selling the manufacturing process to the Gilberta Company, so in the future the hairpins would probably be made in Corinna's workshop, but for now they were all hairpins we had made together.

I had thought that the hairpins would only sell from the end of autumn to the beginning of spring, since outside of winter those with baptism ceremonies and adulthood ceremonies could gather flowers on their own. But traveling merchants drawn to rare products were buying hairpins aplenty.

...I hope they sell today, too. I delicately placed the hairpins onto a tray, taking care to avoid damaging the shape of the flowers. Of the five differently colored flowers on the tray, one had flowers that looked worse than the rest. I laughed a little as I thought about how Myne had probably made that one.

Second bell rang and the gates opened. Customers came in one after another. Some came to sell wool, cloth, and thread while others came to buy the same things before leaving. All of them made the front of the store loud and busy. As a mostly useless apprentice, I was still not allowed to work in the front of the store. The most I could do was carry checked goods to the back.

The lehange that joined in the spring was the son of a large store, so he was used to dealing with customers. He offered them tea, carried their deliveries inside, and basically did work in the front of the store.

"Lutz, could you take this delivery to the back? Give it to Leon, if you would."

"Understood." I took the cloth from him and headed to the back, then searched for the leherl Leon to give it to him. He nodded and put the delivery where it needed to be. Cloth was organized based on quality and color, but I couldn't determine the quality of the cloth by touching it yet. Leon came from a store dealing with cloth and was so skilled with it that despite first signing up as a lehange, he was eventually promoted to a leherl.

...It might not be possible for me to become a leherl, but I needed to at least do a good enough job for my three-year lehange contract to not be ended early.

Everyone else working at the Gilberta Company was from merchant families. As a carpenter's son, I lacked the childhood experience with business that they had. I needed to work much harder than anyone else. I was accepted as an apprentice because I made the paper and hairpins with Myne, but that wasn't really my accomplishment. It was all Myne.

By the time third bell rang, the customers who had entered the city right at second bell had started to leave and were replaced with merchants from within the city. The new lehanges would go to the front of the store when their family arrived and practice dealing with customers. But since nobody in my family came to do business, I had no opportunity to practice. Master Benno said I would have to practice with Myne. But since Myne wasn't a merchant, I didn't think she would make for the best practice.

Fourth bell signaled the end to morning work and the start of lunch. The store closed, and with one person staying behind on watch, everyone went back home or grabbed something to eat from the stands and restaurants on the main street. The bread Mom made me take to work wasn't enough for lunch, so I usually got something at a stand. Having my own money I could spend on myself felt amazing. I owed Myne a lot for teaching me to save money for when I needed it in the future.

It was a pain, but when eating lunch I had to go back to the attic and change clothes again. No matter how hungry I was, I couldn't eat anything while wearing my apprentice uniform. Mark would get mad at me if he saw me walking around chomping on food in uniform.

The food stands closer to the market in the western part of the city were cheaper than the stands by the plaza or to the east. I bought a galette there and ate it on my way back to the plaza beneath the hot summer sun.

Galettes were a mobile form of food made from mixing three kinds of flour together, cooking them for a bit, then wrapping the resulting bread around ham, bacon, sausage, and other kinds of meat. Unlike bread cooked dry for preservation purposes, galettes were easy to eat without soup.

I could eat out today thanks to the clear weather, but on rainy days I had to make do with water and the hard bread I brought from home. There weren't many food stands that operated in the rain, and it'd be a pain to walk outside during bad weather anyway. Basically, the weather was always important.

I finished my galette right as I reached the plaza, and out of habit, wiped my hands on my pants. I jerked in fear and looked around to see if anyone from the store was around.

...*Whew, nobody.* I sighed in relief and hurried back to my attic room. Unlike Master Benno, who loved to have long and slow meals, I had plenty of spare time during lunch break and intended to use the opportunity to do laundry. I wanted to wash my hair today too. I took a washtub and put a bucket, my spare uniforms, a towel, soap, a laundry board, and a jar of rinsham into it before walking down the stairs and heading to the well. It was rough living in an attic room due to all the stairs.

I drew water into the bucket at the well, put in the rinsham, and washed my hair first. I took off my shirt, poured the bucket of rinsham water onto my head over the washtub, put the water back in the bucket, and repeated the process. Getting my hair completely wet then drying it off with a towel was how I washed my hair. My hair was short unlike Myne's, and I didn't have anyone to help me, so this way was the best way for me.

After drying my hair with the towel, I washed it with my clothes. Afterwards, I returned to my room and hung them from some twine to dry. That way they would be dry by the next time I came.

I ran a comb through my hair. My head felt great and my hair was smooth. I pulled a strand of hair and nodded after seeing that it was silky again. With that done, I changed back into the uniform I had been wearing in the morning and returned to the store.

"Oh, I see you washed your hair. It's good that you've learned to do that before I point it out. Keeping oneself clean is very important," said Mark, complimenting me. My efforts being recognized gave me the strength to keep trying my best. I wanted to learn from Mark's example and be more capable of keeping an eye on other people. *That won't be easy.*

Town merchants dropped by the store occasionally throughout the afternoon, but compared to the morning, we were much less busy. This was when Master Benno and Mark went to the Noble's Quarter on days where they had business there.

After fifth bell rang, we newbie lehanges were taught by experienced leherls about the businessmen dropping by the store, ran errands to the Merchant's Guild, and studied to do our jobs better. We had a lot more spare time, and it was the easiest time to ask questions.

"Today we'll be learning about how to write supply orders. Each store writes their orders in somewhat different ways, so forget about how you do it at home. You will need to learn how we at the Gilberta Company write our supply orders."

"…Relearning stuff again? It's so hard to remember all the little differences." The newbie lehanges knew how things worked at their homes, but they had to relearn much of it to work at the Gilberta Company. Learning some things from scratch was hard for me, but it was probably even harder for them to relearn the same thing with slight differences.

"You know how to write supply orders already, Lutz? Looks like these are just how the Gilberta Company writes them. Yep, all good. Try doing the math for these sales reports, then."

"Understood."

Man… Myne really is amazing. Thanks to Myne teaching me how to read, write, and do math on top of us learning how to count money and write supply orders through our business with Master Benno, I was somehow managing to do my job despite lacking the knowledge of a kid raised as a merchant. If not for her, I could imagine that the leherls would have stopped bothering trying to teach me a long time ago.

I clinked the pieces of the calculator around as I did the math. I was still slow with it, but the fact that I was just a little bit of practice away from being as fast as the other apprentices was thanks to how I had practiced using it with Myne.

"Lutz, the master is calling for you. Please go to his office." Mark called out to me and told me to go to Master Benno's office. I stood up and felt the envious glares of the apprentices around me.

"Lutz again, seriously...?"

"Master Benno always calls him the Myne Chief. I bet it's just something to do with Myne again."

I headed to his office while listening to the lehanges murmuring behind me. They weren't wrong. I only ended up as a merchant's apprentice thanks to being Myne's childhood friend and the guy watching over her. Which was exactly why I fully intended to do my job as "the Myne Chief." ...*Nobody else could be her chief but me.*

"There you are, Lutz. It's about Myne," said Master Benno the moment I stepped into the room, looking up from some paper and boards he was checking over. "What's everyone around you saying about Myne joining the temple?"

"I don't think anybody knows she's becoming a shrine maiden except me and her family. Everyone else thinks she's just working at home and coming here like she has been. Her family's not spreading the word since it would look bad from the outside... I think."

Only orphans joined the temple. Those orphans being pre-baptism kids who were abandoned by their families, perhaps, and had no close relatives to look after them. Baptized kids could become live-in apprentices with their employers as their guardians. Their lives would become much harder, but they would keep their jobs and their status.

There were many rumors about kids raised in the temple's orphanage. Some said they were worked to the bone in noble mansions, some said they were trapped inside the temple for the rest of their lives. Nobody would ever hire them, and since they allegedly never participated in baptism ceremonies or adulthood ceremonies, they weren't even counted as citizens of the city. They were treated as unwanted baggage. Myne's family would be mocked and belittled if it became known that their child had joined the temple.

"Myne's going to be treated like a blue shrine maiden, but most people won't understand the significance of that, and we sure don't know what'll happen if she gets involved with a real pain of a noble. Don't say anything you don't have to. I've gotten reports that someone's sniffing around the city for details on Myne, so be careful."

It seemed that Freida had warned him that a man had visited the Merchant's Guild looking for information on Myne.

"Freida just thought he's another merchant Myne's stepped on the toes of, but we know she's entering the temple. It wouldn't be strange for someone on the nobility's side to be gathering information on her. Lutz, it won't be hard for them to find out that you have a magic contract signed with her. Keep an eye on yourself and your surroundings."

Master Benno intended to hide Myne as much as possible, and I intended to do the same. To be honest I had never dealt with nobles, so I didn't know what made them scary or annoying to deal with. But everyone was so on guard toward them I knew I should be too.

"By the way, is Myne about to get better?"

"I think so. It's been three days since she got sick with a fever, so she should be getting better soon."

"Bring her here when you can, I need to talk to her about something."

"Understood." I nodded and left his office, only to see that everyone was closing up the store already.

"Lutz, please put away the unorganized products still in the back room. The bell is about to ring," said Mark, just as the sixth bell began to ring. Sixth bell signaled the closing of the store.

"See you tomorrow."

We lehanges all started heading home. The store was closed by the leherls that had rooms in the upper floors of the store, like Mark and Leon. I needed to go leave soon so the store could close. I hurriedly grabbed my stuff and ran outside.

I then climbed to my attic room to start preparing to go home. I took off my apprentice outfit and threw it into the washtub before changing into my usual clothes. Then I checked the water jug to see how much water it had left. If there wasn't enough water to wash my face there, I wouldn't have time to get more the next morning. ... *Looks like there's still enough.*

I locked my attic door and raced down the steps, then started walking home. Pretty much everyone in the city went home at sixth bell, so the steadily darkening street was filled with people. There was a cool breeze, but the body heat from the crowd rendered it pointless.

...There were never this many people when I was just coming back from the forest. I was stuck walking with the sixth bell crowd now that I had a job, but back when I was gathering in the forest, since the sixth bell signaled that the gates were closing, I only ever saw the fight between merchants trying to force their way into the city and the gate guards trying to close the gates. We kids could slip into small alleyways on our way home, so we could avoid the crowds.

"Ah, welcome back, Lutz." Mom was making dinner when I got home. My brothers were all home too. It was a daily practice for Mom to yell at me to help with dinner, reminding me that everyone else was tired too, and today was no exception.

Our home menu had expanded a bit thanks to Myne's recipes, but many of them required stuff like parues, which only grew in the winter or otherwise took a lot of hard work to make, so our normal eating habits hadn't changed that much. We mainly just ate bread, soup, ham, and sausage.

"Gaah! Ralph! That's mine!"

"Your fault for being slow!" Ralph stole a slice of my ham so I lifted my plate, eyes flared open in anger, but then Zasha came from the side for my sausage.

"You're a merchant apprentice, you don't move around too much. We're carpenters and a lot more hungry than you."

"Stop, Zasha!" roared my mother. "Sit down and eat!"

My sausage was saved thanks to Mom's yelling, but I could tell from their eyes that they were still aiming for my food. If I didn't finish my plate while they were still meek from Mom's glare, they would be back at it again in no time. I scarfed down my sausage and then moved to my soup-soaked bread.

...Gaah, darn it! They're gonna pay for this! Thanks to my savings I had enough money to buy some food for myself, but still, having my food stolen really ticked me off.

Our conflict-filled dinner ended, and I moved right to preparing for bed. I couldn't wake up early if I didn't go to bed early, and in any case there wasn't much for me to do after sunset. Going to bed fast to save on candles was the best plan.

I heard seventh bell ringing, signaling that it was bedtime.

...I think I'll go check on Myne tomorrow. She should be better by now.

The Roots of the Guildmaster's Worries

"Is that all we have to discuss today? In that case, a reminder that we are holding a taste-testing event in the larger meeting room for a confectionery I plan to sell soon. Drop by if you have the time. My granddaughter said that there would be enough for everyone here and their servants. Benno, Freida put her all into this knowing that you would be coming. You wouldn't betray her expectations, would you?" I said, finishing the meeting.

Benno stood up with a visible grimace on the face. I understood that as an expression meaning he would go even though he didn't want to, which filled me with an undeniable sense of satisfaction. His glare felt pleasant to me, and I left the room with a snort.

I went in the opposite direction of the other interested store owners and climbed the stairs to my office before sitting in my guildmaster chair.

Now then. How will it go, I wonder? The taste-testing event was an experiment for me, suggested by Myne and enthusiastically supported by my granddaughter as a challenge to face. The goal was to make it clear that the soon-to-be-sold pound cakes were property of the Othmar Company while also searching for the flavors that would be most profitable and desirable.

I couldn't hear the bustle from downstairs in my office, but I nonetheless strained my ears to see if I could hear any hints as to how it was going.

"Master Gustav, are you curious about the taste-testing event?" asked Cosimo, a long-time servant of mine who could be called my right-hand man, while pouring me tea with a slight smile. He was certainly remembering how, when planning the event, Freida had asked me not to come, as my "strong influence would make all her hard work vanish like mist."

I would have liked to see my grandchildren doing their best, but I had no choice but to quietly step back and let their wings grow. It didn't please me, but Freida was right. If I attended as the guildmaster of the Merchant's Guild, then it would diminish the idea that it was being held by the Othmar Company in particular.

"Lady Freida has certainly been full of spirit lately. I suppose it is all thanks to Myne," said Cosimo joyfully. I thought back to how excited Freida was while preparing the event and felt a small smile of my own form.

Freida, due to the Devouring ravaging her health, had barely gone outside before signing a contract with a noble. Following that she had started taking lessons at home to prepare herself for moving to the Noble's Quarter after reaching adulthood, which naturally led to all the servants living with her to grow quite fond of her.

Freida met a fellow Devouring child named Myne not long before her baptism and had seemingly been moved by Myne's straightforward, unwavering pursuit of her dream. Ever since then she had become quite lively and active. Freida had taken full control of setting up this event, with Myne's advice guiding her. Of course, her family and I helped her to some degree, but she had displayed a sharp mind and management skills far beyond what one would expect from her age.

"I am curious, but I am confident it will end well. All I can do is wait for her report."

"If you say so, Master Gustav, I am sure it will succeed. Your business instincts have never been incorrect. You said that change was coming to Ehrenfest... and indeed it has," said Cosimo with a smile. As he said, my business instincts were rarely wrong.

"...Which is precisely why it hurts that I failed to acquire Myne for myself. Hairpins, rinsham, pound cakes, rumtopf, plant paper... I can see already how Myne's inventions and ideas will bring enormous change to Ehrenfest."

Myne, Freida, and Lutz, under the guidance of Benno, a member of the young generation, were already enacting great change to the markets in Ehrenfest.

Cosimo nodded slowly and looked at me. "Myne's influence is still limited to the commoner sphere of the city. But as you said, she is a small seed that will grow into a large, revolutionary tree. In which case, we will need to maneuver such that she is not crushed by nobles who hate change, and to negotiate as best we can so that she is taken in by a progressive noble who will raise her well."

That went without saying. Such was the duty of the Merchant's Guild, and the Othmar Company with its long and proud history dating back to the establishment of the Merchant's Guild.

The Othmar Company's history stretched far into the past. It existed in Ehrenfest before modern Ehrenfest came to be. Even during the reign of the first Archduke, the Othmar Company had sold food to nobles as the Archduke's favored business.

The new Archduke had brought with him personal craftsmen and artisans to make clothes, furniture, and so on to his taste. It was natural for nobles to bring workers with them to keep their environment to their liking. But food was the one thing they had no control over. Even if they brought a chef with them, they would have to rely on the food that could be grown in the new land.

The Othmar Company bought the best food possible from the surrounding farms and sold them to the nobles and the prior Archdukes. Merchants brought from afar had no way of knowing which seasons were best for which crops, which crops were high quality and which weren't, and so on. It was thanks to these circumstances that the Othmar Company successfully continued doing business even as the Archduke changed with the generations.

At the same time, the Othmar Company was selected to be a third party negotiator between the personal workers brought by the new nobles and the personal workers that had already been serving the old nobles. An organization was needed to manage the entirety of business in Ehrenfest. The result was the Merchant's Guild, which was founded to serve as a window into the nobility and manage business disputes among large store owners.

"Master Gustav, Damian would like to see you." He had likely come to give a report on the taste-testing event. I said to let him in, and once he was in front of my desk I asked for his report.

Damian was my grandson and Freida's older brother. He was not yet an adult, but he had experience in multiple stores as a lehange. My plan was to try sending him to the Gilberta Company once his current contract ended.

"The pound cakes were received very well. Everyone was comparing the flavors with very serious expressions."

"Oh ho... How was Benno?"

Damian forced a smile and shrugged. "The moment he entered the room, he caught Myne and forced her to change into his store's apprentice uniform."

"I had hoped to build up an association between Myne and the Othmar Company, but I suppose that failed, then."

The Roots of the Guildmaster's Worries

The recipes and inventions Myne learned about "within her dreams," according to Leise, were too much for one store to monopolize. The entire city deserved them. The newly reformed Gilberta Company could not handle everything themselves, nor should they. My intention had been to show that the Gilberta Company was not monopolizing the profits of her products, but it hadn't worked.

"Does Benno intend to collapse his store once again?" The hairpins and rinsham were one thing, but I had offered to handle the plant paper for him — changing the name of the Parchment Guild to the more general Paper Guild — but he had kept it to himself. What good would come from him handling products outside of his store's focus of clothing and apparel?

After telling Damian to return to the event, I let out a slow sigh. "A single store like the Gilberta Company monopolizing enormous wealth will be the start of chaos. I do understand that Benno is still operating under the mindset of protecting his store and family, yes. But it is about time for him to open his eyes and see the full picture. Unlikely as that may be, given how much of a hot-blooded youth he is."

The Merchant's Guild was focused on bringing profit to all of Ehrenfest, whereas the Gilberta Company merely wanted to bring more profit and prestige to themselves. Conflict between the two was inevitable. Thanks to Benno's recent unending struggle to monopolize profits for himself, I was spending each day with a headache.

"The conflict between you two arises not only from your different opinions in economic philosophy, I'm afraid. You are in part responsible for this, Master Gustav." Cosimo shook his head while giving an exaggerated sigh.

"...I had only good intentions with that."

"Which means nothing if they don't understand your intentions. It's no surprise that Benno ended up so stubborn when dealing with you."

The Gilberta Company had been growing in influence for a number of decades, but they were not yet a century old. Their name came from the seamstress Gilberta, who once made clothes for nobles. The company started when she married a man who established a clothing store.

It was under the leadership of Benno's father that the store began to grow in renown and size enough to be considered a "large store." Just as everyone was expecting them to continue to grow, Benno's father died outside of the city.

A large store was too much for a young man who had just reached adulthood to handle. Left on its own, the Gilberta Company would no doubt crumble. I would not have liked for a newly developed store to fall after such substantial growth. Furthermore, it would have become difficult to deal with nobles had there been no one to fill the niche in business that the Gilberta Company filled.

My first wife died before me, but I recovered quickly and married not long after her death to preserve a future for the Othmar Company. My second wife also died before me, but our sons had already reached adulthood and my eldest son was well old enough to handle the company if necessary, so I hadn't married again.

It was the perfect opportunity. I offered to wed Benno's mother so as to protect the Gilberta Company. While she was bedridden with sorrow, her inexperienced young son would no doubt let workers slip through his fingers and make errors that would be hard to recover from, if possible at all. It should be clear after some thought that it was more important to protect the store than to be caught in the past mourning the dead.

When I proposed, not only was Benno there, but several of his younger siblings were there too. I thought they would all rejoice that their mother would be remarried and the store would be saved.

That was not the case. The Gilberta Company treated my proposal as an insult. I did not know why they had been so insulted, but those who knew my tendency for such blunders all sighed and shook their heads.

"Women and men do not think the same way. A widow would never think about remarrying so soon after the death of her husband. If instead of proposing immediately you gave time for her sorrow to fade and the hardships of raising a family alone set in, she would have accepted your proposal immediately."

My son and his wife both admonished me, whereupon I understood my mistake. Women and men certainly did approach such issues with different mindsets.

"Perhaps things would have been different had she died instead of her husband..."

As expected, lehanges left the Gilberta Company without renewing their contracts and fewer nobles ordered clothes from them, putting the newly adult Benno in extremely poor circumstances. A skilled leherl hired by his father named Mark helped Benno quite extensively, but even so, the store was entering a swift decline.

Despite being aware of the problem, I as the guildmaster of the Merchant's Guild was tasked with equalizing profit, and could not give indiscriminate backing to one company in particular with no excuse for doing so. Just as I was mourning the sight of a sharp-minded young businessman being crushed before his prime, Benno's fiancée fell sick and soon died.

The sooner one acted to halt the decline of a store, the better. Benno should understand that, after working so hard as the head of the store to save it. So I offered Benno one of my daughters in marriage.

The result was him feeling insulted. I didn't understand. He was a man as well, so why was he insulted?

"They were in love from a young age and spent their lives together. He didn't want to marry her for connections or political reasons. If you offer a marriage proposal to someone so soon after someone that close to them dies, it's only natural that they would get mad."

I later attempted to go through more proper channels and offer an engagement between Benno's little sisters and my sons, but one of them fled outside of the city and the other married a traveling merchant. For some reason, Benno began behaving quite hostile and defiant toward me. Very troubling.

"We went through some rough times, but luckily I've managed to warm my relationship with Benno somewhat by selling him information on the Devouring and selling Myne a magic tool."

"That is quite an optimistic view of things, Master Gustav. For me it is easy to imagine that Benno is becoming even more defensive around you, especially when Myne is involved," said Cosimo, which made me frown.

"...But why? Surely he feels some gratitude toward me after I sold a magic tool I had broken my back to get for Freida."

"Myne might be thankful for you saving her life, but Benno is likely more wary now since you lied about the price to try and trick Myne into your store."

"A panic will arise if Myne continues to produce strange, revolutionary products sold only in Benno's store. The market will collapse if they are kept together, if not worse. Surely he understands the benefits of him being separated from her."

"When it comes to the Gilberta Company and Myne, exactly nothing has ever gone as you planned, so I imagine that will continue to be the case," said Cosimo with a sigh.

Suddenly, a white bird slid into the room — despite the windows and doors being closed. I opened my eyes wide in surprise, since this generally only happened once every few years, and immediately the white bird turned into a letter in front of me. This was the method of communications nobles used for high priority messages.

Under normal circumstances, a commoner working for the noble would carry a handwritten letter. But in situations where time was of the essence, magic tools such as these were used. It was common to receive one after the Archduke Conference, but that took place in spring and I could think of no reason why there would be emergency contact now in the summer.

"What in the world?" I opened the letter and saw that it was a request from the temple, asking for information on Myne. As she would be joining the temple as a shrine maiden, they wanted all the information we had on her workshop, current funds, and so on. Nothing was to be omitted.

"...Myne is joining the temple?" She had been registered as the forewoman of the Myne Workshop just a few days ago, allegedly so that she could make new products under Benno's protection while working from home. There had been no report that she would be joining the temple as a shrine maiden. I had heard from Leise that Myne said she would be stuck dealing with nobles whether she wanted to or not. Perhaps I now knew why.

As Myne lacked magic tools and had no intentions of signing with a noble, she only had half a year or so at best to live. I had gambled that even if Benno kept her inventions monopolized, she wouldn't be able to complete many of them before perishing.

But that was all water under the bridge if she was joining the temple. The temple had divine tools — religious magic tools — and blue priests of the nobility. Myne's life would be saved and she would no doubt be forced into a contract with one of the nobles there.

...Though it was likely that she would be treated with utter cruelty. The temple had an orphanage, and everyone understood it to be where commoner orphans with no guardians went. Nobles were given blue robes, orphans were given gray robes. One needed visit the temple only a few times to see that they received entirely different treatment.

The truth would become clear after donating goods and gold to the temple. The truth that gray robes are treated as slaves by the blue robes. The truth that they are forced into absolute submission, no matter the circumstances.

I would not be able to bear Freida being put under such conditions, so I searched for an honest noble with a warm heart to sign a contract with her. Myne would not be so lucky, doomed to live as she now was.

...Did Benno know about this? Dealing with nobles unprepared was a death sentence for commoners. I reflected on Benno's recent actions carefully.

"Registering Myne as a forewoman and making a new magic contract with her... Did he do all of that for her sake?" Continuing to protect Myne did open avenues for the Gilberta Company to gain new noble connections and sell her products, but the risk was simply too high for such a gamble.

"Benno, you don't know what you're dealing with. Your youthful ignorance wounds me once again." There was no doubt that if the

Gilberta Company made a large blunder here, the Merchant's Guild would be dragged down with them in some way or another. "Ngh. Yet more headaches."

I would have to give up on getting Myne to join the Othmar Company now that she was joining the temple. It was impossible to say what influence she would have on Freida, who would be entering the Noble's Quarter after reaching adulthood. I had chosen Lord Henrik to be Freida's partner based solely on his personality. He was a laynoble and had little influence in the Noble's Quarter. At the very least, I should try to minimize the contact they have until it becomes clear what kind of noble Myne will sign with.

"I feel pity for Freida losing the friend she was so glad to obtain, but her safety comes first." I let out a sigh and started writing my answer to the inquiry about Myne. It would be wise to make her appear as valuable as possible, so that they might treat her just a little bit better. It was true, in any case, that with Myne's vast knowledge of unknown products the temple could obtain sizable wealth through her.

...It was unlikely that this would actually impact how the nobles treated her, but given the political events in the Sovereignty and how the temple is lacking in money and mana, perhaps every little bit counts.

"I will need to summon Benno and ask for the details."

"Should I write a meeting request, Master Gustav?"

"Please do."

Cosimo began writing a meeting request for the Gilberta Company. It was at that point that Freida burst into the room, eyebrows arched in fury.

"We have a problem, grandfather. Benno said that he will begin training chefs of his own! He intends to keep Myne's knowledge of recipes to himself as well! Even though Myne said she would let Leise take care of all her recipes!"

...First he monopolized hairpins that fit into his store entirely, then rinsham that could be forgiven as a beauty product in general, then plant paper entirely removed from his business demographic, and now food as well?!

"He's sticking his hands into every pie he can find. This will not end well. Does Benno wish to collapse his own store?!" I stood up reflexively and yelled on instinct.

Cosimo spoke up. "Master Gustav, please stay calm. Such excitement is bad for your health, and we are relying on your abilities. You must at least remain healthy and fighting until Lady Freida reaches adulthood..."

Benno was continuing to charge forward with his eyes set on monopolizing profit for his own store, while simultaneously attempting to protect Myne as she went into the temple and the world of nobles nigh defenseless. The pressure from the rampaging Gilberta Company all fell on me, as I needed to preserve the balance between the large stores.

...Benno, you brat! Learn to respect your elders.

Afterword

Hello again, it's me, Miya Kazuki.

Thank you for reading Ascendance of a Bookworm Part 1 Volume 3. With this, Part 1 comes to a close.

Myne's life was saved thanks to Freida and the guildmaster, but it wouldn't last forever. She chose to live with her family and try as hard as she could to make a book before her death. Lutz opened up to his mother and showed her how serious he was about becoming an apprentice merchant.

When Myne went to the temple to go through her baptism festival, she discovered a book room — the closest thing to a library she had seen in this world and more or less what she had been longing for this entire time. The book room in the temple was essentially a chained library where the books were protected by sturdy metal chains. In an age where books were as rare as they were expensive, libraries protected them from theft by chaining them. Books even more rare were placed in boxes that needed keys from three separate people used together in unison to open.

Myne wanted to spend the rest of her remaining life to read. She charged forward to make her dreams come true and through a high donation, Crushing the High Bishop, and firm negotiation, she successfully became a blue shrine maiden in the temple.

Myne's adventure continues in Part 2: Apprentice Shrine Maiden. Please look forward to it.

In any case, as I imagine anyone holding this book knows, volume three ended up quite large. Reason being, I fought hard to get all of the short stories from outside of Myne's perspective into this volume. They're heavily involved with what happens in Part 2, so they couldn't be cut, and we couldn't release a volume four of just those short stories, so I did my best to get them into this book together.

In fact, everyone involved with this volume worked hard to get a book with this many pages out. Thank you, everyone at TO Books. Truly.

Also, unlike the prior volumes, the cover art for this volume was done at my request. Thank you You Shiina for drawing an illustration of Myne happy with her family to close off Part 1.

As one last statement, I would like to offer my utmost gratitude to everyone who read this book. May we meet again in Part 2 Volume 1.

J-Novel Club Lineup

Ebook Releases Series List

Keep an eye out at j-novel
    for further new title
    announcements!

ASCENDANCE OF A BOOKWORM

I'll do anything to become a librarian!

Part 2 Apprentice Shrine Maiden Vol. 1

Author: **Miya Kazuki**
Illustrator: **You Shiina**

PART 1 VOLUMES 1-3 & PART 2 VOLUMES 1-4 ON SALE NOW!